Elements of Port Operation and Management

BOOKS BY THE SAME AUTHOR:

(1981) *Elements of Shipping*. 5th edn. Chapman and Hall London.

(1982) *Economics of Shipping Practice and Management*. 1st edn. Chapman and Hall London (2nd edition in preparation).

(1984) *Elements of Export Marketing Management.* 1st edn. Chapman and Hall London.

(1985) *Elements of Export Practice*. 2nd edn. Chapman and Hall London.

(1982) *Dictionary of Shipping/International Trade Terms and Abbreviations*. 2nd edn. Witherby and Co. London (3rd edition in preparation, 8000 entries).

(1984) *Dictionary of Commercial Terms and Abbreviations*. 1st edn. (6000 entries). Witherby and Co. London.

(1986) *Dictionary of Multilingual Shipping/International Trade/ Commercial Terms in English – French – German – Spanish* 1st edn (10 000 entries). Witherby and Co. London.

Elements of Port Operation and Management

ALAN E. BRANCH
FCIT, FIEx., AITA

Shipping Executive / Lecturer / Chief Examiner in Shipping and Export Practice / Shipping, Port and Export Consultant

LONDON NEW YORK
CHAPMAN AND HALL

First published in 1986 by
Chapman and Hall Ltd
11 New Fetter Lane, London EC4P 4EE
Published in the USA by
Chapman and Hall
29 West 35th Street, New York NY 10001

Printed in Great Britain by J. W. Arrowsmith Ltd, Bristol

ISBN 0 412 25250 3 (hardback)
ISBN 0 412 25260 0 (paperback)

British Library Cataloguing in Publication Data

Branch, Alan E.
Elements of port operation and management.
1. Harbors—Management
I. Title
381.1 HE551

ISBN 0–412–25250–3
ISBN 0–412–25260–0 Pbk

Library of Congress Cataloging in Publication Data

Branch, Alan E.
Elements of port operations and management.
Bibliography: p.
Includes index.
1. Harbors—Management. I. Title.
HE551.B52 1986 387.1′068 85–24301
ISBN 0–412–25250–3 (U.S.)
ISBN 0–412–25260–0 (U.S. : pbk.)

TO
PHILLIP AND ELIZABETH

Contents

Preface

Since the publication of my books *Elements of Shipping* and more recently *Economics of Shipping Practice and Management*, both selling in over 130 countries, I have received numerous requests both from home and abroad for a companion volume on seaports.

This book has been written to provide a practical, overall understanding of the elements of port operation and management of a competitive, profitable port authority. It reflects the author's many years of experience in port and ship management, international trade and education. It deals in simple language with the role and function of seaports in a trading pattern, port investment criteria, port tariffs, free ports and free trade zones, port traffic control, budgetary control and marketing, port management structure and dock labour, computerization, cargo-handling equipment, the economics of port design, the role of port cargo-handling organizations, the economics of international trade, finance of international trade, and many other aspects of this extensive subject. The importance of complete professionalism in all areas of port practice as a means of providing the viable, high quality service required to sustain and expand international trade cannot be overemphasized. This book will help towards establishing that professionalism.

The material assembled here is intended not only for students preparing for seaport examinations, but also for persons employed in port authorities. In short, it is an *aide-mémoire* to those engaged in the industry throughout the world and may be regarded as 'the port executive's handbook'.

The book will be useful to students taking seaport, international trade, cargo-handling and transport examinations under the aegis of the Institute of Chartered Shipbrokers, the Institute of Freight Forwarders, the Institute of Export, the Institute of Transport Administration, the Institute of Materials Handling, the Institute of Packaging and the Chartered Institute of Transport. The book will also assist students or port executives taking a short seaport course.

I am greatly indebted to the various organizations listed in the acknowledgements for the assistance they have given so enthusiastically: the fact that so many of them are situated overseas is reflected in the international content and market of the book.

At my request Mr H. B. Jackson BSc (Econ.), FIEx., FIB, former Chief Executive of Barclays Export and Finance Co. Ltd, wrote Chapters 2 and 10 on the economics and finance of international trade, Mr C. A. Rich, Extra Master, M Sc, DMS, FNI, FCIT, MBIM, contributed to Chapters 3, 4 and 5 and Jane Splarn drew the diagrams. I am most grateful for their contribution, which has enriched the contents of the book.

Finally, I should like to express my grateful thanks for the considerable secretarial help given by my lifelong family friends Mr and Mrs Splarn, who have undertaken similar tasks for my six other publications. As always, I wish to record with gratitude the help rendered by my wife in proof-reading and to pay tribute to her tolerance and enthusiasm during many a lost weekend.

19 The Ridings
Emmer Green
Reading
Berkshire

A.E.B.
Senior Lecturer
Faculty of Business and Social Science
Kingston Polytechnic
Kingston-upon-Thames
Surrey KT1 2EE
December 1985

Acknowledgements

The author wishes to acknowledge the generous assistance provided by the following companies and institutions:

Amin Kawar and Sons

Associated British Ports (ABP)

Barlow Handling Ltd

British Ports Association (BPA)

Direct Transport Service (Sweden) Ltd

Dover Harbour Board (DHB)

Eftertayek Förbjudes

Felixstowe Dock and Railway Company

International Association of Ports and Harbours (IAPH)

International Cargo Handling Co-ordination Association (ICHCA)

International Labour Organization (ILO)

International Maritime Organization (IMO)

Lansing Bagnall Ltd

Maritime Service of New South Wales

Port Authority of Dunkerque

Port Authority of State of New York and State of New Jersey

Port of Adelaide

Port of Antwerp

Port of Aqaba

Port of Quebec

Port of Rotterdam

Port of Singapore Authority

Sea Containers Ltd
South African Harbours
St Lawrence Seaway Authority

Diagrams

Tables

CHAPTER 1

Role and function of seaports in the trading pattern of a nation

SCOPE OF BOOK

This book is written to provide a practical overall understanding of the elements of port practice and the management of a competitive, profitable port authority. It deals in simple language with the salient commercial, operating and political aspects of the subject, with particular emphasis on economics and port management. In so doing the book is written not only for the student of the subject, but also for port executives throughout the world. Particular emphasis is placed on the need to strive for complete professionalism in all areas of port operation and management as a means of providing a viable high quality service to sustain and expand international trade passing through the port.

FUNCTION OF SEAPORTS

A seaport has been defined as

> a terminal and an area within which ships are loaded with and/or discharged of cargo and includes the usual places where ships wait for their turn or are ordered or obliged to wait for their turn no matter the distance from that area. Usually it has an interface with other forms of transport and in so doing provides connecting services.

Within the context of modern transport techniques, there is increasing emphasis on the port, not generally as the terminus or end of a transport movement, but as a point through which goods and passengers pass. In other words, by acting as a link in a transport chain, the port makes provision for the concept of the through transport operation. This is found in the container movement or distribution of iron ore involving rail/ship/rail transportation from the ore mine to the steel plant.

A wider definition of ports is provided in the following quotation from an Alderman for the Port of Antwerp:

> The task of promoting the interests of the port knows almost no limitations in time or space. Its aim is to serve the prosperity and welfare of our regional or National community and beyond our borders to make a contribution to improving the quality of life.

This underlines the European philosophy which regards the port as part of the transport infrastructure of the country – to be supported by direct government subsidy. This criterion applies to many other countries throughout the world, while in the UK and the USA particularly the ports are viewed as individual commercial enterprises which should conform to normal financial criteria.

Ports exist as an important and fundamental part of the overall pattern of trade and transport. The four principal roles of a port can be summarized as follows:

(a) Provision of shelter from the elements. This arises when, due to heavy seas and storm conditions prevailing, ships take shelter in the environs of a port and thereby seek safe anchorage.

(b) Cargo and passenger handling. A place where ships can load or discharge their cargo, and/or passengers. This is the prime function of a port.

(c) Support services for ships. This embraces victualling, stores, bunkering, ship repair and so on. In the larger ports such as Dunkerque ship yard/dry docking facilities are available for ship survey and overhaul purposes.

(d) A base for industrial development. This involves the provision of industry and its infrastructure to facilitate the development of trade passing through the port. It may be a steel plant. A more recent development is the free ports concept (see pp. 107–114).

(e) A terminal forming part of a transport chain. Such an interchange point links the shipping service with other transport modes to provide an overall international trade distribution network, often under the combined transport operation concept (see Chapter 9 of *Economics of Shipping Practice and Management*). It may involve rail, road or inland waterways/canal transport.

FACTORS DETERMINING THE SHIPOWNER'S/ SHIPPER'S CHOICE OF PORT

In tracing the pattern of international trade developments during recent years and pointing to future trends one must bear in mind that the paramount consideration is the shipowner/shipper and more especially the market. It is the market which decides whether the goods will pass and this is conditional on many factors as follows:

(a) General world demand for a particular product. An example is oil, which has slumped in recent years compared with the peak of the mid-1970s. This is due primarily to quadrupling of the price in 1973 and the development of alternative forms of energy. In consequence a surplus of oil tanker tonnage has arisen, and under-utilization of tanker berths.

(b) The quality of the overall international trade transport service. If the port is subjected to frequent industrial disputes, low port efficiency particularly in terms of dock labour, sluggish turn-round of ships, absence of modern technology in the port, and so on, the result is likely to be a declining volume of business through the port.

(c) The overall competitiveness of the port. This includes all the aspects of port operation and commercial practice such as tariffs, clearance of cargo, distribution arrangements, hours of working, cargo-handling equipment, port development, and so on.

(d) The port tariff structure in so far as the shipper is concerned. Some port authorities are very marketing orientated and offer negotiated discount rates to volume shippers. Hence a shipowner or shipper generating say 100 000 tons of a particular commodity through a particular berth annually may have a 5% discount on the published port tariff. See also item (a).

(e) The extent of any political or statutory influence relative to port users. Regulations may exist regarding the routing of particular commodities through a particular port thereby giving no choice to the shipper. A further example arises whereby an increasing number of ports, usually by government decree, give berth preference and more favourable tariffs to the national flag. Hence a vessel of country A about to enter a port in country A will be given priority of berth allocation over ships with other national flags, and likewise lower port tariffs. This practice is called 'flag discrimination' (see

Chapter 14 of *Economics of Shipping Practice and Management*).

(f) The overall transit cost. A situation could exist with parity on port tariffs at two ports situated some 100 km apart, but where the overall distance from the port to the shipper's premises favours port A rather than port B. Hence port A is more likely to obtain the business unless port B is willing and able to reduce the port B tariff to a level which will equate to or better the overall transit cost compared with port A.

(g) Climatic conditions. Many ports are affected by climatic conditions. For example, during the winter months a port may be closed owing to ice formation. Other situations include tidal variations imposing draft restrictions, and fog limiting access to and from the port. With regard to the latter, this has largely been overcome in many ports by radar technology.

(h) Origin and destination of the cargo. This will influence the overall transit cost as detailed in item (f).

(i) The nature of the commodity and the volume. Specific cargoes are dealt with at specific ports – which require specific cargo-handling equipment and berths.

(j) Mode of transport. It may be road, rail or canal. If the goods are essentially rail-borne traffic, obviously a rail-link port is required.

(k) Bunkering cost and other port charges to the shipowner. This will influence considerably which port a shipowner uses when he is examining the port options to start a new service, or reviewing an existing shipping service and the ports served. A further example arises where some ports offer discounted bunker tariffs to their national flag, thereby practising flag discrimination.

(l) The range of port facilities available to the shipper and shipowner. This includes agents, bunkering, victualling, stores, ship repair, tugs, lighterage, forwarding agents, cargo-handling equipment, customs, port access both seaward and landward, and so on.

(m) Any agreement with liner conferences, trade associations, shippers' councils relative to the user of particular ports.

It must be stressed that the significance and importance of the foregoing factors will vary with individual circumstances. The basic considerations tend to be the cost, the nature of the traffic, the adequacy of port facilities and the overall efficiency together with the industrial relations record.

FUTURE TRENDS IN INTERNATIONAL TRADE

Against the foregoing background of the factors influencing the shipowner's/shipper's choice of port, we now examine future trends in international trade and especially how they are likely to affect the port industry.

(a) The development of containerization – which first emerged on an international scale in the early 1960s – will continue to penetrate existing cargo liner trades and consolidate further their position in present containerized routes. This will call for further investment in container berths and associated equipment. It will foster the development of the combined transport operation involving road or rail services to and from the port. Moreover, the container encourages the use of the Inland Clearance Depot (ICD) (see *Elements of Shipping*, Chapter 16), thereby transferring away from the port the task of customs clearance and loading/unloading of the container. This reduces the risk of port congestion and, overall, improves the throughput at the container berth.

(b) The concept of the combined transport operation is being developed in many trades involving the through rail, road vehicle or container service. It enables the merchandise to travel under one document covering the various transport modes and permits a through rate to be quoted. The major advantage to the port authority is the unimpeded flow of traffic through the port and ease of documentation and port procedures.

(c) Most industrial seaboard nations now have mechanized cargo-handling techniques and this is being extended to other seaboard nations as their shipping services become modernized. It is important that where there are capital-intensive port transhipment systems, dock labour attains high productivity. The effect will be to place the port in a competitive position and to encourage the development of trade. Countries which do not have modern cargo transhipment systems encourage sluggish turn-round of vessels, increase port charges to the shipper, have longer transit times, and discourage the development of trade compared with countries exporting similar commodities but through a more modern and efficient port and associated shipping service.

(d) Computerization is developing slowly in many ports, but by the mid-1990s it will become a major area of technology in many ports throughout the world. Included will be control and monitoring of containers passing through the port; preparation, issue and despatch of the cargo manifest; collation/preparation of consignment lodgement details to customs for customs clearance, including assessment of the VAT and duty payable – called in the UK a direct trader input (DTI) system (see *Elements of Export Practice*, 2nd edn, pp. 147–148); shipping movement information – the estimated and actual times of arrival or departure; loading berths and receiving dates; billing of customers' port accounts; preparation and issue of port documents through a computer, indicating the charges, name of shipper/agent, commodity description and basis of charges raised; issue of consignment notes, bills of lading, waybills and other documents by the agent/shipowner at the port; booking facilities for shippers with carriers and their agents; computerized master file of all port personnel records, all rates issued to shipper/agent; control and record of port equipment and stores material; preparation of paybills and issue of pay slips to port staff; allocation of berths and cargo-handling equipment to shipowners/agents; and preparation and despatch of accounts to shipowners relative to port used, embracing berth, cargo-handling equipment, dock labour, cargo dues, victualling, stores, and so on. Overall, the major area of development will be the computerized system of customs clearance and consignment information and control at seaports and ICD.

(e) Oil prices dramatically quadrupled in 1973 and since that date the world demand for oil has declined with alternative and less expensive forms of energy being developed. Accordingly, the world oil tanker fleet has declined and numerous ports have experienced a contraction of their oil trade with some rationalization of facilities. An example is the port of Rotterdam.

(f) SITPRO (see Chapter 14 of *Elements of Export Practice*), together with other organizations, including UNCTAD and OECD, continue to strive to reduce the range of documentation used in international trade, and to modernize existing documents. The development of electronic data processing techniques is playing its part in achieving this objective. It is having a profound effect in many ports on customs, documentation, cargo manifest, consignment notes, bills of lading, and so on. Overall, it is helping to speed up the movement of cargo through the port, thereby improving port efficiency.

(g) Ro/Ro. The development of the Ro/Ro (roll-on/roll-off) service in recent years has been dramatic and the growth continues, primarily in the short sea trade, and to an increasing degree in the deep sea trades, often involving the multi-purpose type of vessel. It has a profound effect on port operation, involving the provision of a ramp and associated facilities. The port of Dover is the most well-known ferry port dealing with cars, coaches and lorries travelling to and from the Continent and beyond.

(h) Dock labour. The decline in the dock labour force has been virtually worldwide and this has been due to the introduction of capital-intensive methods of cargo handling. As the development of containerization and especially Ro/Ro services becomes even more widespread in underdeveloped countries, the reduction will become even more pronounced.

(i) Earlier ports built in the nineteenth century tended to be built at the head of the river and close to the hinterland on which the port relied for its markets. An example is London with its four major dock complexes, all of which have now closed. Today, with the provision of vessels having deeper draft, wider beam and greatly increased overall length, the deep water berths/ports tend to be situated at the mouth of the river estuary, as is found at Felixstowe port.

(j) The range and type of ships continue to increase. Accordingly, this has a profound effect on the type and range of port facilities. Such vessels may be a specialized vessel with up to eight decks, to convey up to 8000 import cars/vehicles, or the combi-carrier, classified as a multi-purpose general cargo ship (see Chapter 4 of *Elements of Shipping*). The current tendency is to build more multi-purpose vessels rather than the purpose-built vessel capable of conveying only one type of cargo, to encourage flexibility of ship operation, permitting the vessel to switch from one trade to another, especially in periods of trade depression.

(k) The tendency in recent years in some countries is to rationalize the number of ports and to give priority to the development of those which fit in with modern needs: in particular to those with the ability to raise capital and provide modern berths acceptable to the market and modern tonnage.

(l) Free ports or free trade zones are areas where trade is based upon the unrestricted international exchange of goods, with customs tariffs used only as a source of revenue and not as an impediment to trade development. They are designed to attract overseas traders and manufacturers to set up business. Duty is payable only when goods move into the host country (see pp. 107–114).

To conclude our examination of future trends in international trade, one must bear in mind the growing importance of the general efficiency of ports in sustaining and developing trade. Furthermore, the economic growth of many countries is based on expansion of an export lead. This can only succeed in the long term in a highly competitive market if the international transportation distribution arrangements are efficient. Modern ports attract modern tonnage, which leads to the objective of a country having a low-cost, efficient sea-transport operation. Moreover, port location still strongly favours the port situated on a shipping lane – which thereby provides the most economical deployment of tonnage.

CHAPTER 2

Economics of international trade

In our examination of the elements of the port industry it is important that we view it against the background of international trade and thereby place the role of ports and shipping in perspective. One must bear in mind that ships carry some 99% of world trade in volume terms and almost 80% in value terms, the remainder being conveyed primarily by air. Moreover, there is evidence of a trend towards more political involvement in the international exchange of goods and less freedom of commercial trade, while fiscal policies are becoming more prevalent in the attitude of various governments towards world trade, especially relative to ports and their charging policies. Factors such as these influence the economics of international shipping and the role ports play in such a situation.

FUNCTION OF INTERNATIONAL TRADE

Trade among nations began for a variety of reasons. The haphazard distribution of natural resources around the world is one reason: some nations possess natural ores and chemical deposits in excess of their own requirements while other nations have none. For example, the UK has large reserves of coal but lacks many minerals such as nickel, copper and aluminium, and the Arab states have vast oil deposits but little else. The effects of climate on the cultivation of natural products is a second reason; some products will grow only in the tropics whereas others, such as citrus fruits, require a Mediterranean climate. Thirdly, some nations are unable to produce sufficient of a particular commodity to satisfy home demand; this is true of the USSR's wheat requirement. With the development of industry and technology, however, there arose another incentive for nations to exchange their products. It was found that it made economic sense for a nation to specialize in certain activities and to produce those goods for the production of which it enjoyed the greatest advantages; these were then exchanged for the products of nations which had advantages in other fields, giving rise to trade based on the 'law of comparative costs'.

Economists maintain that it will be advantageous for mankind if people specialize in those occupations in which they have the greatest comparative advantage or the least comparative disadvantage, leaving the production of goods and services for which they have little aptitude to others. This principle of specialization in certain trades and occupations is paramount in the theory of international trade. Nevertheless, complete specialization may never occur even if it is economically advantageous. For strategic or domestic reasons, a country may continue to produce goods in which it does not have an advantage. The benefits of specialization may also be affected by transport costs: the expense of moving goods and raw materials around the world narrows the limits within which it will be profitable to trade. Another impediment to the free flow of goods on the basis of comparative advantage is the possible introduction of artificial barriers to trade, such as tariffs or quotas.

The benefits deriving from the development of international trade are (a) a reduction in the cost of goods owing to the advantages possessed by the supplying country, (b) a greater variety of products, (c) wider markets for the producing country, thus leading to economies of large-scale production, and (d) the overall growth of trade owing to reciprocal advantages.

SURVEY OF INTERNATIONAL TRADE

There is evidence of trading between nations as far back as the sixth century BC. In those early days the exchange of goods was conducted on a 'barter' basis now known as 'compensation trade'. For example, Solomon supplied food to the Lebanon against delivery of timber with which to build the Temple, and early Phoenicians brought fabrics and dyestuffs to Cornwall in exchange for tin. A medium of exchange in the form of coins was introduced early in the fifth century BC; these were exchanged weight for weight where sufficient trust could be placed on their metallic values. This was not a foreign exchange system in the modern sense, however. By Roman times some trading was being conducted by exchange of coin, the first evidence of a foreign exchange system. Money changers such as those ejected from the Temple in Jerusalem were carrying on the dual functions of bullion dealing and foreign exchange that now form distinct but related markets. Upon the decline of the Roman Empire there was a widespread reversion to barter or the exchange of metallic coin by weight, but by the eleventh century AD money changing had once again become an important profession.

In the thirteenth century bills of exchange began to displace coin for trade purposes, creating a financial market that remained almost unchanged until the end of the eighteenth century. The importance of London was increasing throughout this period, although in the sixteenth and seventeenth centuries Antwerp and Amsterdam were probably more important. In the sixteenth century there evolved a system for forecasting future exchange rates, which in Holland, Belgium and Spain mainly took the form of betting. Mail transfers came into being after the French Revolution, but did not dislodge bills of exchange from their dominant position. Forward exchange dealing was developing throughout the nineteenth century, although in this regard London lagged behind such centres as Vienna, Berlin, Trieste and St Petersburg. With the growing influence of Great Britain in world trade, a large proportion of transactions was expressed in sterling, so that London merchants had little cause to buy or sell currencies, while abroad there was obviously need for a market in sterling against other currencies. Meanwhile, banks were developing techniques and services to facilitate the smooth conduct of international trade by establishing worldwide networks for the rapid transfer of funds and providing economic and credit information.

Just as the means of payment developed, so did the means of transport. With clippers giving way to steamers and ultimately oil-fired vessels, and with the more recent advent of container transport, the transfer of goods around the world became quicker and safer. Cargo insurance underwent a parallel development.

As the basic requirements for the growth of international trade were met, there then developed a variety of methods and expertise to assist in the conduct of that trade, for example the services of export houses specializing in certain markets, the appointment of agents overseas, direct selling by travelling sales staff, the establishment of branch offices or subsidiary companies abroad and group marketing to share expenses.

Everything would suggest that the 'law of comparative costs' could operate to its fullest extent to the benefit of all. Unfortunately, the economic and political pressures to which individual nations are subject have tended to create barriers to the free flow of goods. These include the protection of home industries by means of tariffs and quotas, the imposition of customs duties to raise revenue, the prohibition of trade with certain countries – for example, the Arab nations' boycott of firms selling to Israel – and the formation of customs unions such as EFTA and the EEC. On the other hand, the more prosperous countries have also attempted to facilitate the sale of primary products by developing countries.

COMMODITY TRADES

Any article of commerce, that is to say anything offered for sale, may be regarded as a commodity. In modern marketing, however, the term is used in a more restricted sense to describe any primary product or raw material marketed internationally, either in its original state (e.g. mineral ores, corn, cotton) or after initial processing to make it acceptable as an industrial raw material (e.g. metal ingots); this definition therefore excludes manufactured goods.

As mentioned above, the essential factors of climate, topography and accessibility have led certain areas of the world to export commodities produced in excess of local requirements. Primary producers are increasingly aware of the importance of studying the requirements of their customers and adjusting their products accordingly. Whereas producers of manufactured goods are involved in the marketing of their wares and often deal direct with retailers, very few primary producers go further than to place their produce on the market through intermediaries such as merchants, brokers or jobbers. Moreover, the 'market' for manufactures is the nationwide chain of retailers, but for commodities there are market places where buyers meet the sellers (or the merchants or brokers acting on their behalf) and bargains are struck in conformity with the self-imposed rules of the market.

Some of the most important commodity markets of the world are situated in Great Britain, and particularly in London. The prices fixed in the London markets are reported daily in the financial press, which also comments on dealings in foreign terminal markets such as New York (e.g. coffee).

Three different types of sale are practised in the London markets: sale of actual bulk of physical goods, sale by sample and sale by specification. Fruit, fish and other perishables are sold in bulk after inspection; imported frozen meat is sold by auction against sample at Smithfield; wool from Australia and New Zealand is auctioned on the Wool Exchange after inspection at the warehouse; and at the daily meeting of the London Metal Exchange members buy and sell such metals as copper, lead, tin and zinc by specification. The bullion market meets twice daily, with dealers both buying and selling gold and silver on behalf of their clients; all orders are tabled and the price is fixed to reflect the forces of supply and demand.

In markets where sale is by specification, the members' associations have devised standard specifications for various commodities. On the Metal Exchange lead is defined as 'good soft pig lead' and on the Baltic Exchange there are international standards for grain. Rubber is in the form of 'latex' or 'sheet' conforming to standards laid down by the Rubber Trading Association.

Members of any of these exclusive markets are required to comply with an established code of conduct, which takes the following form:

(a) Transactions are conducted verbally, but where the commodity is not immediately transferred to the buyer against payment, written confirmations are exchanged. These take the form of standard 'contracts' that have evolved over time and must be employed by all parties.

(b) Any dispute between buyer and seller is submitted to arbitration as laid down by the market authorities.

(c) Where any commodity is sold by specification, the actual consignment is inspected and the price adjusted to take account of any divergence from standard.

Many of these markets have evolved an important form of 'futures' contract, usually for three months ahead. A 'future' is a contract by which the seller undertakes to deliver and the buyer undertakes to accept a stipulated quantity of a standard commodity at a future date, the date and related price being fixed at the time the contract is concluded, thus enabling dealers to guard against the risk of price fluctuations.

Two types of intermediary operate in the markets – the merchant and the broker. The merchant buys from one or more suppliers and on-sells to his clients in the same way as an export merchant, while the broker buys and sells on behalf of a principal and is paid a 'brokerage'. In some markets there are separate brokers for buying and selling. Where the commodity is sold by auction, the auctioneer is considered to be the agent of both buyer and seller. In many commodity transactions the goods are sold while still in transit, so that in effect the buyer purchases the documents of title and not the goods themselves. The main document involved is the bill of lading (for further details see *Elements of Shipping* and *Elements of Export Practice*).

FLOW OF MANUFACTURED GOODS

As the developed countries began to specialize increasingly in manufacture, they reached a point where they no longer produced enough raw materials for their industries or food for their peoples. In consequence, they exported manufactured goods in exchange for raw materials and foodstuffs. The increase in specialization and the growth of technology resulted in the exchange of technical products between the more industrialized countries, so that manufactures were exported not only to buy raw materials and food but also in exchange for other technical products.

Scientific research and technological development have brought about an enormous increase in the volume and variety of manufactured goods. This has led to a rapid growth in the exchange of manufactured goods between industrialized countries, but it has also resulted in the development of synthetic substitutes for many natural products, such as synthetic rubber, plastics and man-made fibres. As a consequence, many primary producers have sought to acquire manufacturing expertise and to become at least partly industrialized.

The growth and direction of international trade are thus influenced by a multiplicity of factors: comparative advantage, which will encourage a country to specialize in certain products; political factors, where governments seek to control the movement of goods either to protect the value of the currency or for strategic reasons; the desire to diversify the economy, especially where the country has been dependent on a single product; and finally, a monopoly of the supply of an essential product by one country.

MULTINATIONAL COMPANIES

As world trade and its attendant risks increased, many firms realized the need to adopt an international strategy. Whereas previously they had built plant overseas whenever an export market reached sufficient size to support the investment, now they ensured that they had a plant wherever market analysis indicated a potential need. This change in policy has led to the creation of large multinational companies. As one company put it, 'We are no longer a British company with some international business but a British-based international organization'. The economic factors which have influenced the development of multinational corporations are (a) the use of local products, (b) savings in freight costs, (c) the availability of cheaper local labour, (d) tax concessions and available finance, (e) technical collaboration to spread development costs and secure new products, (f) the provision of more reliable demonstration, installation, delivery, repair and maintenance services from local facilities and (g) higher profits. These are coupled with strategic considerations such as (i) the need to control facilities of a certain size so as to gain market power and avoid the dispersion of resources, (ii) economies of scale in central services and research, (iii) fiscal advantages obtained by transferring goods at the most advantageous prices in order to minimize taxation, (iv) the existence of investment grants and (v) the possibility of shifting liquid capital to hedge against currency devaluations. Host countries welcome the establishment of subsidiaries of multinational companies because they bring employment, new technology and increased growth. They may or may not increase exports or imports. At the same time, host countries are wary of the possibility of price manipulation between members of the group, particularly in order to show profits where tax is lowest.

Shipping has played a major role in the development of multinational companies. Many such companies own or charter their own fleet so that they may convey raw materials and/or manufactured goods at cost rather than at liner conference rates. Moreover, they have complete control over schedules, with many of them owning or operating their own maritime terminals. All these factors aid the competitiveness of the product in the international market-place. The development of new activities and the expansion of existing ones by multinational corporations have added the exchange of skills and technology to the exchange of goods and services which make up international trade.

MAJOR TRADING AREAS OF THE WORLD

There are three main types of economy:

(a) Free enterprise economies, where government control is at a minimum and trade and industry are run largely by private enterprise; the best example is the USA, but many of the developing countries also have this type of economy.

(b) Mixed economies, where some industries are state owned but many others and most trading activities are in the hands of private firms. The UK provides a good example of this type, although in fact all advanced nations and many developing countries have at least some state-run industry.

(c) Planned economies, where the state runs all industry and commerce except for tiny pockets of free enterprise, such as the smallholdings on which peasants are allowed to grow a few vegetables to sell for cash. This sort of economy is generally communist controlled and its international trade is conducted by state trading enterprises.

Trading patterns have gradually changed since the end of the Second World War. In the past, Western nations specialized in industrial products to exchange for the raw materials and food they required, while primary producers relied upon their sales of natural produce to buy industrial goods. Some countries with a favourable climate were able to combine industrial growth with the production of much of their food requirement.

The UK is probably the best example of a country which relied almost entirely on the export of its manufactures in exchange for raw materials and food. Under the colonial system this was a very satisfactory arrangement for Britain, but with the end of the Empire the newly independent nations began to cast their net more widely in seeking buyers for their produce and suppliers of their industrial needs. At the same time they sought to diversify their economies and develop some industry.

The basic geographical pattern of produce remains largely unchanged for reasons of climate and the location of raw materials – that is, Western Europe and North America for industrial goods;

South America for coffee and rubber (Brazil), wheat and beef (Argentina) and minerals such as copper (Peru); the Near East for rubber and tin; Australasia for wool and mutton; and Africa for timber, cocoa and vegetable oils. However, these divisions are no longer as sharply defined as they were previously. Japan has entered the list of manufacturing countries in a big way; the Arab nations have developed their oil production; and countries in South America, Africa and the Near East have begun to establish industries. At the same time, the Western nations have attempted to come closer to self-sufficiency in food and to intensify the search for minerals at home; examples of this are the encouragement of agriculture and the search for oil in the UK and the development of fruit and vegetable cultivation in countries bordering the Mediterranean. The interchange of goods between nations is thus expanding, diversifying and moving away from the previous clearly defined paths.

PREFERENTIAL TRADING GROUPS

Since the very beginning of international trade, certain trading groups have felt a desire to join together for mutual protection and assistance. An early example of this was the Hanseatic League founded in northern Germany during the thirteenth century, an arrangement that came to an end upon the disintegration of Germany as a result of the Thirty Years War (1618–48).

The more important preferential trading groups of modern times may be summarized as follows.

British Commonwealth

This was a free trade area of considerable importance, comprising the members of the British Commonwealth of Nations. As their economies became more highly developed, however, member nations ceased to maintain the system of preferences and sought a wider sphere of trading activity. The vestiges of the Commonwealth preferences system disappeared when the UK joined the European Economic Community in 1973.

European Free Trade Association (EFTA)

The UK was disinclined to join the EEC at its inception in 1957, as the member states wished to go far beyond the removal of customs barriers. Accordingly, Great Britain, Norway, Sweden, Denmark, Portugal, Austria and Switzerland signed the Stockholm Convention in 1959 establishing the European Free Trade Association, whereby they agreed to reduce import duties among themselves and to maintain their individual tariffs towards non-member countries. Finland became an associate member in 1961 and Iceland a full member in 1970. Now that Denmark and the UK have joined the EEC, the significance of EFTA has declined considerably.

European Economic Community (EEC)

As the reconstruction of Europe was beginning after the end of the Second World War, there emerged the idea of a supranational European community based initially on economic union but developing towards political union. It evolved through the following stages:

(a) Belgium, the Netherlands and Luxembourg formed the Benelux Customs Union in 1948.

(b) The European Payments Union was set up in 1950 to help solve the balance of payments problems of individual countries.

(c) In 1952 six countries – Belgium, France, West Germany, Italy, Luxembourg and the Netherlands – joined together to form the European Coal and Steel Community.

(d) In 1957 these six nations signed the Treaty of Rome by which they agreed to form the EEC, which came into existence on 1 January 1958.

The Treaty provided for the removal of customs barriers and other obstacles to trade between member states, the introduction of a common external tariff towards third countries and common policies for agriculture and transport. Plans were also made for the harmonization of taxation; for example, the French VAT system was to be adopted by the other members.

On 1 January 1973 the UK, Denmark and Ireland became full members of the EEC. Current membership includes: Belgium, Denmark, France, Greece, Ireland, Italy, Luxembourg, the Netherlands, Portugal, Spain, the UK and West Germany.

Council for Mutual Economic Aid

Set up in 1949, the Council for Mutual Economic Aid (CMEA or Comecon) groups together the USSR, Poland, Romania, the German Democratic Republic, Czechoslovakia, Hungary, Bulgaria, Mongolia, Cuba and Vietnam. Although not a member, Yugoslavia enjoys special status that enables it to participate in certain spheres of Comecon's activities. The Council aims to attain self-sufficiency through the complementary development of member countries' economies on the basis of central planning. In its early years it contented itself with co-ordinating the foreign trade of member countries, many of which have been reluctant to agree to further proposals for integration.

The benefits to be derived from free trade areas stem from the increased market opened to members, especially where the area has an affluent population. Their advantages were soon appreciated, and free trade areas have been set up in various parts of the world; it is estimated that about two-thirds of world trade is already conducted between such groups.

Besides EFTA, the EEC and Comecon, the following free trade areas have been created:

(a) Latin American Free Trade Association (LAFTA), comprising Brazil, Bolivia, Mexico, Argentina, Colombia, Peru, Venezuela, Chile, Ecuador, Uruguay and Paraguay; in 1983 LAFTA was replaced by the Latin American Integration Association (ALADI), a less ambitious and more flexible form of co-operation.

(b) Central American Common Market (CACM), whose members are Guatemala, El Salvador, Honduras, Nicaragua and Costa Rica.

(c) Caribbean Free Trade Association (CARIFTA), the forerunner of the present Caribbean Community and Common Market (CARICOM) which comprises Antigua, Barbados, Belize, Dominica, Grenada, Guyana, Jamaica, Montserrat, St Christopher–Nevis–Anguilla, St Lucia, St Vincent, and the Grenadines, and Trinidad and Tobago.

The activities of these various trading groups (with the exception of Comecon) have to conform to the principles laid down in the General Agreement on Tariffs and Trade (GATT) which requires its signatories:

(a) To concert together to achieve a mutual reduction of tariff barriers and preferences

(b) To avoid discrimination by means of tariffs against foreign products which compete with home products

(c) To abolish quantitative controls and

(d) To remove existing restrictions imposed by exchange control.

Although several of these rules have been given practical application as trade has been liberalized, it is unlikely that the general requirements of GATT will be implemented in the present state of world trade.

CHAPTER 3

Economics of port design and layout

This chapter outlines the basic factors that are likely to influence the design of modern ports and their infrastructure compatible with the market needs. It is not a technical assessment but primarily an evaluation of the economic and related factors relevant to efficient port design; it should be read in conjunction with Chapter 7 which deals with port investment criteria. The latter part of the chapter examines various types of berth.

INFLUENCE OF COST, CONSTRUCTION AND SAFETY FACTORS

Let us first review the trends stemming from developments of the past decade which will influence port design and its infrastructure – especially berths – in the 1980s and beyond, and later the berth and cargo-handling factors.

(a) Extensive legislation has been adopted during the past 20 years regarding the design of port facilities and their scale of operation including the transport units involved in both ship and road/rail/waterway distribution. Particular emphasis has been placed on the control of pollution, movement of dangerous cargo, annual survey of cargo-handling equipment, conditions of employment of dock labour, certification of container, and so on. Organizations closely involved include the International Labour Organization (ILO), the International Maritime Organization (IMO) and the International Cargo Handling Co-ordination Association (ICHA), all described in Chapter 13.

(b) The level of dock labour will continue to fall in the next decade with greater emphasis on the versatility of dock labour employment and capital-intensive cargo-handling technique and cargo unitization.

(c) Dock labour employment conditions will become more stringent, with better staff accommodation provision and more safeguards on working conditions under the aegis of 'safety at work'.

(d) Cargo-handling equipment is subject to increasing stringency in terms of certification and annual examination of equipment to ensure that it is operationally safe.

(e) Regulations regarding areas where dangerous classified cargo may be handled and the requisite quantities/operational requirements/handling precautions are becoming more stringent.

(f) Port control systems as described in Chapter 8 are an essential feature of modern port management techniques involving both port operators and ship management. Radar and computers feature prominently in the more modern systems.

(g) Computerization (see pp. 223–225) now features more and more in the efficient management of the port. It is involved in all areas of the business and is closely involved in container berth operation relative to the monitoring of the container unit.

(h) The development of the combined transport operation involving Ro/Ro units and containerization will influence port layout and design and encourage more traffic to be customs cleared at an inland clearance depot away from the port area.

(i) The provision of purpose-built berths for particular bulk cargoes such as coal, oil, chemicals, and so on will continue to be made and existing ones modernized (see pp. 32–44). This may involve extensive storage facilities at the berth which may be leased from the port authority.

(j) Maritime canals and inland waterways are likely to play a more important role in the 1980s and beyond. This is particularly so in the Western European ports of Rotterdam, Antwerp, Dunkerque, Caen, Rouen, and so on. Similar remarks apply to many African and Asian ports where overside loading into lighterage forms a large part of the general cargo business. Likewise it applies to LASH and BACO barge carrier concepts (see pp. 69–71).

(k) The size and carrying capacity of many types of vessel is likely to continue to increase. Port authorities must give particular attention to this area through the development of longer and deeper berths of greater handling capacity. Coal carriers are an example, reaching a capacity of 300 000 d.w.t. as the world market for coal grows (see pp. 35–36). Similar remarks apply to the Ro/Ro vessel, many of which are now over 10 000 d.w.t.

In our consideration of the berth and general cargo-handling factors one must bear in mind that in general terms traffic through a port will be either 'general' or 'bulk'. The latter is easier to define; the former covers greater variety. General cargo is heterogeneous, both in type and shape, but in many cases unitization, involving the formation of such heterogeneous loads into unit form, has been introduced to make handling easier, particularly by mechanical means.

Increase in tonnage per man-hour has come from these 'new', quicker methods of cargo handling – mechanization and unit loading – both of which give greater economies in scale and faster operations on the general cargo berths.

Mechanization of handling of general cargo has meant changes in the layout of our terminals, notably the basic parameters associated with the design of transit sheds and warehouses (from a commercial operations rather than a civil engineering point of view) and their location on the terminal.

Basically a transit shed is provided for goods in transit, not storage. The use of mobile trucks, fork lifts, mobile cranes, etc. has changed the optimum layout for sheds and port areas requiring the following:

(a) Wider, larger quay aprons.
(b) Flat paving on aprons and other working areas.
(c) More shed space for single-height short-term storage.
(d) Single-storey transit sheds where land availability permits.
(e) Layout of shed for cargo space and ease of cargo-handling equipment movement.
(f) Covered loading areas for lorries or railway wagons.
(g) Easily operated sliding doors of suitable size for cargo-handling equipment access and through movement.
(h) Fewer internal (pillar) supports.
(i) Location of offices, etc. off the shed floor.
(j) Better lighting and ventilation.
(k) Adequate fire protection and control.
(l) Development of computerized techniques where practicable and viable.

The transit shed should be cleared as near as possible at the end of each shift: the maximum time for any goods in the transit shed should be 72 hours with financial incentives to the importer for less and demurrage payments when the period is exceeded. Damaged or disputed goods must be cleared away from the quay apron as soon as possible to lessen disputes on demurage and so on.

Transit sheds encompass the following facilities: general cargo areas; customs control areas; cargo separation areas; dirty cargo areas; lock-up for high value cargo, mails, etc; and special stow items, which may include a bonded area.

It is unusual for transit sheds to be used for such items as refrigerated goods, firearms, explosives, contaminants, livestock, chemicals, and so on.

Many ports still use direct delivery from the ship to the inland transport system, which means that the road/rail vehicles must be on the quay apron to receive goods directly from the discharge hook crane. This practice should be limited to special circumstances as it may lead to: congestion problems of road/rail vehicles intermingling with the 'on berth' mechanical handling equipment; problems with documentation and clearance of the goods; and hold-ups in general caused by disputes on quantity and actual condition of cargo being loaded onto road/rail vehicles. Most general cargoes being discharged/loaded on the ship will require checking (tallying)/sorting and these operations would best be carried out away from the immediate quay apron, probably inside a transit shed. However, direct delivery from the ship is practised in many ports with little adverse effect – in fact it speeds up cargo discharge arrangements.

Two types of warehouse are available for the covered storage of imported cargo: the general and the bonded warehouse. Both are situated outside the port working area. This imposes the minimum of interference to the smooth flow of goods from the ship working area to clearance of the dock gate.

The general warehouse prime function is the storage of goods. It may also offer a sampling and packaging service. Many warehouses are managed by the wholesaler/importer – in some countries this is a marketing board using the accommodation as a distribution depot to convey their goods to the market/retailer. An increasing number of such warehouses are cold stores (see pp. 36–37).

A bonded warehouse is under customs surveillance and houses dutiable cargo such as spirits, carpets or tobacco which may be stored on importation and withdrawn at the importer's convenience on payment of the relevant duty. The importer pays the customs duty only at the time of withdrawal of the goods. This enables the importer to import substantial quantities of highly dutiable cargo at favourable prices. By so doing he eliminates the heavy financial burden of paying customs duty at the time of importation. The importer is thus able to withdraw the goods at a time convenient to himself, at which stage the duty is paid only on the goods released from the bond. Such warehouses also provide a sampling and processing of goods service such as bottling of spirits which have arrived in container tanks. Many importers also use the accommodation as a distribution point for their clients. It is stressed that the bonded warehouse is under strict customs surveillance and only when the cargo duty has been paid are the goods released from the customs bond.

Weighing facilities in the form of a weighbridge are normally supplied at the port. In some cases this is a requirement of the government in an attempt to control the axle and total weights of road vehicles when the goods are being imported in container units and Ro/Ro traffic.

The port authority would not normally decide on the type of inland transport vehicle used but obviously the importer/exporter would have to ensure that his vehicle can be handled satisfactorily. It is most important that good internal road systems in the port area together with vehicle parking systems must be provided by the port authority. Marshalling areas, good signposting and traffic control are imperative to the modern port.

In more recent years there has been a growing preference for road rather than rail distribution in many ports, especially with general cargo and containerization. With the newer developments of Ro/Ro and container services together with inland sorting depots, this trend is likely to continue in many ports throughout the world.

Port authorities give a service to any user, but obviously can influence the inland transport mode by giving an incentive to pre-pack goods before arrival in the dock area. An example arises in palletized consignments.

Traffic through a port may be classified as 'general' or 'bulk'. The specialist port, unlike the general cargo port, in order to obtain maximum efficiency tends to cater for a single (or at least related) commodity. Economically such specialization has its advantages because both manpower and capital can be channelled to only the specialized ships and cargoes using the port. Quicker turn-round for ships and reduced handling costs for cargoes are the main aim of the port management. Clearly, the first and most vital aspect for a specialized port is the continued availability and world importance of its specialized traffic.

There are basically two types of specialized port: the terminal and the through port.

There are very few cargoes which actually terminate in the port area but there are many which are transformed into some other related commodity in seaboard industries. These may be defined as:

(a) Those with processing plant located within or very near to the port area.

(b) Those that act as a partial storage area only and use some other transport media to move goods/passengers to processing plant or destination.

In both cases above it is necessary to have some form of storage area to maintain stocks and to use the port itself as a header tank to maintain an even flow of raw materials. Development has been towards larger specialized ships and quicker turn-round, i.e. greater utilization of the port facilities. However, this has brought with it the need for a much better service from inland transport services.

In many cases the owner/user of the specialized berth owns/operates his own inland transport system. Such terminals may be container, Ro/Ro, or passenger. The container, Ro/Ro and passenger terminals require speed of ship turn-round and limited storage area. The maintenance of a steady traffic flow is the important consideration in all the four terminals. The oil terminal, however, requires extensive storage facilities.

The modern specialist port uses a new area for development and in most cases the operators have not made any attempt to utilize old existing port structures. If we consider the traditional port operation it becomes obvious that it does not fit into the modern concept of specialist port working. This is due to the type of ship handled, cargo-handling equipment, dock labour organization and so on. Redevelopment of existing port areas is usually confined to unit load/passenger operations where storage areas need only be relatively small and existing inland transport terminals may be used.

Most specialized ports are highly capital intensive as they have special equipment for the fast moving of a particular commodity and have a low in number but very specialized manpower resource.

Port development will almost certainly aim to accommodate the larger, specialized bulk carriers. Investment in specialist facilities at deep water harbours will be justified as industrial users of bulk raw materials concentrate new developments in the port areas. Partial processing for raw materials has and will increase the unit value of bulk cargoes by reducing the waste element in the shipments, such as pelletization of iron ore.

An increasing degree of integration of raw material production, partial processing, deep sea transportation, terminal development and larger scale manufacturing complexes will be seen in the major bulk trades. The port is just part of the total process of moving the goods from producer to manufacturing unit.

We will now examine the factors which must be considered in the layout of a berth and in so doing the reader must have regard to the foregoing analysis.

FACTORS DETERMINING BERTH LAYOUT

In considering the range of factors which determine the layout of a berth, it is important to bear in mind that it tends to be classified as a general cargo or bulk cargo berth. This classification can be varied to be either 'general' or 'specialized'. The specialist port, unlike the general cargo port, in order to obtain maximum efficiency tends to cater for a single (or at least related) commodity. However, numerous factors – which we will now examine – determine a berth layout. In examining them it is suggested that the reader reconciles these factors with the berth layouts of differing types found on pp. 32–44.

Type and size of vessel using the berth. In particular the overall length of the ship; the type/classification of the vessel such as whether it is a container vessel or bulk carrier; the draught of the vessel; shipboard cargo-handling equipment; and speed of ship turn-round time.

The availability of land, which includes reclaimable land. Land availability at a port tends to be limited and the best use should be made of it.

In berth layout design particular emphasis should be placed on catering for future development and expansion. This may include land reclamation. It also takes in new technology, including computers.

The depth of water serving the berth. Port dredging is an expensive operation and the tendency is for vessels to become larger and of deeper draught.

The type/classification of cargo to be handled at the berth. It may be containers; bulk cargo such as oil, grain, ore; Ro/Ro vehicles; general cargo (break bulk); chemical carriers; and so on. Alternatively, it may be a multi-purpose berth. For dangerous classified bulk cargo, special precautions are necessary, requiring for example the oil terminal operations to be isolated from the general cargo berths and to be some distance away from any residential property. Passenger terminals require extensive facilities for immigration and customs needs together with passenger lounge amenities. The passenger terminal layout will largely depend on the volume and nature of the passenger traffic handled including cars, coaches, cyclists and foot passengers, and on whether it is subject to seasonal variations.

The organization of the dock labour needs. With the growing development of the capital-intensive berth operation involving extensive cargo-handling mechanization and limited dock labour content, the tendency has been for far fewer cargo-handling staff on the berth/quayside but with higher technical specialized skills.

The volume of cargo to be handled at the berth, its classification; the nature of handling required such as containers, Ro/Ro vehicles; loose cargo; and a detailed analysis of the quantity each week or working day. This will determine the resources needed to handle such cargo in terms of dock labour, customs, distribution arrangements, cargo-handling equipment and so on.

The overland transport system will have a direct bearing on the design of the terminal/berth. This includes the volume of cargo to be handled through the overland transport system; the distance from/to the inland cargo source to the port location; the availability of existing land transportation resources; the geographical port location; the type of ship using the berth such as a container vessel, oil tanker or Ro/Ro ferry will largely determine the overland transportation arrangements; the nature of the cargo/product; the climatic conditions which could very much influence the working hours of the dock labour at the berth; and finally the stock pile requirement of the shippers. With regard to the latter point, the more frequent the service the less the need to carry large stocks by the shipper with the attendant risk of obsolescence and stock deterioration. Such a practice is called inventory control.

Traffic analysis is an important factor and requires to be carefully evaluated to determine seasonal variations and the resources required to handle such merchandise. Particular attention should be given to the traffic variations by individual commodity and likely future trends.

The nature of the cargo-handling equipment required and likely changes in the future in terms of technology.

The degree of overside loading/discharge involving lighterage. This will help speed up the turn-round of vessels in port and reduce the volume of cargo passing over the quay/berth. Some vessels like LASH (see pp. 69–71) convey the barge throughout the voyage and release them on arrival at the destination port.

The customs requirements and whether the customs examination is undertaken at the port or whether the cargo passes through the port under bond to an ICD/CFS.

The amount of capital available and the method of funding. It may be by bank loan; using the port authority reserves; a government loan; a government subsidy or grant; and so on. The tendency today is for the port authority to bear the cost of the berth provision and lease the cargo-handling equipment.

The method of discharge from the vessel and the degree of customs examination ashore. For general cargo the cargo is discharged and placed on the berth/quay/transit shed pending customs examination/clearance which is dependent on availability of documents. Following customs clearance the cargo is despatched to the importer/buyer/consignee, which usually involves a clearing agent undertaking the customs clearance arrangements. This can take several days. Meanwhile the cargo is occupying valuable berth/quay/transit shed space. It may be a container; loose break/bulk cargo; road trailer; pallet; and so on. Modernization of cargo-handling techniques involving capital intensive methods, and more unitization of cargo, coupled with computerization of documentation and customs, should speed up the customs clearance process. In some situations involving bulk cargo shipment, such as rice, the ship can be cleared by customs quickly after arrival at the berth, and thereafter direct delivery from the vessel to the barge, road vehicle or railway wagon may proceed. The speed of cargo discharge in this situation is very much dependent on available transportation resources and on how well they are organized. Adequate pre-planning is essential.

The role of the port and its infrastructure within the national and international economy. Port efficiency is essential: it aids development of a country's economy and fosters trade expansion. Many ports throughout the world are owned and operated by government or subject to government funding. Thus governments are taking a greater interest in their ports to help develop their economy and provide adequate funds for their continuing modernization and expansion. Accordingly they feature in a nation's economic plan, which may be of five years' duration.

The total cost of the project. It may be a new berth, or modernization of an existing one. Usually various options are evaluated to decide on the most acceptable berth layout and infrastructure. Consultation usually takes place with the port users and special attention is paid to future trade/operational developments and needs. The financial evaluation takes account of both short-term and long-term requirements to operate the berth on a profitable basis. It takes account of cost savings achieved through closure of any other berth(s) and likewise the reduced handling cost inherent in the berth modernization.

Competition with other ports. Where a port authority is keen to remain competitive with other ports in the area/country it will endeavour to have the facilities and berth layout which will be competitive and acceptable to the market.

Statutory regulations. Extensive legislation exists in the provision and operation of ports. This includes particularly health and safety aspects, safe working loads of cargo-handling equipment, berth construction, equipment maintenance, and so on. The legislation varies by country and circumstance.

Close liaison must be maintained with the port users and in most ports a liaison committee exists which meets to discuss common problems with a view to solving them to the mutual satisfaction of all concerned. This involves trade associations, shippers' councils, chambers of commerce, port users' associations, liner conference, government agencies, customs, port security, marketing boards, shippers' associations, and so on. Such organizations should be consulted on port modernization and development to ensure thereby that the most acceptable layout is provided. In many situations a liner conference or trade association may have requested improved or new berth facilities to cater for the modern tonnage with its attendant improved port efficiency and potential trade development. Port users include agents, shipbrokers, customs, police, stevedores, shipowners, road operators, railway companies, lighterage/barge companies, ship repair companies, ship chandlers, pilotage associations, P & I clubs, and so on.

Consultants' reports and recommendations and market research reports should be considered in any port improvement scheme. Some major ports commission consultants to undertake a study of the existing port facilities/berth layout and make recommendations with regard to future improvements. This may extend to undertaking market research to determine existing port users' views and potential traffic development.

Major port authorities tend to have a three or five year business plan featuring investment schemes. Any berth layout improvement should be included in such a business plan to ensure adequate capital provision is available.

The berth layout should be so designed as to avoid or reduce to a minimum any contra-operational movements as these tend to slow up the smooth flow of cargo to or from the ship and thereby create an impediment to smooth working. Most general cargo berths deal with both export and import cargoes.

Climatic conditions. These will influence or determine access to and from the port by the vessels and the periods during which ships can be loaded or discharged in conditions of safety. For example, some ports are ice bound in the winter, while in the Middle East, dock working ceases during the period of noon in the summer owing to the extreme heat.

Adequate back-up facilities should be available for specific berths such as those dealing with containers, Ro/Ro traffic, break bulk cargo and palletized consignments.

In concluding our review of the factors influencing port layout it is appropriate to mention that as port modernization progresses in the next decade it will bring special problems. It will require specialized dock labour low in number, but adequately trained. As dock labour requirements are reduced it will bring social problems and the need to find such labour alternative work, probably outside the port environment. Furthermore, as technology develops further it may pose environmental problems, especially the handling of dangerous classified cargoes and the location of berths dealing with such commodities. Undoubtedly, governments will become increasingly involved through discussion with various international organizations to resolve such problems.

Finally, one must strive to design the most efficient berth layout having regard to the traffic flow, overall cost and likely developments. This includes the ongoing development of the combined transport operation.

TYPES OF BERTH

We will now examine a number of types of berth and their salient features.

Bulk dry cargo berths

These are designed for one particular product or a range of dry cargo products.

An example is found in Durban harbour, where the multi-purpose multi-product berth specializes in the handling of dry cargo commodities ranging from 1000 to 5000 ton lots. The berth is equipped to handle both exports and imports.

The terminal handles both agricultural and mineral products which, depending on their density and handling characteristics, can be shipped at a rate ranging from 500 to 1000 tons/hour, and discharged at 200 to 350 tons/hour. Twenty silos are available with a total capacity of 30 500 tons for agricultural products including rice, maize, wheat, malt, sunflower seeds, animal feed pellets, and so on. A bagging plant facility exists for both import and export cargoes.

The mineral section has a series of eleven covered concrete bins providing a total storage capacity of 60 000 tons for minerals at a density of 1.75 tons/m^3. Typical products handled include fluorspar, cement, clinker andalusite, vanadium slag, sponge iron, clays, etc. A number of small bins are used to provide the flexibility required in handling of the different grades. A third storage plant for soda-ash imports has two silos with a total storage capacity of 12 000 tons and a bagging facility. The terminals are well served by both rail and road.

Bulk dry-and-wet cargo berth

Another berth in Durban harbour is equipped to handle both dry and wet cargoes in bulk.

The dry cargo storage comprises 18 concrete silos of varying sizes, the largest being 67 m high, all specially designed to handle products with difficult flow characteristics. The silos are divided into two sections, the one for agricultural products being capable of receiving 7000 tons by road or rail. Shiploading of dry cargoes is undertaken by conveyor belts operating at 230 m/min to achieve a loading rate of 650 tons/hour.

On the liquid cargo side, there are some nine tanks with a total capacity of 5564 m^3 for the handling of vegetable oils both for export and import. Cargo can be received/despatched by both road and rail, and vessels are loaded/discharged at 250 tons/hour. Pipelines link the storage tanks with some three berths. The berth draught is 10 m, thus permitting a vessel of 37 000 d.w.t. to be handled.

Cargoes handled include maize and maize products, sorghum, ground nuts, sunflower seeds, oil cakes, wheat bran, citrus pulp, bagasse, soya beans, chrome ore, andalusite, anthracite, phosphates and vanadium slag. Liquid cargoes include maize, groundnut, sunflower, soya and rapeseed oil.

Bulk liquid berths

The volume of bulk liquid trades has increased substantially in recent years and this trend is likely to continue. Ports have played a major role in the development of these markets through the provision of specialized berths to handle one particular product with its associated infrastructure, especially storage plant, or a multi-purpose, multi-product berth with modern handling techniques.

An example of a bulk liquid/storage facility is found at Table Bay Harbour, Cape Town where Cape Chemical Storage (Pty) Ltd have such a facility. It is operated on a common user basis both for handling and storage facilities. The chemical carriers dock at the oil tanker berths and the product is transferred by stainless steel pipeline to the bulk chemical storage tanks. The storage tanks are provided with metering measuring equipment and can be blanketed with an inert gas if required. The three tanks have a capacity of 2500 m^3 and are epoxy lined. The product can be moved into or out of the tanks by road, rail or sea. Any chemical with a high flash point in shipments of about 3000 tons each can be handled at a discharge rate of 400 tons/hour.

At another site in Table Bay Harbour a total of 57 tanks of

varying sizes are provided. They handle chemical products of both high and low flash points. The tanks are connected by pipeline to some four common user berths. Facilities available include heated, coated and lined tanks, nitrogen blankets, product driers, filtration, blending and drumming, together with a bonded storage.

At the Port of Felixstowe the main tankship berth is suitable for tankers of up to 180 m (600 ft) in length and up to 25 000 d.w.t. in a least depth of 9.1 m (30 ft) LWOST; a second berth for tankships of up to 20 000 d.w.t. in a least depth of 7 m (22 ft) LWOST is also available.

The bulk liquid storage terminal can offer facilities for all types of bulk liquid products passing through Felixstowe. Three tank farms are operational. Number one tank farm, with an aggregate capacity of 12 000 Cubic Metres (CBM), contains tanks with various capacities down to as low as 30 CBM; some of these are lined while others are insulated and fitted with heating coils. This area is used for storing high-flash-point products and the tanks are particularly suitable for the storage of vegetable and fuel oils, emulsions, detergents and fatty-acid-type products. Tank farms number two and three are of more recent construction and have been designed specifically to take low-flash-point products.

Tank farm number two contains tanks fitted with mild steel pipelines which are mainly suitable for clean products. A section of this farm contains a number of small tanks holding speciality products moved in and out only by road tanker, mainly via Ro/Ro ferries using the port. Tank farm number three contains mild steel tanks fitted with stainless steel pipelines, a system which offers considerable flexibility. The tanks can be readily adapted by applying internal coatings of lacquer, or some suitable coating, in order to store sensitive or aggressive products. The pipelines may be easily and efficiently cleaned after use, making the installation particularly suitable for short-term use or spot hire. Over the whole installation tank sizes vary from 20 to 5000 CBM, providing a total capacity in the three tank farms of approximately 100 000 CBM in 166 tanks.

Additional tanks are made of glass fibre reinforced polypropylene, externally insulated and heated, using hot water circulated through internal stainless steel coils, and they are used to store food grade products. All tanks, especially those of 200 CBM and below are equipped to receive products from road tank trailers or container tanks, arriving off the Ro/Ro ferry services using the port. Number three tank farm also contains a modern petroleum loading system for road tankers; high-speed loading pumps are provided, each loading point being fitted with ticket printing facilities.

The facilities of the bulk liquid storage terminal include one 100 mm (4 in) and three 150 mm (6 in) bore stainless steel import/export pipelines, which are provided with up-to-date piping equipment, together with steam cleaning and flushing arrangements. Other petroleum solvents and industrial spirit import pipelines connect the tanker jetty to the tank farms and will be extended to connect up with future tankage. Among the facilities are: provisions for loading and discharging road tankers; demountable tanks; drum filling; extensive import duty approved hydrocarbon spirit bonded warehouses, including a Customs-approved compound for the storage of drummed products; provision for nitrogen blanketing and transfers between tanks; modern steam-raising plant with facilities for steam cleaning and cold or hot water washing for road tanks and containers.

Coal berths

The world market for coal is likely to rise substantially in the next decade and the capacity of the coal carrier could rise ultimately to 300 000 d.w.t. By 1985 the largest coal carrier was 175 000 d.w.t. with the most common capacity varying between 60 000 d.w.t. and 80 000 d.w.t. Many vessels, however, are less than 40 000 d.w.t. and are playing a major role in coal distribution worldwide. The coal is conveyed either in a bulk carrier or combined carriers of the ore/bulk/oil type (OBOs).

The most modern method of loading the coal carrier is by conveyor system. This may be situated at the berth/quayside or at a jetty, the latter being likely to be industrially owned and managed. Coal would arrive at the port by railway wagon.

An example is found in Richards Bay coal terminal in South Africa. The two berths total 700 m long and are situated at a terminal comprising a railway exchange yard of 36 ha and a 67 ha coal stacking site. Two tandem truck tipplers operate on parallel tracks to deal with the two 84 wagon unit trains. Each tippler, on which the wagons are placed, empties a pair of wagons in 90 seconds, so that the 84 wagon long train can be unloaded in 1 hour. From the tipplers the coal is transported by a conveyor belt to the stacks.

The various types or grades of coal for each shipment at the loading berths are reclaimed from the stacks by a stacker/reclaimers, and dropped into a yard conveyor belt which feeds into a surge bin or silo. Here the coal is picked up on the wharf conveyor belt to the shiploaders at which stage it is spread by chute into the holds of the waiting ships and is thus trimmed simultaneously. Each shiploader has a capacity of 6500 tons/hour so that a 100 000 d.w.t. vessel can be loaded in less than 24 hours.

Modern coal discharging berths exist in the Port of Rotterdam. Coal discharge is undertaken by grabs which have a lifting capacity of 85 tons. Each crane is equipped with a grab which can handle 4000 tons/hour. Vessels having a draught ranging from 11 to 21 m may use the four coal berths available.

Among the coal exporting countries Australia has a port where vessels of over 100 000 d.w.t. can load. An example is Hay Point in Australia, which is equipped to handle coal carriers of up to 150 000 d.w.t. The coal trade from the USA is confined to vessels from 60 000 to 80 000 d.w.t. because of the limited depth of the East Coast ports and the restrictions imposed by the Panama Canal. Poland has coal ports for carriers up to 100 000 d.w.t.

Short-haul coal carriers do exist, as, for example, those operated by the Canadian Transport, which are equipped with self-unloading machinery in common with many other lakes vessels in Canadian waters.

The coal is distributed from the port by road, rail and barge – the latter two methods being the most popular and economic. However, an increasing proportion of coal is now being transported overland or subsea by pipeline in North America, in the form of coal slurry.

Cold store terminal

The development of refrigerated cargoes tends to be very much on the increase and a growing number of ports are equipped with a cold store. An example of one is found in Kuwait, which has twenty cold rooms independently operated with a total volume of 30 000 m^3 and an artificial banana ripening plant. Another cold store plant is provided at Jeddah. At Riyadh, Saudi Arabia the 12 000 m^3 cold store is fully computerized. Facilities in hot climates such as those described provide the most exacting conditions under which cold stores operate. Such cold stores operate in conjunction with refrigerated container or purpose-built refrigerated vessels.

Container berths

Container handling equipment is fully explained in Chapter 5 but it is appropriate to consider a modern container berth. Such a facility exists at the Port of Felixstowe – Languard Container Terminal – a brief description of which now follows.

Opened in 1967, this was the first operational container terminal in the UK; in 1983 it was re-equipped and reorganized utilizing rubber-tyred gantry cranes in the container parks in place of straddle carriers. These machines have a 35 tonne capacity and are each capable of stacking containers six wide and one over three high. Felixstowe was the first UK port to utilize such a system and the first in Europe to change to a solely mobile gantry system. Further capital investment was made in 1981 with the introduction of a computer-assisted container control system. A new control building was completed in 1984.

The terminal has a quay length of 469.4 m (1540 ft) and is equipped with one 40 tonne and two 30 tonne capacity rail-mounted quayside cranes capable of handling 20 ft (6.10 m) 30 ft (9.15 m) 35 ft (10.70 m) and 40 ft (12.20 m) containers on automatic spreaders. A fourth crane was introduced in 1984. The quay has a depth of water alongside of 10.15 m (33.3 ft) LWOST which is dredged annually. Adjacent to the quay is a 20.6 ha (51 acre) container park for the storage of preshipment and discharged containers and other unit cargoes. Storage space is provided for 6750 Twenty feet equivalent units (TEU)s of import/export containers. In addition there are facilities (208/440 V) for over 100 refrigerated units. The terminal is also rail served.

In common with the other container terminals a large fleet of fifth wheel tractor units and 50 tonne trailer transport boxes between the quayside and adjacent storage and handling areas are provided. Groupage facilities are available close to the terminals and also at the East Anglia Freight Terminal on the port perimeter which has a covered area of 13 935 m^2 (150 000 ft^2).

Ferry berths/ramps

One of the leading ports worldwide in the handling of vehicular traffic is found at the Port of Dover, England. It offers services conveying cars, coaches, road haulage vehicles, passenger and general freight to Belgium and France. In the peak of the season it deals with some 110 sailings daily. A feature of the service is the quick turn-round of the vessels conveying vehicles, which varies from 45 to 90 minutes. A modern vessel using the port would have a capacity of 1800 passengers and some 400 cars or 60 road-haulage vehicles or other combination of vehicle traffic including cars, coaches and road-haulage vehicles (see *Elements of Shipping*, pp. 54–55). The vessel length would be 130 m and beam 22 m. Such vessels have both bow and stern loading and vehicles are loaded/discharged over a double-deck shore-based ramp.

A layout of the port is shown in Diagram I and the following points are relevant.

(a) The port is served by passenger trains at the marine station alongside berth 3 found in the inner harbour.

(b) A Jetfoil service berth is provided in the inner harbour, providing a year-round daily service to Belgium.

(c) Also found in the inner harbour is the Hoverport, which is the Hovercraft service terminal to France providing daily services throughout the year.

(d) Ship repair facilities are available at Wellington Dock.

(e) At Dover Eastern Docks in the precincts of the eastern arm is found the most modern terminal, dealing with Ro/Ro vehicles, coaches, cars and passengers. Berths 3, 4, 5 and 6 are two tier, thereby permitting simultaneous loading or discharge from the ship's two vehicular decks. Areas immediately behind the berths accommodate the customs-processed traffic awaiting shipment (outwards/export).

(f) The Import Freight Building/Area deals with the imported road haulage traffic. Customs clearance is very quick, varying from 2 to 6 hours, and is fully computerized, using the direct trader input (DTI) system (see *Elements of Export Practice*, pp. 147–8).

(g) At the Export Freight Building road haulage traffic is received and processed through customs prior to shipment. The system is very quick and within 1 hour of arrival the vehicle can be loaded on to the ship.

(h) Motorists, cars, coaches and passengers are processed through immigration and customs examination in the purpose-built passenger accommodation. Separate facilities are provided for cars, coaches and passengers. The processing for both inward and outward traffic is very quick.

The foregoing is just a brief commentary on a modern port

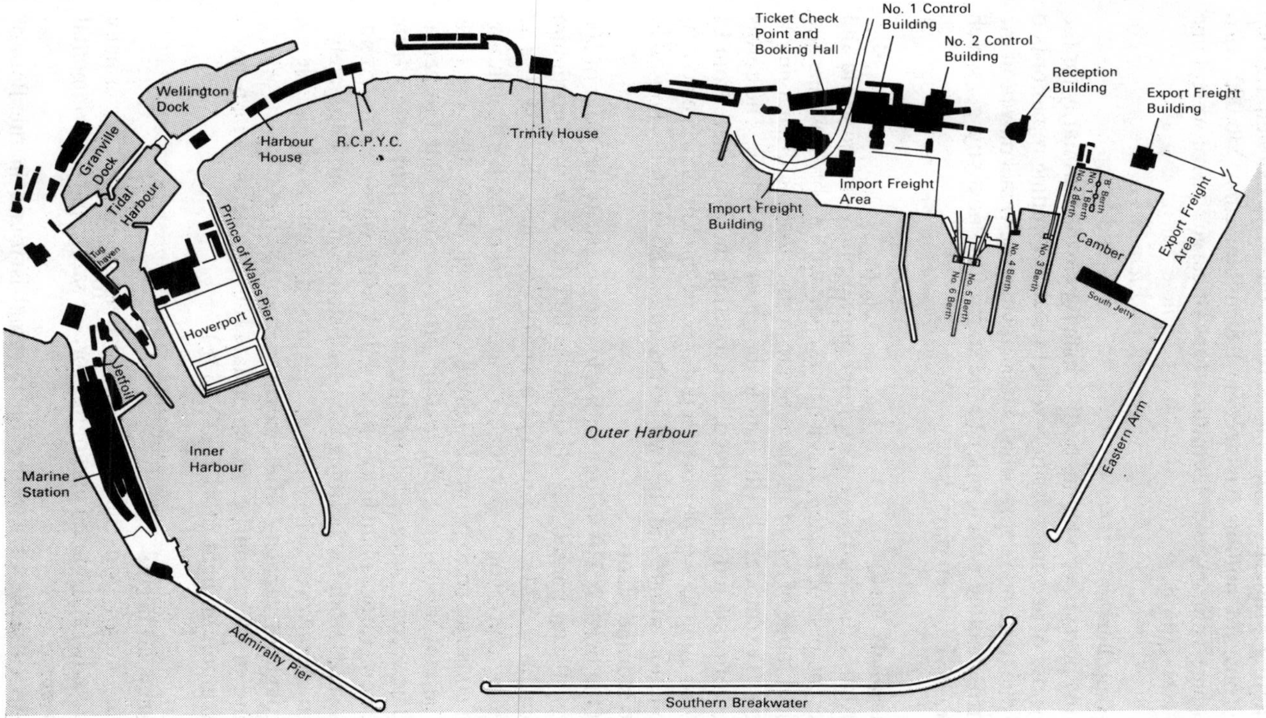

Diagram I   Dover Harbour (reproduced by kind permission of Dover Harbour Board)

handling primarily vehicular traffic. In 1984 it handled 120 000 coaches, 14 million passengers, 1.6 million cars, 740 000 road haulage vehicles and 8.9 million tons of cargo. There were some 28 000 sailings.

Lay-up berths

Many ports have a lay-up berth which is provided primarily for the purpose of accommodating a vessel which is awaiting repair or laid up due to a trade depression. Alternatively, the vessel may be at the berth awaiting a crew prior to the start of the next voyage, which may be in seven days' time.

Phosphate berths

Jordan is the third largest exporter of phosphates in the world and uses the port of Aqaba. It is a natural port with no breakwaters and a tidal range of only 1 m, thereby facilitating loading/discharging of ships. Two modern berths handle the phosphate traffic. The berths are both rail and road served, transporting the phosphate from El Abiad mine to Aqaba port – a distance of 250 km. Storage accommodation situated at the two berths totals 180 000 tons, housed in two storage plants.

One berth is 210 m long with a loading capacity per hour of 500 tons. It can handle vessels up to 15 000 d.w.t. with a maximum draught of 30 ft (9.15 m) and beam of not more than 54 ft. The loading conveyor is extendable seawards from the berth, but was not constructed to permit longitudinal travel. Hence the vessel has to be moved/shifted as the loading proceeds from hatch to hatch.

The second berth is 180 m long and has a conveyor system from the new storage plant involving mobile loaders whose boom extends seawards from the berthing face – a distance of 26 m. Ultimately a second conveyor belt system will be provided which will double the throughput capacity. Bulk carriers of up to 50 000 d.w.t. with a beam of 50 m can be accommodated at the berth, which has a maximum draught of 41 ft (12.45 m).

Marine oil berths

Many major ports have marine oil berths and they are usually situated in an isolated part of the port for safety and environmental reasons.

An example of a major oil terminal is found in the Port of

Singapore, which has some six installations each operated by different international petroleum organizations. A brief description of each is given below.

Singapore is a modern oil port with modern storing, blending, refining and distributing facilities for all grades of mineral oil. There are six international petroleum organizations presently operating in the Republic, each with its own installation situated close to the harbour.

British Petroleum

BP Refinery Singapore Pte Ltd owns and operates a refinery situated at Tanjong Berlayer. The refinery has a capacity of 27 000 barrels of crude oil per day or 1.35 million tonnes per year.

The import of crude oil and export of refined products and the bunkering of vessels are handled over three jetties, two for coastal vessels and one for ocean-going tankers up to 33 000 d.w.t. length overall (LOA about 214 m, maximum draft 11 m), or 80 000 d.w.t. tankers (LOA about 259 m, maximum draft 8 m). The first coastal tanker berth can accept up to 5000 d.w.t. tankers (LOA about 137 m, maximum draft 9 m), while the second coastal tanker berth accepts up to 2400 d.w.t. tankers (LOA about 91 m, maximum draft 6 m).

Caltex

Caltex operates a marine terminal at Tanjong Penjuru, covering an area of 12 ha and with a storage capacity of 982 000 barrels for all petroleum products.

The terminal comprises two offshore berths over 670.7 m long with draft 13.7 m. Berth 1 is capable of handling vessels of any size; while berth 2 can handle any vessel exceeding 91.4 m flat sides, up to 32 000 displacement tons and length not exceeding 182.9 m.

Esso

Situated at Pulau Ayer Chawan, an island 2.4 km south of Jurong Industrial Complex, the Esso refinery has a refining capacity of 231 000 barrels per day and a lubricant plant with a capacity of 5000 barrels per day.

The jetty has an overall length of 982 m and consists of four loading and bunkering berths.

Berth No.	Maximum d.w.t. (tonnes)	Limits on size: Length of vessel (m)	Limits on size: Depth alongside (m)
1	1 700	82.4	7.6
2	25 000	198.0	10.9
3	48 000	244.0	12.8
4	140 000	305.0	16.1

All grades of bunker fuel are available to vessels up to 140 000 d.w.t. load or light load. Ballast disposal facilities are available. Fresh water can be supplied with bunkering at 24-hour service. There is also an off-shore single buoy mooring system capable of accommodating VLCCs up to 252 000 d.w.t.

Mobil

The refinery has a total production capacity of 180 000 barrels per day. It manufactures gasoline, aviation turbine fuel, kerosene, diesel fuel, fuel oil, LPG (liquefied petroleum gas) and sulphur. It has a maximum storage capacity of 9.6 million barrels (crude and product).

Mobil Oil Singapore Pte Ltd provides five berths measuring 1040 m long for vessels up to 85 000 d.w.t. at Jurong.

Shell

The Shell refinery is situated at Pulau Bukom, about 4.6 km off the south-west coast of Singapore.

Shell Eastern Petroleum (Pte) Ltd has ten berths and a single buoy mooring for ocean-going vessels.

The refinery has a refining capacity of 25 million tonnes per annum. It manufactures LPG, petrol, aviation turbine fuel, kerosene, gas oil, diesel fuel, solvents, fuel oil, lube oil and bitumen for local and overseas markets. There are 200 oil storage tanks with over 3 million tonnes capacity. All grades of bunkers are available 24 hours a day.

Berth No.	*Maximum draft (m)*	*Maximum length (m)*	*Maximum displacement*	*Remarks*
1	9.75	173.7	33 000	Continuous
2	9.75	91.4	33 000	jetty
3	10.95	82.3	33 000	
4	12.19	189.0	43 000	
5	12.50	193.6	45 000	
6	14.63	243.8	92 000	Minimum
7	12.34	185.9	65 000	length
8	12.95	230.1	65 000	acceptable
9	13.10	198.1	33 000	172.2 m
10	15.54	265.0	84 000	
SBM	22.36	–	352 990	

Singapore Petroleum

Singapore Petroleum Co Pte Ltd (SPC) provides three berths for bunkering and other services on Pulau Merlimau, an island approximately 1.2 km off the south-west coast of Singapore.

Berth No.	*Maximum draft (m)*	*Maximum size of vessel (d.w.t.)*	*Maximum LOA of vessel (m)*
1*	15.5	90 000	260
2*	15.5	90 000	260
3	10.6	17 000	158

* Berths 1 and 2 can accommodate vessels up to 100 000 d.w.t. in light loaded condition and subject to a maximum LOA of 300 m. Approaches to berths are restricted by tide to vessels drawing more than 11.9 m up to a maximum of 14.3 m.

The refinery has a refining capacity of 65 000 barrels daily. In addition, SPC operates five self-propelled bunkering barges for carrying gas oil, fuel oil and marine diesel oil.

Ro/Ro berths

An increasing volume of trade is now conveyed on Ro/Ro vessels which may operate in the short or deep-sea services. The port of Felixstowe handles such services and a description of the four berths involved is given below.

Berth 1 with a draught of 7.1 m (23.3 ft) LWOST is available for bow and stern loading vessels up to 137.2 m (450 ft) in length. The berth consists of a floating pontoon 45.7 m (150 ft) in length and 27.4 m (90 ft) wide and is connected to the marshalling area by two steel girder bridges each 4.9 m (16 ft) wide. An upper deck loading ramp enables units to be driven on or off the upper decks of the vessels. The 109 m (360 ft) quay is equipped with a 32 ton capacity electric travelling crane, capable of spanning 19.8 m (65 ft) wide ships.

Berth 2 has a bridge 29.3 m (96 ft) long by 6.7 m (22 ft) wide with a capacity of 140 tons, and is raised and lowered by hydraulic rams. In common with berth 1 an upper deck loading ramp capable of carrying units of 32 tons has been added to the capability of this bridge. Vessels with bow or stern loading may be accepted up to 24.4 m (80 ft) beam while the berth is dredged annually to 7.71 m (25.3 ft) at LWOST. Berths 1 and 2 are backed by 7.3 ha (18 acres) of open storage for trailers in addition to 4849 m^2 (52 200 ft^2) of covered storage.

Berth 3 is available at all states of the tide for bow and stern loading vessels up to 152.4 m (500 ft) in length with a beam of up to 24.4 m (80 ft) in a least depth of 7.71 m (25.3 ft) at LWOST (dredged annually). The bridge is raised and lowered by hydraulic rams and is 43.6 m (143 ft) long, 9.1 m (30 ft) wide, with an end width of 17.1 m (56 ft), and is designed to carry two lanes of traffic with loads of up to 140 tons. The 137.2 m (450 ft) long quay is equipped with an electric travelling crane with a capacity of 35 tons at 29 m (95 ft) radius.

Berth 4, with a least depth of 10.15 m (33.3 ft) at LWOST (dredged annually), can accept vessels up to 213 m (700 ft) in length and 24.4 m (80 ft) beam, for bow, stern, side or quarter ramp loading arrangements. The bridge is raised and lowered by hydraulic rams and is 43.6 m (156 ft) and is designed to carry two lanes of traffic with loads of up to 104 tons. Berths 3 and 4 are backed by a large marshalling area, a purpose-built container park, a transit shed and warehouse, with space for future covered storage.

PORT FACILITIES

In our examination of the economics of port design and layout, it is appropriate to examine briefly some of the port facilities available at a major modern port. Accordingly we have chosen Singapore. It is an important shipping centre in South-East Asia and also a commercial and financial centre of the region. It handles a minimum of 200 ships daily and provides international shipping links to over 300 ports around the world. It is stressed again that the facilities available at any port, and their layout, will vary with individual circumstances. The diagrams provided are merely a broad outline of the berths and their salient features.

A 24-hour berthing service is provided by most modern ports including Singapore. Vessels can be berthed at any time, subject to minimal limitations of tidal flow. The 24-hour service also enables vessels to be taken out at night immediately after cargo has been worked so that the berths can be made available for other vessels. This arrangement makes it possible for conventional general cargo vessels to be turned round after an average stay alongside of 44 hours, and for container vessels, 15 hours, in the port of Singapore.

Bunkers are available at Keppel Wharves, Container Terminal and any of the 28 terminal berths at Pulau Bukom, Pulau Ayer Chawan, Pulau Merlimau, Tanjong Berlayer, Tanjong Penjuru and Tanjong Sakunyit, which are owned and operated by Shell, Esso, Singapore Petroleum, British Petroleum, Caltex and Mobil respectively. These companies also operate bunkering barges to refuel ships at anchorage.

Pilotage is compulsory in the western sector of the port and in the East Johore Straits. The eastern anchorage also requires compulsory pilotage for vessels of more than 10 000 Gross Registered Tonnage (GRT). In addition, every chemical and gas carrier of more than 75 GRT moving within the pilotage districts in the western anchorage, eastern anchorage or East Johore Straits will have to be under pilotage by a Port of Singapore pilot unless exempted. Although pilotage is not compulsory in the other areas, most vessels still take advantage of the service. Most major ports including Singapore provide round-the-clock pilotage services with licensed pilots for operations at all docks, oil terminals and anchorage within the port area.

The port of Singapore operates a fleet of 14 tugs which includes seven Fixed Kort Nozzle conventional tugs ranging from 700 to 1200 h.p. and seven Voith Schneider Propulsion tugs with 2520–3200 h.p. In addition, there are five leased tugs to cater for peak periods.

These tugs are available to assist in berthing, unberthing, towing, shifting and hauling of vessels. Some are equipped with fire-fighting and anti-oil pollution equipment. Tugs are also used in LASH operations and salvage work.

Round-the-clock waterboat services supplying water to vessels and offshore islands are provided by the Port of Singapore. A fleet of nine waterboats with capacity ranging from 207 to 465 tonnes is available.

The Port of Singapore offers about 700 000 m^2 of covered storage area, of which 255 000 m^2 is outside the free trade zone (FTZ). Storage space is available on a lease or common-user basis, for long and short terms. Port users can lease special modules of covered space in which they have complete flexibility of usage, such as storing, rebagging, repacking and consolidation. The largest of the complexes is the Pasir Panjang Warehousing Complex, which houses 250 000 m^2 of warehousing space. This development aims at integrating terminal and warehousing services, thereby providing a regional warehousing and distribution centre in the region.

Three blocks of 11-storey warehouses involving a multi-storey complex have been constructed on a 15 ha piece of land at the junction of Alexandra and Pasir Panjang Roads. The complex has 150 730 m^2 of space available for leasing to manufacturers, forwarders and traders. The processing, packaging, reassembly and bagging of cargo is undertaken at this complex together with many other similar activities.

The offshore supply terminal renders services to foreign companies engaged in oil exploration activities around the South-East Asia region. Its facilities include coastal berths at Telok Ayer Wharves; and 22 220 m^2 of covered storage space and 14 820 m^2 of open storage area at Pasir Panjang Wharves. Services offered are shipping expertise (e.g. freight-booking and forwarding) documentation, palletization, storage and stevedorage.

A modern five-storey cold storage complex is available at Keppel Wharves, providing a total warehouse space of 27 980 m^3 with a 10 000 tonne chiller and freezer storage capacity. It has a temperature range of -30°C to $+15$°C, and is the largest in the Far East.

Loading facilities are available at Keppel Wharves for shipping liquid commodities in bulk. Presently, there are four installations for latex and two for vegetable oil.

A bulk liquid storage terminal – GATX Terminals (Pte) Ltd at Tanjong Penjuru, Jurong Town – has facilities for the storage and handling of chemical and other liquid products. Blending, processing, specialized packaging services and warehouse storage of packaged liquid products are also available at this terminal.

The terminal has two deep-water berths to handle the discharge or loading of liquid products from coastal and ocean-going vessels. Berth 1, with 22 pipelines, can accommodate ships up to 85 000 d.w.t. while berth 2, with 10 pipelines, can accommodate ships up to 5000 d.w.t. An additional finger pier can berth two mini-tankers or tank barges up to 1000 d.w.t. each.

The Port of Singapore Chemistry Department is available to provide a wide range of technical services and advice on scientific matters to the shipping community. Some of the main services are as follows.

(a) The Chemical Analysis Department has two analytical laboratories. The central laboratory at the Bulk Installation Centre caters for the testing of flash point of petroleum, slop oil, oil spill dispersant, palm oil, drinking water and other miscellaneous analyses. The other laboratory at Pulau Sebarok provides on-the-spot testing of slop oil, which is necessary for the efficient running of the Slop and Sludge Reception and Treatment Centre.

(b) A team of chemists, called Petroleum Inspectors, provide round-the-clock service on gas-free inspection of tankers at the various anchorages so that these vessels can proceed with minimum delay to shipyards for repair. This team of chemists also inspects vessels for 'hot work' as well as atmospheric content in confined areas to ensure safe conditions for workmen.

(c) The Inspectorate of Dangerous Goods provides technical services to port users on the classification of dangerous goods, carries out daily spot checks on dangerous goods in the Port of Singapore premises and advises officers and workers on the proper handling of dangerous goods.

(d) A fumigation unit, under the Chemistry Department, provides fumigation services using both methyl bromide and hydrogen cyanide gases. For land fumigation, methyl bromide gas is used for fumigation of cargo in containers as well as inside the transit sheds. Hydrogen cyanide fumigation is carried out onboard vessels for the main purpose of issuing deratting certificates.

A dangerous goods landing jetty at West Coast Road for the handling of explosives and other dangerous goods is available. The jetty, with 2.1 m draft, has a 41 m ramp which can be used for Ro/Ro operations.

No dangerous goods shall be removed or discharged without the prior written permission of the Port Master or the Traffic Manager at the Port of Singapore.

In order to promote the ship-repairing industry and to prevent oil pollution, the Port of Singapore inaugurated de-slopping facilities on Pulau Sebarok. This project was promulgated to prevent indiscriminate discharge of oil and refuse into Singapore waters.

The treatment plant containing the slop facilities can now receive 300 000 tonnes of slop and dispose of 25 000 tonnes of chemically contaminated slop and 10 000 tonnes of sludge annually. Tankers up to 45 800 displacement tonnes with a maximum depth of 12 m are dealt with.

There are also seven de-slopping barges of varying capacities from 400 m^3 to 1500 m^3 and two tankers of capacities 20 000 m^3 and 1600 m^3 as floating facilities to collect slop from larger tankers that could not berth at Pulau Sebarok.

Port security is provided continuously, involving police both on land and sea.

The Police Force has a Criminal Investigation Department responsible for investigation and prosecution of all crimes and offences committed in the port, a marine section for seaward policing, and an arms and explosives section to supervise and control the movement and security of arms and ammunition as well as dangerous and valuable cargo arriving by ships.

The Police Force is supplemented by a Security Guard Unit whose primary task is the guarding of warehouses, godowns and other port properties.

The Port of Singapore is equipped with modern fire engines and ancillary equipment. The two purpose-built fire-fighting launches are available continuously while other launches are equipped with fire-fighting equipment for use in emergencies.

Consultancy services, periodical inspection and servicing of fire extinguishers and hosereels are also conducted by the Fire and Safety Department of the Port of Singapore.

The Environmental Control Unit is responsible for the cleanliness of port waters and the environment within the port of Singapore premises and properties. Services provided include sea garbage collection from vessels in port waters. In addition, special services can be provided upon request by the vessel on a minimum charge per trip basis.

The Port of Singapore also provides passenger as well as vehicular ferry services. Passenger ferries, with capacity for 40 to 400 persons, ply between Southern Islands and Singapore mainland and operate from the World Trade Centre Ferry Terminal and Clifford Pier. The vehicular ferry transports vehicles from Tanjong Berlayer to Southern Islands.

The Training Department caters for operational, technical and management training in the port.

The World Trade Centre, Singapore is provided to promote world trade through Singapore.

The single building has a floor area of 144 000 m^2, and is a unique blend of commercial, recreational and marine terminal facilities. It provides within one location all the facilities and services businessmen require to conduct international trade.

Exhibition halls, a World Trade Centre Club, restaurants, an auditorium, conference rooms and ample car parks are also housed within the complex. General facilities available include banking facilities, postal services, telex and overseas telephone services, as well as trade information and library services.

The port of Singapore is a major world port and the range of facilities just described demonstrate the range of modern facilities provided. It also places increased emphasis on the need to attain a very high level of efficiency in all areas of the business. The range of facilities provided at a smaller port would be much reduced.

We will now examine in broad terms a number of wharves/berths and some of the facilities found in the Port of Singapore.

General plan of container terminal (Diagram II)

Facilities provided at this terminal include the following:

	Berth Nos.	*Length (m)*	*Draft (m)*
Main berths (including	49, 50, 51	914	13.2
a Ro-Ro berth)	53, 54	640	12.0
Feeder berth	52	238	9.4
Cross berth	48	213	10.4
Container berth	42, 43	535	12.2
Container berth	55	355	12.2

Container yard: Total area – 51 ha and 2.12 ha of hard standing for chassis operation

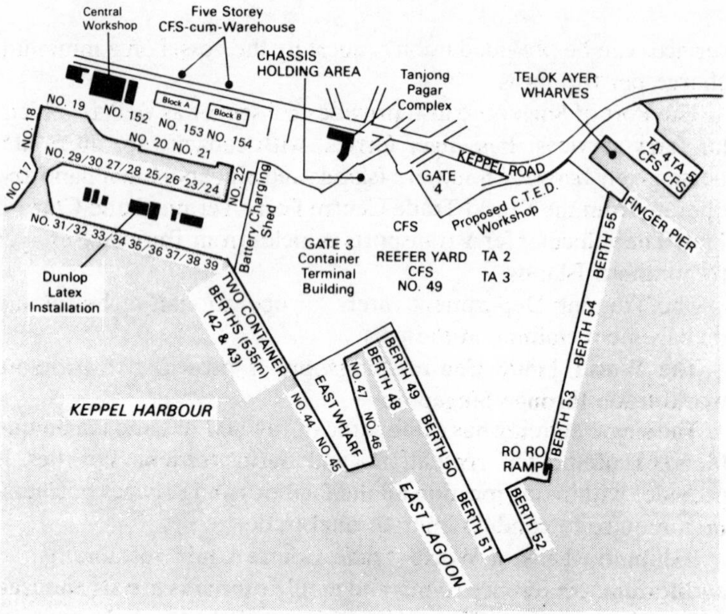

Diagram II Container terminal: Port of Singapore (reproduced by kind permission of Port of Singapore Authority)

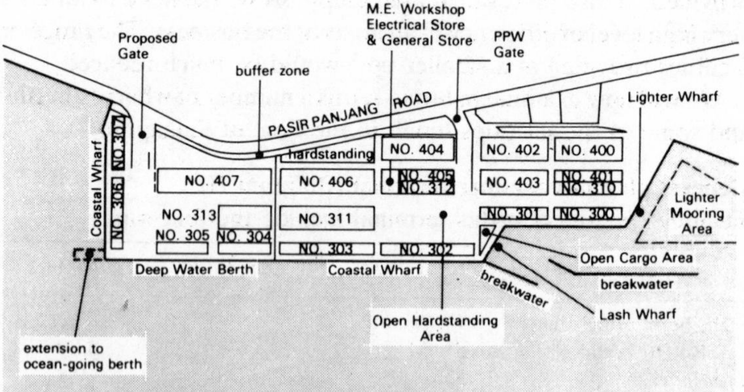

Diagram III General plan of Pasir Panjang Wharves – Port of Singapore (reproduced by kind permission of Port of Singapore Authority)

Storage area

Covered storage area container	Three container freight stations	22 000 m²	for LCL containers on the ground
	One container freight station	7000 m²	for LCL containers on chassis
	Four back-up sheds	10 000 m²	
	Total	48 000 m²	
Open storage area		2000 m²*	
Total storage capacity		31 000 TEUs	

* Excluding stacking yard.

Mechanical equipment

Type	*Capacity*	*Units*
Quay cranes	30.0–35.0 tonnes	12
Straddle carriers	30.0 tonnes	20
Transtainers	30.0–35.0 tonnes	20
Forklifts for Ro/Ro operations	22.5–25.0 tonnes	5
Forklifts	10.0 tonnes	8
	2.5–3.5 tonnes	78
Prime movers	30 tonnes	71
Skeletal trailers and semi-trailers	6.1 and 12.2 m	100
Weighbridges		4

Particular attention should be paid to the range of mechanical equipment and the storage area available. In a Western European container berth, it would be rail served.

General Plan of Pasir Panjang Wharves (Diagram III)
This berth is available for general cargo vessels, particularly coasters, with extensive covered area embracing transit sheds. Facilities provided at this terminal include the following:

Berths

(a) 480 m of deep water wharves with draft of 10.03 m.
(b) 986 m of coastal wharves with draft of 6.4 m for ten coasters.

(c) 132 m of transitional wharves with draft of 2.6 m for four LASH barges.

(d) 553 m of lighter wharves with draft of 2.3 m for 23 lighters.

Mooring basin

Capable of accommodating 120 lighters.

Storage area

Covered storage area	5 transit sheds	44 400 m²
	1 back up-shed	22 300 m²
	2 warehouses	14 200 m²
	Total	80 900 m²
Open storage area		35 200 m²

Equipment

Type	*Capacity*	*Units*
Fork lifts	2.5–3.5 tonnes	129
Mobile cranes	8.0 tonnes	6
	60.0 tonnes	1
Tractors	50.0 tonnes	4
Trailers	40.0 tonnes	8

Other services/facilities include the following:

(a) Direct supply of water to vessels alongside the wharves.
(b) Ship-to-shore telephone services.
(c) Palletization.
(d) Removal and trucking.
(e) Repacking and rebagging.
(f) Container stuffing and unstuffing.
(g) Lashing.

General plan of Sembawang Wharves (Diagram IV)

This wharf deals with conventional ships, but primarily timber carriers. Facilities available include the following:

Berths

Five berths totalling 822 m for conventional vessels of which one is a

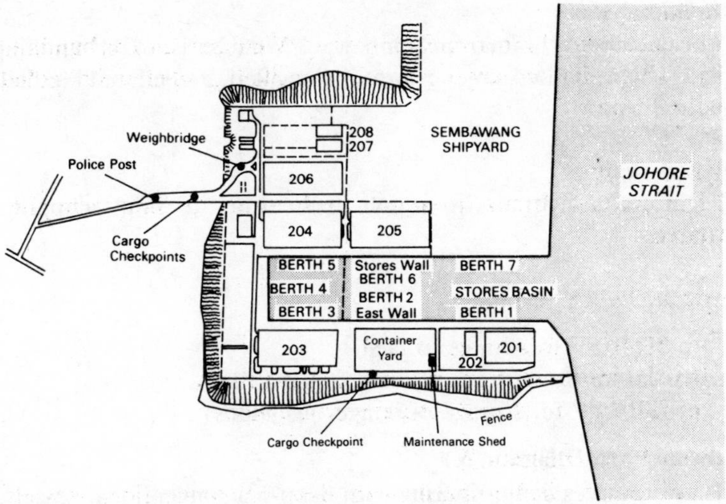

Diagram IV General plan of Sembawang Wharves – Port of Singapore (reproduced by kind permission of Port of Singapore Authority)

priority berth for container vessels which operate on a chassis system.

Draft
8.13 to 10.4 m.

Storage area

Covered storage area	4 transit sheds	26 400 m²
	5 back-up sheds	24 500 m²
	Total	50 900 m²
Open storage area		46 000 m²

Container yard
An area of 21 000 m² of hard standing to accommodate 338 35 ft containers on chassis.

Container freight station
One container freight station of area 4645 m² for packing and consolidation of containerized cargo.

Bundling yard
Located about 10 km from Sembawang Wharves is an 8 ha bundling yard where timber may be sorted, stencilled, graded and bundled before export.

Water supplies
Eight water hydrants to supply fresh water to ships alongside wharves.

Special storage facilities

(a) 1350 m^2 for storage of acid.
(b) 250 m^2 for storage of distress signal flares.
(c) 2800 m^2 for storage of dangerous goods.

Jurong Port (Diagram V)
These wharves deal primarily with deep-sea conventional vessels. Details of the port are given below:

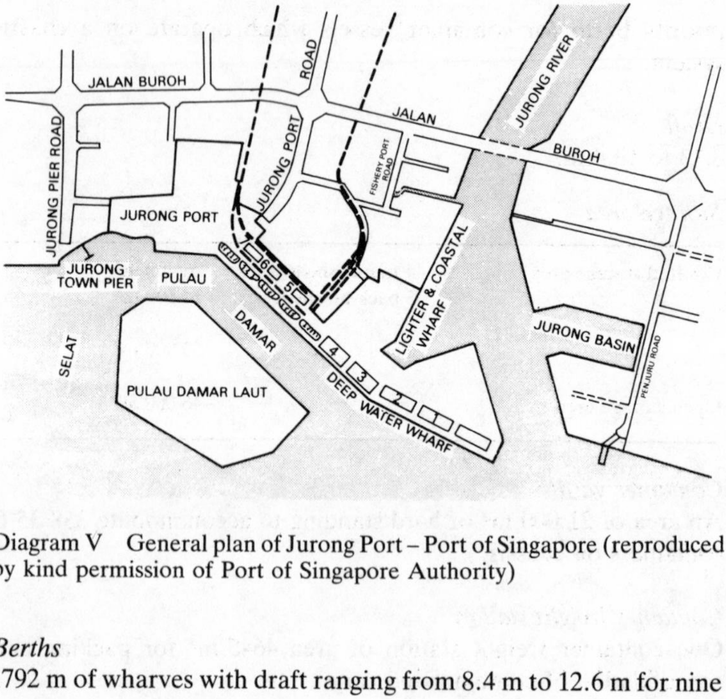

Diagram V General plan of Jurong Port – Port of Singapore (reproduced by kind permission of Port of Singapore Authority)

Berths
1792 m of wharves with draft ranging from 8.4 m to 12.6 m for nine

ocean-going vessels; 172 m of wharves with draft 3.1 m for coastal ships.

Berth No.	*Wharf marks (WM)*	*Channel approach depth (m)*	*Depth alongside (m)*	*Maximum loaded draft allowed (m)*
1	0–183	8.4	12.3	8.1
2	183–366	8.4	12.6	8.1
3	366–549	10.5	12.6	10.2
4	549–720	10.8	12.3	10.5
5	720–903	10.8	11.0	10.5
6	903–1124	10.8	11.0	10.5
7	1124–1320	10.8	11.0	10.5
8	1320–1517	10.8	11.0	10.5
9	1517–1792	10.8	8.4 (at WM 1557) 9.9 (at WM 1617) 10.9 (at WM 1694)	9.6

Storage area

Covered storage area	3 storage warehouses (NFTZ*)	22 600 m²
	5 storage warehouses (FTZ†)	27 600 m²
	5 transit sheds	34 550 m²
	Total	84 750 m²
Open storage area		226 600 m²

* NFTZ = Non-free trade zone.
† FTZ = Free trade zone.

Equipment

Type	*Capacity*	*Units*
Unloader cranes	450.0 tonnes/hour	3
	300.0 tonnes/hour	1
Suction type unloaders	100.0 tonnes/hour	2

CHAPTER 4

Cargo-handling equipment

Cargo handling is an extensive subject and primarily involves the interface between the ship and port. The degree of efficiency attained to maximize cargo throughput at a berth, quicken ship turn-round time in port and minimize cargo-handling cost overall affects the development of international trade and cost of the international distribution of goods. Port managements throughout the world are becoming more conscious of the need to provide modern equipped berths with their attendant capital-intensive cargo-handling techniques involving low labour content as a means of increasing their general competitiveness and encouraging trade through their port. Modern berths with modern cargo-handling systems attract modern tonnage, thereby offering competitive international transport distribution services. Failure of a port to modernize its berths and attendant cargo-handling systems will encourage shipowners and shippers to use other ports where practicable/possible.

FACTORS DETERMINING TYPE OF CARGO-HANDLING EQUIPMENT

In our examination of cargo-handling systems we will consider the aspects which have led to the present era of rapid technological and organizational change in international trade distribution and the factors which influence the determination of the most suitable types of cargo-handling system. These are as follows:

(a) The nature of the cargo. It may be bulk shiploads – dry or wet cargo; general cargo involving conventional break-bulk handling methods; unitized cargo involving containers or pallets; vehicular cargo shipments involving road trailers requiring a ramp access to and from the ship; heavy lift cargo such as a transformer needing a high lifting capacity crane; livestock needing adequate provision to be made; dangerous cargo requiring isolation and special handling requirements; overside loading into barges, and so on.

(b) Handling cost, general safety and reliability. This is usually based on a per ton or cargo unit/container rate (see Chapter 5). A labour-intensive system tends to be much more expensive than the capital-intensive system.

(c) Resources available at the seaport including shore-based equipment, dock labour and their productivity and shipboard facilities such as derricks.

(d) Weather conditions. Bad weather can seriously interrupt loading/discharging operations and delay the scheduled departure of the vessel.

(e) Evaluation and cost of alternative cargo-handling systems, including their maintenance and operational availability. This for example may involve the extent to which lighterage is engaged to speed up cargo unloading and/or the use of the ship derricks to quicken cargo discharge to the berth.

(f) Competitive situation compared with other ports. This could influence the tariff level to remain competitive and the attitude of the port authority to providing the most modern cargo-handling facilities/techniques practicable.

(g) Type of vessel. This is a decisive factor. It may be a combi-carrier, Ro/Ro vessel, OBO, VLCC, fruit carrier, cement carrier, refrigerated vessel, and so on.

(h) Distribution arrangements. Efficient distribution arrangements are a paramount need and will influence the cargo-handling equipment requirements. It may be by rail, road, inland waterways or pipeline.

(i) Tidal conditions. Tidal variations can influence the efficiency of cargo handling and interrupt the transhipment arrangements through excessive movement of the vessel while at the berth. The closed dock system eliminates such a risk.

(j) Development of the combined transport operation is encouraging modern cargo transhipment techniques.

(k) International trade. Market conditions are requiring quicker overall transits, which demands faster cargo transhipment arrangement.

We will now examine the various types of cargo-handling systems.

CONVENTIONAL BREAK-BULK HANDLING

The conventional break-bulk cargo-handling technique is operative in the deep sea and coastal trades within the ship capacity range of 200 to 16 000 d.w.t. The great majority fall between 8000 to 16 000 d.w.t. The handling technology employed involves the lifting of cargo in units of between 1 and 3 tons with a considerable amount of manhandling on shore, in the ship's hold, and in the port transit area in the making up and breaking down of these units and in the stowing of cargo. The handling rates/speed achieved varies to about 10 tons per hook (crane) hour for homogeneous (of the same cargo type) cargo in bags or bales, and for bulk cargoes handled in tubs.

For general cargo the port transit function is infinitely more complex than it is for bulk cargoes because a large number of items have to be individually identified and located. Import cargoes have to be taken to transit sheds or open dock areas (depending upon requirements for protection from the weather), sorted to marks, and stacked. At the same time consignees or their agents have to complete the payments and documentation procedures required to enable the goods to be released. These are concerned chiefly with customs clearance and the payment of port dues and charges. Finally, the goods have to be retrieved from their position in store and loaded to some mode of inland transport. On the export side operations are often simpler because, in many cases, there are no export duties, documentation can be completed before the ship arrives, and the cargo allowed on the berth only when the ship is loading. Handling rates at the berth are very sensitive to transit area operations. Congestion in import sheds can slow down discharging, and the way in which export cargo comes forward and is presented to the port has a very important effect upon loading rates.

Similar considerations apply to stowage in the ship. For bulk cargoes this may be very simple (see *Elements of Shipping*, pp. 237–9). However, in the case of general cargo each parcel has to be stowed in such a way as to allow the ship to work as many hatches as possible at each port of call while keeping restowage to a minimum. At the same time the physical characteristics of the cargo, as they affect the stability and safety of the ship, have to be taken into account. Other major factors which affect the performance of the conventional system are the number of shifts the port will work and stevedoring practice. The number of shifts can vary between about six and fourteen a week and stevedoring practice has a major effect upon loading and discharge rates.

There are a number of different pieces of equipment used for lifting general cargo into, or out of, a cargo vessel. Factors influencing the choice of system to be used for a particular cargo-handling operation include initial cost, general reliability, maintenance, availability of replacements, operational availability having regard to maintenance schedules, productivity of the systems, flexibility of the equipment, expected lifespan and safety. These include ship's equipment, derricks or cranes and shore equipment, portal level luffing cranes or various gantry arrangements, each of which we will now examine.

A popular one is the derrick system rigged in 'union purchase' with one derrick (boom) over the ship side plumbed over the quay and the other over the ship's hatchway. A guying system holding the derricks in place and cargo lifted from the hold of the ship on the cargo 'fall' before being transferred to the shore 'fall' for discharge.

The 'union purchase' system is a very efficient handling arrangement for small units of approximately one to two tonnes and where there is very little spotting requirement in the hold or dock area to identify the cargo to be lifted. There are various arrangements for increasing the safe working load (SWL) of this equipment by doubling up the gear, i.e. putting a purchase on the cargo fall; by utilizing an equalizing beam on two derricks or by increasing the purchase and using a single swinging derrick.

Shipboard cranes are now commonly used for handling general cargo. The cranes are installed on either side of, or on, the centre line of the ship. When installed on the centre line it is with the intention of one crane being able to work both sides of the ship and also one end of two adjacent hatchways. However, if the crane is so sited it must be much larger in order to provide ample reach over the ship's side. The shipboard crane is not as fast at handling small general cargo units of one to two tons as the traditional union purchase rig but it has a number of advantages over such a system. These include the fact that the spotting area for a crane is considerably better; due to the lack of guys, supports, stays, etc. the ship's deck remains completely clear of the wires – hence the safety factor is considerably increased; the crane, with the minimum of driver training, is simple to operate; the crane is frequently of greater safe working load than the union purchase rig derrick system; and finally, maintenance is less as there are less working wires, etc. but may be more technical.

The level luffing dock crane is commonly used in the ports of Western Europe (see also pp. 72–76). The cranes, frequently of a safe working load of 3 to 5 tons, rest on wheels on the quay apron and are usually tracked along the length of the quay. The crane jib can slew and luff, hence the crane can pick up a load from any point in the square of the hatch and deposit it anywhere on the quay apron within reach of the jib. Utilization of the quay crane is usually considerably higher than for the shipboard crane owing to the lesser amount of 'down time' while the ship is at sea, which is the main argument against shipboard equipment. The strongest argument against the dock crane is usually associated with its track system because this interferes with the safe and efficient working of fork lift trucks on the quayside.

The gantry crane is usually associated with bulk handling of raw materials, container handling, etc. (see also pp. 77–106). The crane is mounted on a structure which spans the whole of the quay apron with a retractable boom which projects out over the ship, alongside the berth, horizontally. A trolley runs along the length of the boom carrying the operator's cabin, winch and falls supporting the cargo handling heads. The capacity of these gantry cranes far exceeds the capacity of the luffing cranes, ranging from 10 to 50 tons safe working load.

Practice shows that the average daily throughput of a break-bulk general cargo berth worldwide varies widely from port to port, from less than 300 to more than 1500 tons per ship. The average productivity of stevedores also varies from 10 to more than 30 tons per gang-hour. This divergence confirms that ports with poor performance lack efficiency rather than physical capacity and have great potential for improvement. On many liner routes handling mixed cargoes involving 'tween-deck tonnage, ships spend up to 50–60% of their time in port, and berth throughputs of over 100 000 tons/annum are comparatively unusual.

TYPES OF GENERAL CARGO-HANDLING EQUIPMENT

A wide variety of types of equipment exist for use with the ship's derrick or shore-based gantry or luffing quayside crane which we will now examine.

A number of packages of cargo placed together and loaded into or discharged from a ship is known as a 'set'. A sling is a length of cordage (Diagram VI) or a steel wire rope (SWR) used to bind and lift the set. It is ideal for hoisting strong packages, such as wooden cases or bagged cargo, which is not likely to sag or damage when raised. Similarly, snotters or canvas slings are suitable for bagged cargo. Chain slings, however, are used for heavy slender cargoes, such as timber or steel rails. There are many different types of sling and the following is a selection of the more common ones.

Endless rope sling

It is made from a length of cordage with the two ends joined by a short splice (Diagram VI). The nominal length of an endless sling is the distance which the sling spans when stretched and closed. In our examination of the various types of sling it is appropriate to describe the pre-slinging technique. It is usually the simplest and cheapest to implement and most suitable for low–medium value goods or low–medium density. It speeds up ship turn-round time considerably as all slings should be 'made up' prior to the vessel's arrival for loading. To achieve maximum benefit, slings must be left on the cargo within the ship to facilitate rapid discharge. There is little point in breaking down slings within the ship at loading only to make them up again upon discharge. This is time and labour consuming. This system appears to operate best when the slings are made up and broken down within the port where the dockers are practised in the art of making up slings. It is not therefore generally a door-to-door service, but most ideal if suitable cheap labour is available at each end of the transport operation. Also, fewer slings are lost if worked within the port area. Special design of slings, etc. may be necessary dependent on the commodity being handled, vessel lifting ability, etc.

Endless SWR/Sling

It is made of a form of grommet by short or 'talurit' splicing together of the two ends of a length of SWR. In very long slings of this type a long splice may be used, but in the shorter slings it would take up too much rope. The short splice should be well served with spunyarn. Its method of use is the same as that of the corresponding cordage sling (see also pp. 62–67).

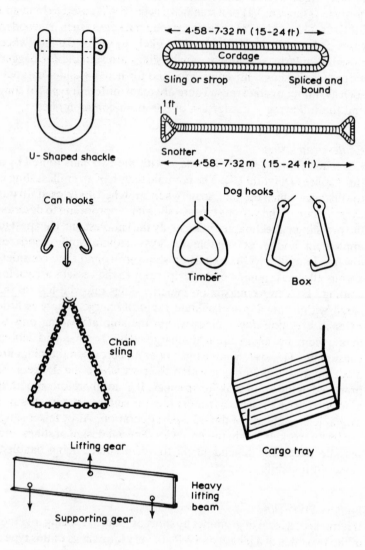

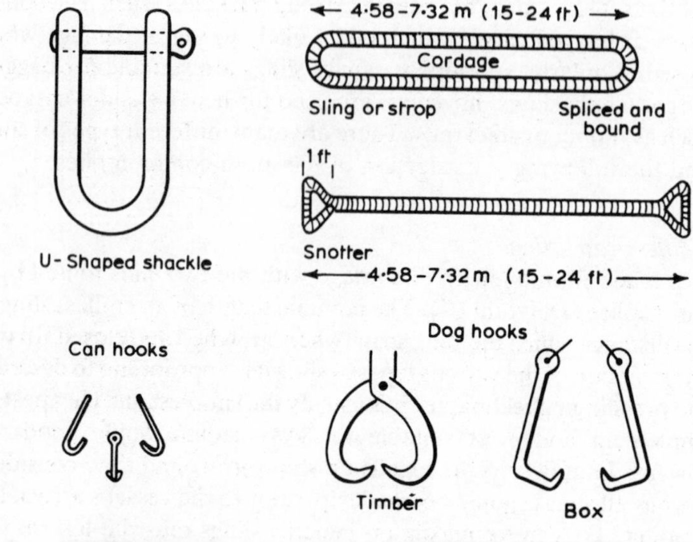
4·58–7·32 m (15–24 ft)
Cordage
Sling or strop
Spliced and bound
1 ft
U-Shaped shackle
Snotter
4·58–7·32 m (15–24 ft)
Dog hooks
Can hooks
Timber
Box
Chain sling
Cargo tray
Lifting gear
Heavy lifting beam
Supporting gear

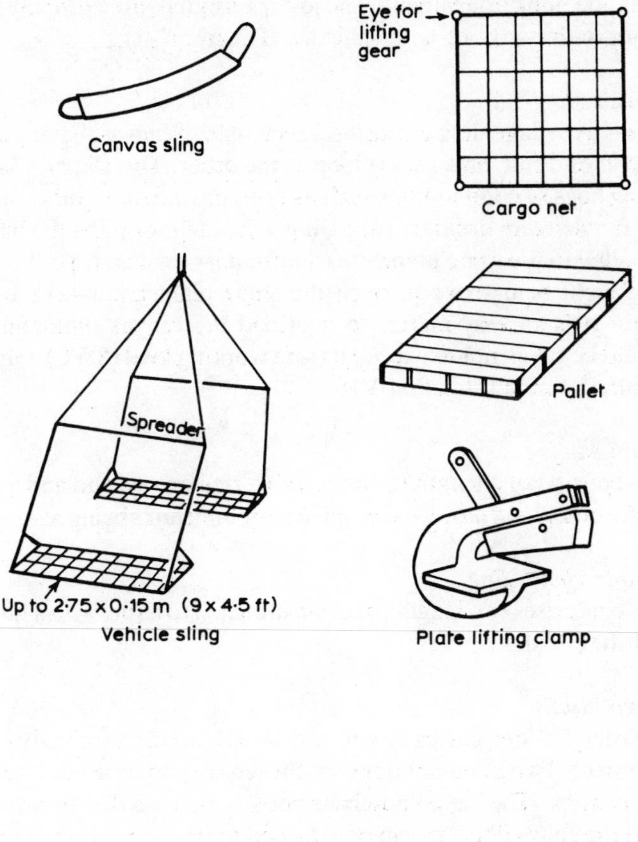

Diagram VI Cargo-handling equipment

Multi-legged sling

This comprises a two- or three-legged sling with a single ring as the upper terminal for attachment to the crane hook. Four-legged slings (or quads) have two intermediate rings joining the legs to the ring for crane hook attachment. The lower terminals are normally fitted either with hooks or with shackles (Diagram VI).

Canvas sling

This is a cordage sling enclosing a rectangle of canvas, having a long loop at one end, and a short loop at the other. This sling is used for lifting bags of commodities such as flour or cement or other similar cargo, where an ordinary rope sling would tear or burst the bags. It is loaded in the same manner as an ordinary endless rope sling, the long bight being rove through the short bight and placed on the hook. It is an easy matter to overload the canvas sling and care should be taken not to exceed its safe working load (SWL), which is usually 1 tonne (Diagram VI).

Chain sling

This consists of a length of chain with a ring on one end and a hook on the other, or a link at each end, one or both links being reversable.

Double chain sling

This comprises two lengths of chain attached to a ring with a hook at each free end.

Cargo hooks

A variety of designs exist and are usually made from galvanized mild steel. Two popular hooks are the lenion purchase hook and the swivel hook. The lenion purchase hook is made so that two runners from the ship's derricks can be attached to the same hook. Another item of equipment is the U-shaped shackle (Diagram VI) which links the crane or derrick with the form of cargo-handling equipment being used. The shackle is joined at its open end by means of a loose pin to form a link. For most lifts a hook is used. The role of the swivel hook is to ensure that the load does not spin as soon as the weight is taken by the crane or winch.

Case hooks and dog hooks

This consists of an endless length of chain 7.9 mm (5/16 in) in diameter, running on which is a pair of clamps. The clamps are spread out to the width of the case and the spikes pushed firmly into the sides of the case. As the weight is taken, the clamps grip the case. Overall such dog or case hooks, and case and plate clamps (Diagram VI), are suitable for transhipping cargo to railway wagons or road vehicles, but not to or from the ship, except to facilitate transhipping the cargo in the hold to enable suitable cargo-handling gear to be attached. Dog hooks are not suitable for frail cases and should only be used to enable slings to be placed.

Can hooks or barrel hooks
These are used to pick up barrels or drums (Diagram VI). They consist of a length of chain, cordage or wire rope, about 3 m long, each end of which is attached to a ring. The two hooks are free to run on the chain.

Cargo net
This consists of a cordage net about 3.6 m square by 20 cm mesh made of 20 mm cordage with 26 mm boundary ropes, which are taken out from each corner to form lifting eyes (Diagram VI).

Cargo tray
This is a rectangular board reinforced on the underside with diagonal iron bands that are turned upwards at the corners to form eyes (Diagram VI). A number are of steel/aluminium construction throughout. Cargo trays and pallets (Diagram VI) are ideal for cargo of moderate dimensions which can be conveniently stacked, such as cartons, bags or small wooden crates or cases.

Additionally in Diagram VI is found the heavy lifting beams suitable for heavy and long articles such as locomotives, boilers, railway passenger vehicles, and so on.

To conclude our review of the traditional cargo-handling systems it is paramount that stevedores and port operators constantly reappraise their traditional cargo-handling methods to determine whether any improvement can be realized. Given overleaf is an example of break-bulk cargo arriving at a port by rail or road, and overall involves six stages from the time of the cargo arrival until loaded on to the vessel.

Stages					
1	2	3	4	5	6
Truck or rail	Men	Fork lift and pallet	Transit shed	Fork lift and pallet	Men and ship

The flow of cargo can be improved by:

(a) Increasing the use of fork lift trucks (see pp. 77–81).

(b) Changing the landward side of the reception area to a suitable height in order that fork lift trucks can move directly on to the bed/platform/floor of the inland transport vehicle.

(c) Changing the packaging system to a unit load system such as palletization.

Additionally, stage two may be eliminated by the following measures:

(d) Improved planning to reduce the need to use the transit shed or combine the movement of goods through the transit shed (see pp. 73–77).

(e) Improve the lifting arrangements on to the ship:
- (i) Union purchase – still fastest for small loads, 1 to 2 tons in weight (see pp. 62–65).
- (ii) Swinging derricks (Hallen, Stulken, etc.).
- (iii) Introduction of cranes to ship.
- (iv) Greater use of shore-level luffing cranes.
- (v) Gantry cranes aboard ship – Munck, etc.
- (vi) Portainer gantry cranes on shore.

(f) Increase efficiency of loading aboard ship:
- (i) Larger hatchways.
- (ii) Motive beam 'tween decks for wing stowage.
- (iii) Twin and triple athwartship hatchways.
- (iv) Flat, strengthened, steel 'tween deck lids for fork lift truck stowage of cargo.
- (v) Introduction of Ro/Ro container ships.

(g) Introduction of longer working day, i.e. shift system, to docks to obtain greater utilization of any capital-intensive equipment.

(h) Gradual introduction of totally containerized handling of those goods which are suitable.

To eliminate stage four the following is required.

(i) Complete reappraisal of port working practices, including labour relations.

UNITIZED CARGO-HANDLING SYSTEMS

Emerging from our example there was considerable scope to improve the performance of the conventional system. Ships' time in port had to be reduced and the efficiency of port/inland transport interface increased. It is often the complexity of the transit area and stowage operations inherent in the traditional liner operations that cause the problems. Management is complex and there is often a split between the port and shipping sectors, consignees and consignors and their agents, and various outside agencies such as customs. The short-term interests of some of these groups often conflict. For example, the desire of consignors to ship as soon as possible often delays ships loading export cargo due to cargo arriving at the berth for export at the last moment, while the wish of consignees to obtain cheap storage tends to clutter up transit areas unless special disciplines are enforced. Some outside agencies, such as customs, are not interested in fleet or port operations, although their activities may have a significant effect upon both. Finally, the organization of the liner trades into conferences had a significant influence. Although liner conferences offer protection from outside competition (see Chapter 10 of *Elements of Shipping*) there were often influences within the group which were a barrier to rationalization or to the imposition of disciplines which would tighten up operational performance.

Bulk cargoes, Ro/Ro traffic, containers and pallets all require special facilities. The trend to larger vessels has meant an increasing need for rapid and efficient handling apparatus. Many ports have invested in new facilities to accommodate these demands. Goods may be stacked on pallets, which are wooden platforms or trays, or packed into containers, which are large metal boxes, temperature controlled, if necessary, and measuring 8 ft or 8.5 ft in height, 8 ft in width and 10, 20, 30 or 40 ft in length, according to International Standards Organization specifications. Container and unitized cargo-handling berths usually require large stacking areas behind the quays and special cargo-handling machinery, including transporter cranes, which are designed to handle a range of container lengths (see pp. 77–106). As many ships are specially designed to carry container traffic the introduction of containers has reduced the time spent handling goods in port and ships' turn-round time and costs. Many ports have improved their internal road facilities to cope with container-carrying lorries and at some ports rail terminals have been built from which rail container services operate to and from industrial centres.

There are a number of different unit load systems, each of which has its own characteristics and handling capability. Overall the unit load system aims to provide a number of benefits. These include the more effective utilization of capital equipment; the provision of a more favourable operational system in which profit margins can be improved; the improvement of the overall quality of service involving faster transit times and less risk of damage and pilferage to cargo; help in stabilizing cost with a capital-intensive rather than a labour-intensive system; making better use of overall resources throughout the system; introducing a more simplified system overall; encouraging the single carrier concept through the combined transport operation, and finally providing a door-to-door service.

One of the problems when introducing any new system is to persuade shippers and receivers that they should use it and will benefit. Areas of possible savings for those who have been persuaded to change their shipping methods may include packaging; insurance; handling – all aspects of labour saving; freight cost; inventory costs; transit time and documentation.

Many of these costs are difficult to break down and analyse closely for comparison purposes, but before choosing a new system the following questions must be answered for each type being considered:

(a) What are the actual details of conventional cost?
(b) What will be the cost of the new unitized system?
(c) To what extent will unitization reduce the value of in-transit and inventory costs, the latter involving less stock piling and risk of obsolescence?
(d) Will the new system reduce packaging, transit repair costs, pilferage, cargo deterioration, etc., and if so, to what extent?
(e) Are the shippers' and consignees' premises and equipment suitable for dealing with the new system? If not, what capital outlay will be required to make them so?
(f) Will the new system increase or decrease documentation?

(g) How will insurance be affected? Premiums are likely to be reduced.

Only after answering these and possibly many other questions and evaluating on the basis of them can a proper decision be made.

The operation of an intermodal transport system is intended to give the shipper a door-to-door service and make it simpler to assess the delivered cost of goods.

There is no one complete answer to any general cargo trade requirement, regarding which systems to implement, but by considering all points a reasonable optimum solution can be arrived at. There may well be operators of systems at the present time who are not entirely convinced that theirs is the best, but have implemented it because of the actions of competitors and for fear of being left behind. An examination of Table I will indicate some of the major factors which have to be considered.

LASH (LIGHTER ABOARD SHIP)

The LASH (lighter aboard ship) type of ship emerged in the late 1960s and a limited number are now operating throughout the world. The ship is 44 000 d.w.t. and has a capacity of 73 barges with about 27 000 tons of cargo – each lighter has a capacity of about 400 tons of cargo. This type of ship enables lighters to be carried from one port to another, thus combining inland waterway with ocean transportation. Each lighter is hauled on board over the stern by a 510 ton travelling crane and then dropped into the desired position on the ship. The holds can be converted quickly so that the LASH vessel can carry up to 1400 standard ISO 20 ft (6.10 m) containers. The vessel has a speed of 19 knots and two such ships would serve a fleet of 400 barges. After off-loading in the ports the barges are towed along the various inland waterways, providing a form of door-to-door service with quick delivery. Advantages of the service include through rates/bills of lading; no intermediate handling during transfer to and from the ship, thereby reducing cost and permitting competitive rates to be quoted and faster transits attained; lower insurance premiums; less risk of damage/pilferage; low risk of cargo delay as the barges are lowered into the water immediately on arrival at each port and likewise the barges are loaded on the LASH vessel, thus reducing time spent in port or its

Table I Factors affecting or determining the suitability of cargo-handling systems

Column 1		*Column 2*		*Column 3*		*Column 4*		
Commodity density	*System*	*Commodity value*	*System*	*Commodity type*	*System*	*National characteristic*	*System*	*Problem trade*
Low	Pallet Container Pre-sling	Low	Pallet Pre-sling Barge	Manufac-tured General	Pallet Ro/Ro Barge Container Pre-sling	Low wage	Pallet Pre-sling	Minimum capital intensity
Medium	Pallet Container Barge Ro/Ro Pre-sling	Medium	Barge Ro/Ro Container	Vegetable produce	Pre-sling Pallet Open container	Medium wage	Any	Maximum capital intensity
High	Barge Ro/Ro	High	Barge Ro/Ro Container	Refrigerated bulk	Various Barge Container	High wage	Maximum mechaniz-tion	

Table I outlines the major factors to be taken into account and indicates which system 'may' be suitable. For example: a medium density, high value, manufactured general commodity moving between high wage areas needs a system with maximum mechanization and of maximum capital intensity: very simple in that particular case, but not so in many.

environs to a minimum. Moreover, through the individual barges serving a variety of ports, it permits the LASH vessel to rationalize severely the ports of call to maintain good ship utilization. Overall, its prime aim is to obviate the need to use costly port facilities. A number of variations to the original have been made, including the Lykes Line See Bee class.

LASH is most suitable for trading between ports served by a good inland waterway system (river or canal) where industry is established near the waterway preferably. It is suitable for all types of general minor bulk or unitized cargo, but is highly capital intensive, which reduces its viability in many trades. Overall it is not always labour reducing to a large extent, but saves ship's time and is sometimes a 'total distribution' system in itself. Its investment requirements reduce its applicability in many areas where it could probably provide a rationalized and improved service. It would seem that 'mini-LASH' are likely to appear on the scene in the near future and the comparable BACAT system is already in operation on some short sea trades.

Examples of successful implementation include the Gulf ports of USA to Europe with paper products returning with general cargo.

ROLL-ON/ROLL-OFF (RO/RO) VESSELS

The Ro/Ro vessel is usually designed to carry a wide variety of cargo loaded in various unit forms but mainly on the road trailer (see *Elements of Shipping*, pp. 54–6). The designs of Ro/Ro ships are much more varied than those of container ships: space can be allocated in varying proportions to containers, cars, trucks, trailers, low loaders, heavy lifts and pallets. The ships are fitted with either ramps or lifts, whereby the various units can be rolled directly into their stowed position in the ship without further lifting.

Loading and discharging may be via bow, stern or side doors; ramps and Hyster-type fork lift or freight trucks are frequently employed. Increasingly the development trends in this field tend to be towards the 'hybrid' ship, i.e. a combination of the Ro/Ro cellular vessel. Particular developments are occurring in this field with respect to 'specialist bulk handling', e.g. car carriers, timber and product carriers. A further development includes the combi-carrier (see *Elements of Shipping*, pp. 47, 48 and 57).

BULK HANDLING SYSTEMS FOR RAW MATERIALS

The handling of dry bulk commodities is characterized by a number of factors. There is a need for a stable flow of the commodity to achieve the maximum efficiency in handling; the system is capital intensive in that mechanical handling is a necessity to achieve the high handling rates required; there will be a relatively low in number, but highly specialized labour force; there is a necessity for berths to be able to handle large ships yet be flexible enough for small ships, as required by different trade routes.

Most of the raw materials handled by bulk handling systems are of relatively low intrinsic value and transportation and distribution costs amount to a very high percentage of the total delivered cost of the material. It is therefore necessary to carry these goods in the largest possible units/ships to ensure the maximum of the 'economies of scale'.

It should also be noted that the provision of high productivity in loading/discharging operations on bulk cargoes requires a high level of mechanization and automation of control of handling machines and procedures. A high rate of cargo-handling operations can no longer be achieved by the individual capabilities of an operator as they are unable to withstand the pressure of high rate, repetitive working. Automation is necessary for both the crane systems and the continuous-feed conveyor-belt systems.

The technology of bulk handling in sea ports is governed directly by the direction of cargo traffic, i.e. whether it is being loaded or discharged from the ship. With few exceptions materials in bulk should be supplied to the purchaser at a uniform rate and back-up storage areas or stockpiles should be provided within the transportation chain. This also assists the ship operation (probably the most costly item) because storage capacity at the ports would normally be such that loading and discharging equipment can operate at highest output during the majority of the time the ship is on the berth.

Various berthing systems exist and from a civil engineering point of view it is important to distinguish between berths designed for imports as against those for exports. Vessel size is clearly significant for the design of any facility, but other aspects must be taken into consideration; these are detailed as follows (see also pp. 21–32).

Export berths

Usually bulk exports are handled by conveyor belt systems of one kind or another and it is often not necessary to have the vessel tied securely to a quay wall. In principle it would be possible to put the ship on dolphins to load and use a supporting structure, clear of the ship's forces (land possibly clear of ship contact), to carry the outreach loading booms and chutes.

This configuration may be considered because the system uses a gravity feed from the conveyor belt end into the ship. As can be seen from Diagram VII, the equipment may be parallel loaders, fixed

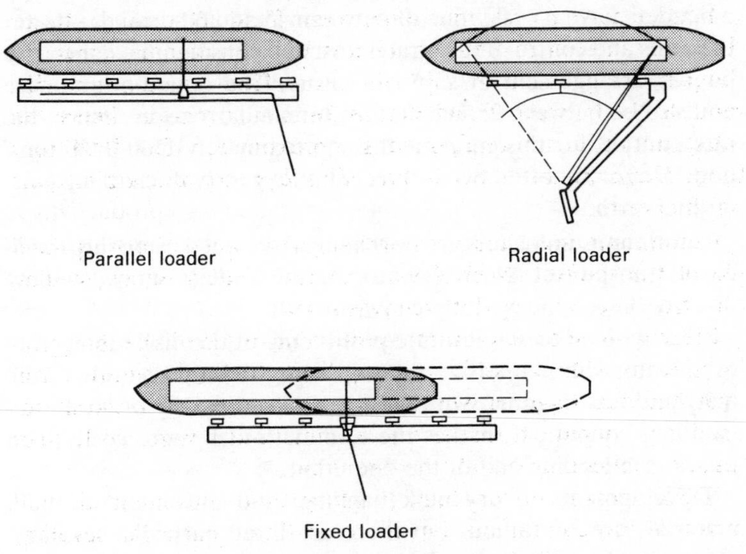

Diagram VII Bulk loading equipment

loaders or radial loaders. The radial loader is probably the most common system adopted and on the berths where 100 000 d.w.t. and over bulk carriers are loading it is usual to have twin radial loaders for flexibility and speed of loading. These loaders have a capacity in excess of 10 000 tons/hour, depending on stockpile and conveyor belt configuration and capacity. The bulk material is usually reclaimed from a stockpile using a bucket wheel reclaimer, fed through a hopper system to ensure continuity of supply to a conveyor belt, hence to the ship loader.

Import berths

In this instance gravity has an adverse effect and the port has to supply equipment to physically lift the bulk material from the hold of the ship. Considerably more power is required for this operation with the result that equipment is much heavier in construction and supporting structures more complex and costly. Grabbing devices are essentially a batch type of discharge equipment, but will, because of their efficiency in overcoming the gravity aspect, remain the most used discharging device for bulk material handling. As can be seen from Diagram VIII, the grab-type dischargers are basically of two types, the slewing clam and the shuttle clam. Modern unloaders have a cycle time of between 45 and 60 seconds – faster than this and control of the grab is lost and considerable damage to hopper arrangement or ship will ensue. The optimum grab size tends to be between 25 and 30 tons for similar reasons, hence the rated output for this equipment is approximately 1500–1800 tons/hour. There are often two or three shuttle gantry discharging units on the berth.

Continuous unloaders are now being developed using the principle of the bucket wheel elevator or the endless screw, feeding directly on to a heavy duty conveyor belt.

Clearly, in all cases accurate positioning of the discharging grab or elevator will necessitate the ship being tied up securely to the quay and this, together with the size and complexity of the shore-handling equipment, makes the terminal much more costly than that at the loading end of the operation.

Developments in dry bulk handling and movement of bulk materials are continuous but there are three particular developments which are likely to affect shipping and ports considerably in the future, detailed as follows:

(a) Part processing of raw materials. In many cases this is the first part of the processing of the material and clearly does three things: (i) it reduces waste materials, hence these are not shipped to the consumer, therefore reducing shipping cost; (ii) it increases the value of the material being shipped; (iii) it provides the exporting country with employment in the plant where the part processing takes place. Probably the best example of part processing of a raw material is the pelletization of iron ore in Peru before shipment to the steel-making plants in Japan.

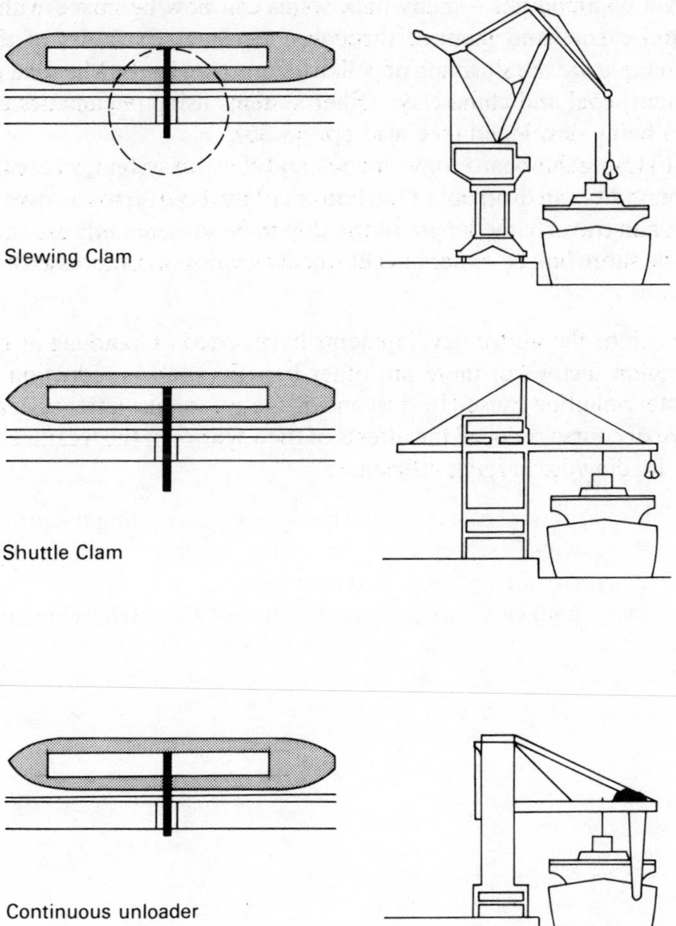

Diagram VIII Bulk discharge arrangements

(b) Slurrying of many commodities. Pipelines have been used for many years as a relatively inexpensive transportation system for liquid commodities – many bulk solids can now be mixed with a liquid carrier and pumped through a pipeline. Examples of this technique are the slurrying of pelletized iron ore by the Marcona jet system, coal and china clay. Other systems using pneumatics are also being developed (see also pp. 35–36).

(c) Using shipboard conveyor belt and elevator system, where the commodity can drop out of the bottom of the hold on to a conveyor belt and traverse the length of the ship to be subsequently elevated to the shore link by either bucket wheel elevator or compressed belt system.

Each of the above developments have speed of handling as the common factor but there are other benefits such as reduction of waste, pollution caused by dust and dirt, etc., and the latter systems have of course reduced the effects of the vagaries of the weather on the loading/discharging efficiency.

CHAPTER 5

Container-handling equipment

With the continuing growth in the use of containers worldwide, the need for reliable and efficient machines with which to handle them also increases. Many ports throughout the world have now evolved into using handling equipment, some of which is complex – and most expensive – but it is essential that it is reliable and economical in use if the profitability of the terminal is to be ensured/attained.

This type of equipment varies widely from straddle carriers to transtainers and rail-mounted gantry cranes. But the only machine that can rightly claim to be capable of being used in every facet of the container-handling operation is the fork lift truck.

It can be used to stuff and strip containers, handle them while empty, part laden and fully laden, stack them from ground level up to three or four containers high, and so on.

This chapter deals with palletization, fork lift trucks, container-handling equipment, and stowage techniques within the container.

PALLETIZATION – FORK LIFT TRUCKS

The fork lift truck, and such equipment as the pallet and pallet truck, operate on the basis that goods at first handling are placed on boards or pallets. The fork lift truck inserts its fork through or under the pallet, situated in a transit shed factory, freight depot, container, warehouse, quayside/berth, raises the load and carries it to the specified place. It may be the stuffing, stripping of a container, stacking cargo on the quayside/warehouse, or from/to the ship's side. With regard to the latter, the pallet is then used as a sling and hoisted direct into the ship's hold where the contents are stowed. The fork lift truck can also be used to tier cargo in a shed or on the quay. This system is called palletization. To a much greater extent it is used in the stuffing and stripping of containers, and more especially the process of handling cargo on the quayside and transit shed/warehouse/freight depot.

The pallets are usually of a standard type, 1000 mm × 1200 mm, constructed of metal, wood or fibre, and with a lifting capacity of up to 1500 kg. Larger and higher lifting capacity pallets are also available. Each pallet has a four-way entry for the fork lift trucks. Palletization is very versatile and relatively cheap to implement. It may be used on a door-to-door or port-to-port basis. Problems of control, repairing, replacement, etc. do exist, and pallet pools are being developed to cope with situations that arise. The pools are often set up by the port authorities. Many 'pallet owners' have been averse to the principle of disposable pallets in the past, but this is now being accepted as a viable principle in many trades as the disposable pallet can be produced cheaply and their cost written off. It frequently proves cheaper than the alternatives.

Pallets can be used either on conventional shipping, particularly between industrialized and non-industrialized countries, where a container system would be felt to be 'too complex' and not cost effective, or as part of a sophisticated pallet ship total system.

It is necessary in most cases to secure/strap the cargo on to the pallet. Plastic shrink wrapping is frequently used in conjunction with plastic or metal taping – the shrink wrapping also assisting in the weather protection for the goods.

More recently, following the growing development of cargo unitization, larger sized pallets – often of steel construction – are being used. This requires a larger fork lift truck of up to 4000 kg compared with the smaller pallet of about 1000/1500 kg lifting capacity.

Fork lift trucks are battery, electric, diesel or gas operated and fitted in the front with a platform in the shape of a fork or other device. The prongs lift and carry the pallet either by penetrating through specially made apertures or by passing under it. The platform, affixed to a form of mast, can be raised and tilted and the truck can travel with its load at any height up to its maximum. It is very manoeuvrable and can stack cargo up to a height of 5 m. Two main types of truck exist on the market today. Those dealing with the palletized consignment and those handling containers. We will deal first with the palletized or unitized/packaged cargo.

The fork lift truck lifting capacity varies from 1000 kg to 12 000 kg. The range of such equipment has been much extended in recent years to cater for the growing development of unitized cargo. It applies to the container, the freight depot warehouse, ICD, CFS, berth/quay, ship's hold, and so on. Not only does it extend to the pallet which may be stowed in a container, stacked in a warehouse/quayside/berth/transit shed, but also to handling unitized package cargoes as paper rolls, packaged timber, steel rods, pipes, steel coils, and so on.

A variety of fork lift truck types exist with a lifting capacity ranging from 1000 kg to 3000 kg and details are given below, as found in Diagram IX.

(a) The conventional fork lift truck is fitted in the front with a platform in the shape of two prongs of a fork. The prongs lift and carry the pallet either by penetrating through specially made apertures or by passing under it.

(b) Barrel handler. Designed to handle barrels and similar shaped commodities. Ideal for loading/discharging containers, and operation in a warehouse, transit shed, berth, and so on.

(c) Crane jib. Operates on the same basis as a crane.

(d) Boom handler. Ideal for the handling of carpets, and similarly shaped products.

(e) Squeeze clamps. Designed to handle newsprint rolls, and articles which would not be crushed through this method of handling.

(f) Drum holder. Ideal for the handling of drums and similarly shaped objects.

(g) Side shift mechanism. Equipment fitted to the fork lift truck to permit it to operate also sideways on and thereby aid flexibility of operation when handling palletized consignments.

(h) Extension forks. Likewise, the extension fork enables the fork to penetrate the aperture or pallet a greater distance, thereby permitting long pieces of palletized cargoes to be handled.

(i) Hand pallet truck. Used to facilitate handling/stowage of palletized cargo in confined spaces.

An example of a fork lift truck is the Hyster Space Saver truck, manufactured by Barlow Handling of Maidenhead, England. It has a lifting capacity of 2500 kg and is gas powered. It is equipped with three stage masks for low collapse height in its container stuffing role. It is equipped with side shifts for accurate load handling and quick release couplings for attaching the paper roll grab. It can unload a 10 000 kg container of 250 kg unit rolls of paper in half an hour.

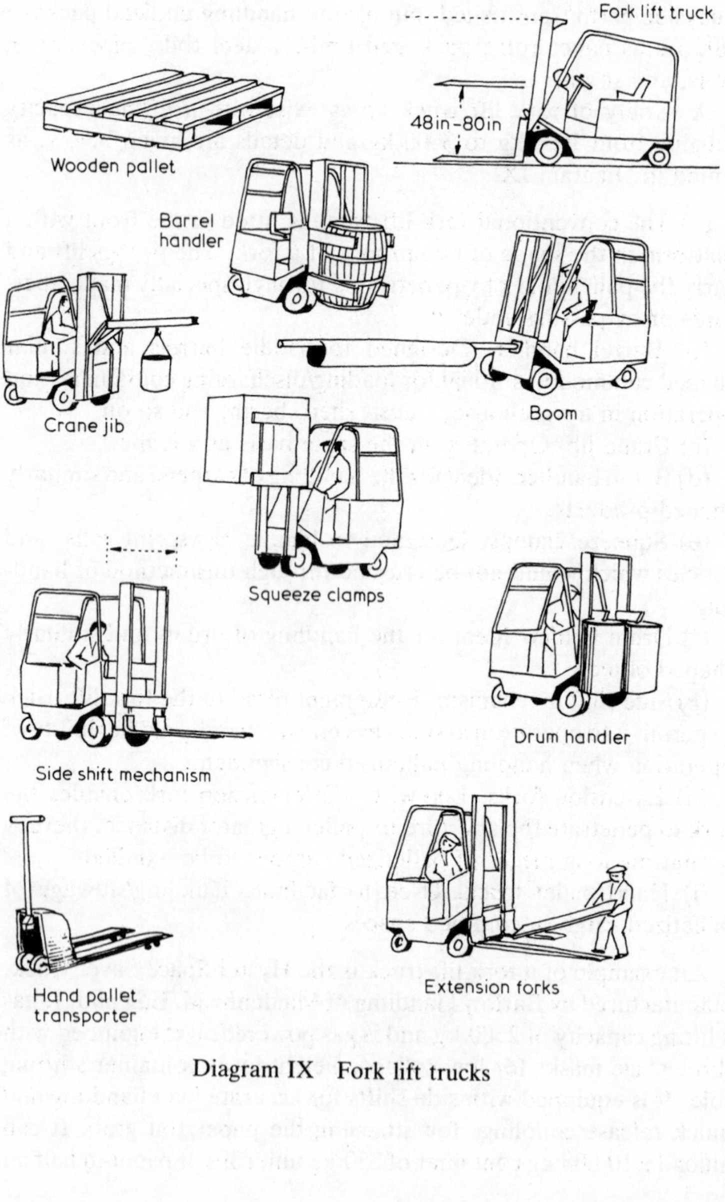

Diagram IX Fork lift trucks

The larger lifting capacity trucks are called freight lifters and have a lifting capacity ranging from 3000 kg to 12 000 kg. They are hydraulically operated. Such trucks tend to have the same range of lifting attachments, albeit on a larger lifting capacity scale. A number can lift transport/handle ISO containers.

An example of a modern freight lifting truck is the Hyster H250E. It has a lifting capacity of 12 000 kg and is capable of quick conversion from one type of attachment to another in minutes. The range of equipment attachments is found in Diagram IX. For example, it may be from the straight-sided bale clamps for 2000 kg lifts of wood pulp to curved clamps for handling board and paper rolls. Fully laden the truck can travel from the dock side to the warehouse. It has the capacity to stock four units high and has good manoeuvrability in loading transport. A further type is the Hyster 580B stevedoring truck, with three stage masts used on 'tween-deck vessels to move paper rolls into the square of the hatch for hoisting by crane. These special trucks have removable counterweights so that lower capacity cranes on smaller ships can lift the trucks aboard.

CONTAINERIZATION

Undoubtedly, containerization is the most important development within the general field of unitization to date (see Chapter 16 of *Elements of Shipping*). It is capital intensive and highly sophisticated when operated as a door-to-door system, which is the most common. In the highly developed trades, it is estimated that some 70% of containers move door-to-door on the FCL (Full Container Load) basis; LCL (Less than Container Load) shipments being 'stuffed' and 'stripped' at container bases, which may be inland or on the berth, dependent upon company policy, market conditions and common user terminal arrangements. By 1990 some 90% of all liner cargo trades are likely to be containerized.

Container systems involve an immensely greater investment in cargo-handling equipment than other unit load systems but they do achieve added benefits. Two of these, which have received a great deal of attention, are the capability of achieving very fast rates of handling (associated with a high rate of throughput per man, which gives large savings in stevedoring costs); and simplification of intermodal transfer, in which the large size of the unit helps to reduce the costs of inland distribution. However, the container system also incorporates a new approach to ship stowage and port transit operations.

Container ships differ from conventional vessels in the hull design and structure and are equipped with special devices and appliances providing high efficiency of handling operations. The engine room on such a ship is located aft; this feature allows us to devote for holds the most suitable parallel middlebody of the ship's hull. The whole upper deck of the container ship consists, in fact, of hatch openings. The cross bulkheads are spaced about 40 ft (12.20 m) apart. The hatch openings are closed, with hatch covers of a caisson type about 40 ft (12.20 m) long. The hatch width is 80 to 85% of the ship beam, so allowing direct access to the cargo spaces. In spite of this it may still be difficult – in container handling terms – on multiport itineraries. Hence, some simplification on routes and rationalization of a number of ports has taken place. Most of the companies are tending to operate a simple route pattern at the expense of incurring quite high costs in inland transport and feeder services. This does, however, allow high ship utilization and achieve high rates of loading and discharging.

The port transit operation has been changed by virtue of the size of the unit, the fact that it provides its own protection from the weather, and that it can be moved with comparative freedom in the container park/container standage area. There has been very varied practice in port transit areas: at one extreme there is the system of containers on trailers in the park, which give random access to any box in the park. Where the trailers used in the park can also be operated in an inland transport, this system is particularly simple to operate. At the other extreme there are the high stacking systems, which make savings in the amount of space required and in the distances travelled within the park, but at the cost of increasing the complexity of operation and the problem of retrieving the individual box required. Where the stacking system is used ribbon type of stacking is required when straddle carriers are the main handling system while herringbone stacking is used when side loaders are operated. Transtainers, a mobile, rubber-wheeled gantry-type crane, usually spanning the whole, or at least one section of the container park, are now being brought into operation as they can be used for the park handling, shifting as well as the park/inland transport interfaces.

The organization of a full container service is a large administrative problem, particularly in the areas of berth arrangements, control of the containers and documentation. Great efforts are being made to reduce these problems with the aid of computers. It involves many companies/people as detailed below:

(a) *Export end*: Producer, dispatch/forwarding department, haulier road or rail, port operator, loading stevedore, freight forwarder, shipping agent, export customs, plus ship's master/ship owner.
(b) *Import end*: Ship's agent, discharging stevedore, port operator, consignee's agent, import customs, delivery haulier road or rail, receiver's warehouse and consignee's buying office.

In consequence, the need for computer control and techniques becomes paramount in the interest of overall efficiency.

RANGE OF CONTAINER-HANDLING EQUIPMENT

The success of the freight container stems from standardization: knowledge of the maximum gross weight, the plan dimensions and the disposition of lifting points enables handling equipment to be designed largely without reference to the type of cargo and to be marketed throughout the world. A paramount continuous need is the demand for enhanced performance, together with an evolving requirement for proper overall control of many items of plant working together as a co-ordinated system. A need for some measure of uniformity in the specification of handling equipment is recognized by manufacturers to help reduce cost and improve reliability by concentrating on a limited range of broadly defined classes of machine. The port operator will be looking for simpler and cheaper maintenance procedures and greater interchangeability among mixed plant.

During the past 15 years terminal operators have been looking for reliability and flexibility qualities in their container equipment. They require equipment which works continuously in return for moderate maintenance effort and which can be deployed in a variety of roles to suit changing traffic demands. If the number of marine container terminals in the industrialized countries diminishes, with flows concentrated through fewer interchange points, there may be an increased requirement for less versatile equipment that can achieve greater efficiency in more limited roles. In that situation the products developed for the marine terminal would become even less applicable to the small inland terminal than they are today, whereas the need for efficient inland transport systems to concentrate the exports and disperse the imports would become more pressing. Developing countries are likely to invest *ab initio* in a limited number of major container ports, backed up by improved rail, road and water transport, with an emphasis on local employment using equipment appropriate to the technical skills available.

While the maritime container-carrying systems of the developed countries have been undergoing a gradual process of refinement and rationalization, with an emphasis on major routes/trades and a limited number of high capacity transfer points, there is at the same time an increasing interest in the inland sector of the throughput movement, and indeed in inland combined transport. This requires dispersed rather than concentrated access to the trunk carrier and hence calls for equipment to serve low flow transfers and sporadic demand. The machinery developed for use in maritime container ports has of necessity been put to work inland, in the same way that available plant was originally used to handle containers through ports. In the next few years the main growth of container transport will be combined transport, which will encourage the diversity of container-handling equipment to be developed.

Current container-handling equipment can be classified in many different ways, including: capacity, speed mechanical principle, height of lift, type of suspension, and so on. An analysis of such equipment is found in Diagram X. The main division is between the rubber-tyred and rail-mounted equipment; within these groups the different types of machine are listed according to their mobility and work rate. Most machines handle loaded or empty containers as the need arises, but some techniques are appropriate only for empty boxes, e.g. lifting a container by one side rather than by the top or bottom.

CONTAINER LIFTERS AND MOVERS

The function of these devices is to lift a container from ground, stillage or trailer, to move it to a new location, and to place it on ground, stillage or trailer. Some of these machines can be described as low cost, low rated, straddle carriers. Other devices in this

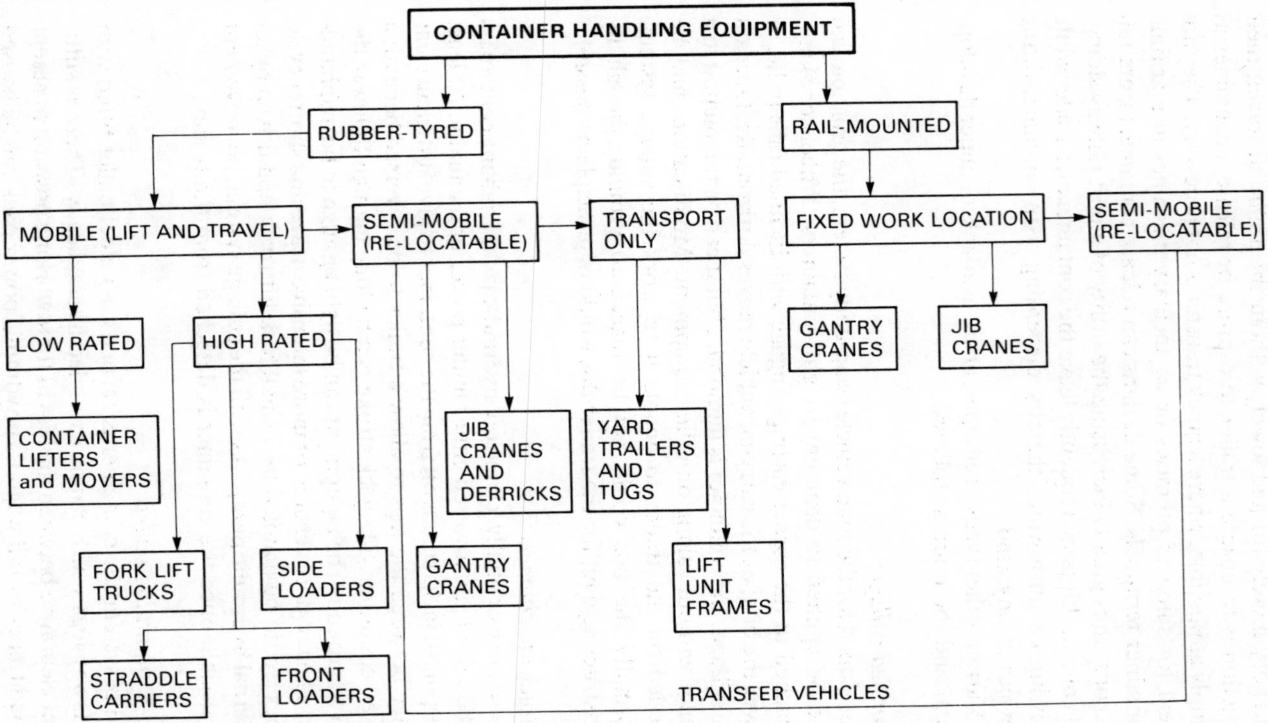

Diagram X Container-handling equipment categories

category merely lift and lower, without the ability to travel; their function is to enable a trailer to capture or release a container as simply as possible, where a quick transfer is not necessary. They are ideal for shippers premises or as ancillary machines in maritime container terminals. Some designs can release containers from rail wagons, thus greatly increasing the utility of a port railway siding. Of course, shippers frequently leave the container on a trailer while stowing or unstowing, thereby dispensing with container-lifting devices of any kind.

Various other types of equipment are available or under development and these are as follows.

Ramped stillages

Developed for the road vehicle swap-body system, the principle can also be applied to demount freight containers. Wheels or skates attached to the corner castings engage with inclined rails to lift or lower the box, as the carrying vehicle moves horizontally. Once on the stillage, the container is immobile, but it can be remounted to a trailer without calling on other equipment. Modifications may be needed on the trailer to enable it to work the stillage system. Normally the box could not be placed to ground, though by constructing a pit for the trailer this would in principle be possible.

Corner attachments

These are essentially 'clamp on' hydraulic jacks enabling containers to be raised and lowered either under power or manually. At least one pair of jacks stands off from the container to give sufficient clear space between the legs to allow a trailer to be reversed beneath a raised container. The jack stroke can be long enough to lower the box to ground. The equipment can be light enough to be manhandled; a heavy-duty version for more intensive usage and shorter cycle times would be handled by a small fork lift truck and driven by an external hydraulic pump. As with the stillage system, no movement is possible once the container is detached from the trailer.

Self-demounting pallets

In this system the container is carried on a steel pallet fitted with foldaway legs which can be extended hydraulically. There is sufficient clearance between the legs in their working position to accept a road trailer or rail wagon. A hydraulic power pack can be housed within the pallet, requiring only an external 24 V d.c. supply to operate the extending legs. Road/road or road/rail transfers can be effected, but the pallet cannot be let down to ground level.

Self-loading trailers
A specially-adapted road trailer gathers the container from ground level or from some form of docking stand or stillage. The container is tilted during acquisition from ground level, and the method would not be suitable for all cargoes. Trailer mechanisms typically include a tilting platform and rails or guides along which one end of the container is drawn as the road vehicle reverses, and possibly a pair of short-stroke rams at the rear end of the trailer. The process is rather slow, but the additional weight is less than that of more elaborate self-loading systems.

Mobile lift frames
These machines resemble the straddle carrier, but without its high-stacking ability and its capacity for extended travel at reasonable speeds. There are a number of configurations and different degrees of elaboration, but in all cases a mobile steel structure is positioned astride the container, which is lifted on the top or bottom four twist locks. Box lengths of 20 ft (6.10 m) to 40 ft (12.20 m) can be handled, and alignment over the load is made less critical by incorporating chains or sideshift in the hoist. Hoisting is by means of hydraulic rams, in some cases enabling containers to be stacked two-high. Power for hoist and travel can be provided by a tug master or by an engine fitted to the machine. These are the most versatile of the low-rated container-movers. Their cost is claimed to be less than one-fifth that of a conventional straddle carrier and they do not require specially reinforced paving.

A wide variety of container-handling plant is usually employed in a marine terminal, the predominance of one type or another depending on the operational system adopted. Before looking at the present-day capabilities of the major items of equipment, it may be useful to examine what happens within a marine container terminal.

The primary function of a container terminal is the transfer of containers between ships and land transport vehicles. Secondary function is the reception of less-than-container load (LCL) export cargoes and its consolidation into containers and the unpacking of LCL import containers and the dispatch of the unpacked cargoes by land transport. This activity, the stowing and unstowing of containers, requires covered storage space and weather-protected loading bays, the whole facility constituting a container freight station (CFS). Other secondary functions may include container and vehicle maintenance and repair workshops and the storage of empty containers. Some container terminals perform only the primary function within the area of the terminal proper, relegating any secondary functions to less valuable land within a short distance of the berths. Other terminals accommodate LCL facilities and repair/maintenance shops on land adjacent to the quays. In all cases there are buildings for administrative and control functions, where information on the export and import containers is assembled; movements through the terminal are planned, the documentation prepared, etc.

There are important differences between import, export and empty containers, which influence the way in which each type progresses through the terminal. Except for some short-sea traffic in which containers may be transferred directly from ship to rail or road vehicle, there are always two steps in the transfer process: import containers are first taken from the ship and placed on the ground or on a wheeled trailer (slave trailer, or terminal chassis), from there they are moved to a stacking area which is often not directly adjacent to the berth, and they are later (usually after several days) lifted from this stacking area and placed on road or rail for delivery to inland destination. Export containers will arrive over a period of many days before the ship closing date, and will be stacked in an area adjacent to the loading berth but not within the reach of the quay container crane; from this stack they will be extracted in a pre-planned sequence and transported to the area under the quay crane, to be lifted and placed in an allotted space in the vessel. Empty containers being shipped out will be dealt with in the planning for export containers; empty containers arriving by sea or land will usually be separated from import containers, and stacked in a special storage area. The disposition of import containers on the terminal is further influenced by their mode of onward delivery: rail destined, road destined and LCL containers will follow different routes through the terminal and may be segregated as soon as they leave the quay crane.

The three categories of container differ in the following ways:

(a) In the predictability of their future movement through the terminal. Ship arrivals are more reliably predicted than (say) container collections by customers, and the order of stowage on a vessel is planned at the same time as the location of stowage in the export stack whereas the order of collection from the import stack is virtually unpredictable. Export containers may thus be stacked four or five high without much risk of the lower boxes being needed before the upper ones, but import containers must be accessible more or less at random, which limits the height of the stack to one or two boxes at most if much repositioning within the stack is to be avoided.

(b) In the timing and accuracy of received information about individual containers. In general, information about export containers is received earlier and is more easily verifiable than that about import containers. Essential information about export containers includes container number, weight, size and conditions, destination port, shipping line and vessel name, IMO class of cargo. These data will normally be obtained and checked before the container enters the terminal. A space will be allotted within the appropriate bay of the export stack, where the box will remain until the ship calls. Similar information about import containers is provided in advance of the ship's arrival, but may be incomplete and is not verifiable until the containers are actually being unloaded. In practice it is not uncommon to find errors in ship stowage plans, which has led some operators to plan the movement of import containers on the basis of what is actually found rather than what the advance information says should be found. Thus, instead of planning to move a container from a particular cell in the ship to a particular position on the terminal (which could be done if the stowage information were error free) the number and size of the next one or two containers to be lifted will be given to the computer, which will match with its stored information and will reply either with movement instructions or with an error message. Incomplete or incorrect information, e.g. relating to contents (LCL, hazardous cargo) or onward delivery (road, rail) will give rise to delays and additional costs.

(c) In their weight. Empty containers can be handled by machinery (e.g. mobile cranes) and by techniques (e.g. gripping two lower and two upper corners) which are unsuitable for loaded containers. Empty containers are also restricted to low stacking heights or to locations beneath loaded containers because of instability of an empty stack in high winds.

There are three available techniques for accessing the container stacks in a high throughput situation: the rail-mounted gantry crane with cantilevers beyond both legs; the rubber-tyred gantry crane without cantilevers; and the straddle carrier. The rail gantry achieves the fastest rate of working and provides the highest stacking density (five high, 14 rows). It can be highly automated. The rubber-tyred gantry is a slower machine and provides less stacking density (four high, six rows) but it can be driven from one stack to another so that several parallel stacks may be served by one machine. The straddle carrier is the most flexible but slowest machine. It will stack up to four high, and will typically produce between five and ten lifts per hour. It requires alleys to be left between all rows of containers. It can load either road or rail vehicles, and it can be used to carry containers between the stack and the quay crane; this practice is not favoured, by some operators. The use of the straddle carrier solely as a transfer (not transport) machine is often preferred but this requires additional equipment and manpower for the tractor–trailer link being preferred. Diagram XI demonstrates the various stacking options and degree of space utilization employing the straddle carrier, fork lift truck and Shifter crane – the latter described on pp. 101–103.

Transport to and from the quay crane is sometimes by straddle carrier, more often by slave trailer, and occasionally by rail. One container crane may be served by three slave trailers and tractors: one under the crane, one at the stack, and one travelling between.

The modern high-speed terminal cannot work economically if the flow of information about container moves to be made is slower than the physical movement of the containers. Without adequate advance information delays to road and rail vehicles, congestion on the terminal, and unnecessary double handling cannot be avoided. For this reason the newer terminals use computers to store updated information, and to make it quickly available where it is needed for operational planning and control purposes.

For a dedicated container berth the rail-mounted gantry crane is unchallenged for moving containers between ship and shore. For

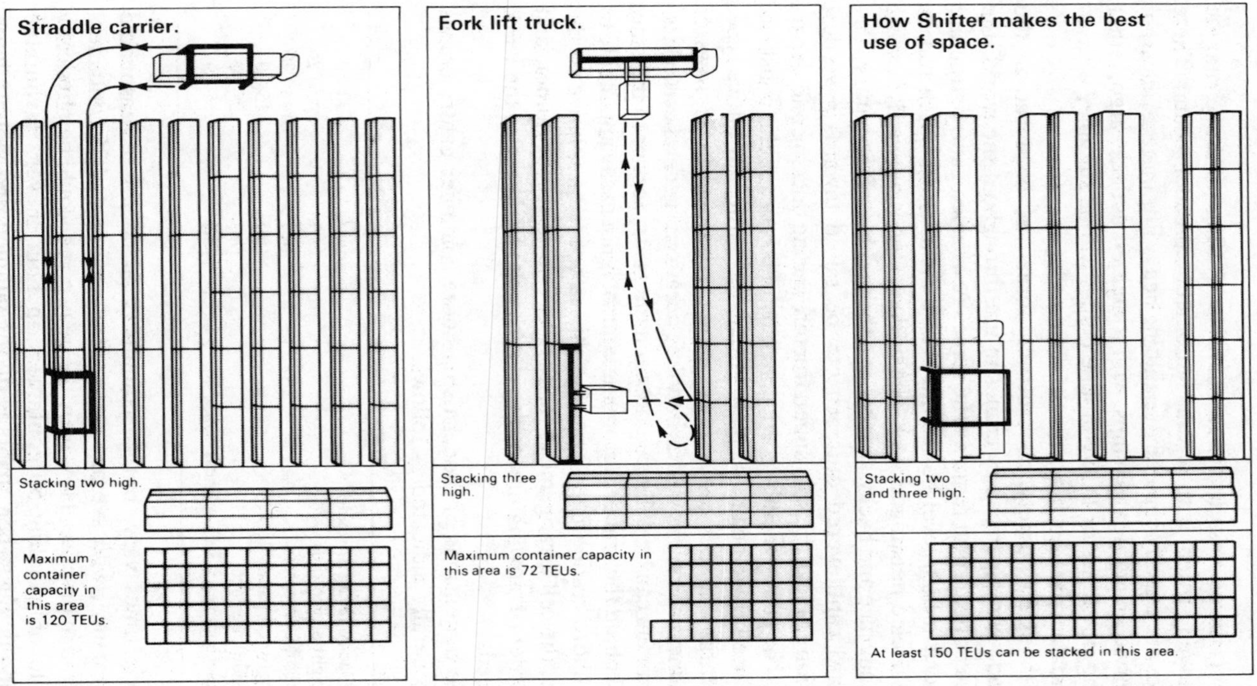
Straddle carrier.
Stacking two high.
Maximum container capacity in this area is 120 TEUs.
Fork lift truck.
Stacking three high.
Maximum container capacity in this area is 72 TEUs.
How Shifter makes the best use of space.
Stacking two and three high.
At least 150 TEUs can be stacked in this area.

Diagram XI Container parking space utilization options using the straddle carrier, fork lift truck and Shifter-type crane (reproduced by kind permission of Sea Containers Ltd)

serving mixed vessels the rail-mounted luffing jib crane may be employed, fitted with a fully automatic spreader beam. These cranes are equally capable of handling heavy lifts or general cargo. To service general cargo ships, with containers as deck cargo, either luffing jib cranes or heavy mobile cranes will be suitable, with an automatic spreader beam for handling containers.

Although a variety of structural forms are displayed in the 750-odd container gantry cranes in use throughout the world, the basic configuration remains the same. A wheeled gantry structure supports a high-level horizontal bridge beam along which travels the wheeled hoisting trolley. The bridge extends outwards beyond the quay face and backwards beyond the rear legs of the gantry. The forward cantilevered outreach can be raised towards a vertical position to clear the ship superstructure during docking and departure. The gantry members are generally of box or tubular construction, the bridge beams of plate girder, box girder, or lattice type. The largest cranes can service ships carrying up to 13 rows of containers across, as well as handling occasional general cargo lifts. Containers can be delivered between the gantry legs or to the quay area behind the crane. Automatic control is not easily applicable to ship–shore crane operations: the ship is not fixed relative to the crane, the cell arrangement varies from one vessel to another, and the order of stowing/unstowing is subject to variation as the work proceeds.

The dimensions of modern ship–shore container gantry cranes are generally indicated as follows:

Lift capacity under spreader	(tonnes)	30–50
Lift height above rails	(m)	up to 25
Lift height below rails	(m)	up to 15
Span between gantry legs	(m)	15–30
Waterside outreach	(m)	25–40
Landside backreach behind near rail	(m)	5–25

Cycle times vary, but 25 containers an hour is a reasonable performance, with average rates of between 15 and 25 containers achieved in practice. However, the quay crane would be physically capable of handling 50 containers an hour in very favourable conditions, e.g. when stripping deck containers and without landside delays. One assessment concluded that quay cranes on average operate at less than 70% of some standard capacity, being a work-rate that could realistically be achieved by reducing delays and interruptions. Since the quay crane is the most expensive item in the handling system, and because its rate of working directly affects the time a ship spends in port, it is important to minimize delays at the interface between the quay crane and the back-up services. In other words, the quay crane should not have to wait for a space to deposit an import box, and should always find an export box correctly positioned ready to be lifted. One way of achieving this is to create a small moving buffer store of containers between the quay crane and the landside services, thereby decoupling the work cycles of the different handling systems.

In the USA such a system has been introduced by Matson Navigation Co. at some of their terminals, where the container stacks are serviced by rail-mounted gantry cranes. The quay crane is provided with a horizontal conveyor extending from a point between the gantry legs to beyond the backreach of the crane. This conveyor holds up to five containers side by side, and can be moved forward intermittently to put an empty space at the reception end and a container at the delivery end. The yard gantry crane is fitted with a short cantilevered extension to its trolley beam, overhanging the conveyor, and is thus able to acquire containers from the quay crane without intermediate quay surface transport. The system can in theory dispense with all vehicles on the berth, in which case a high degree of automation could be achieved in yard operations.

A vertical system to create the same sort of moving buffer, but accessed by trailers at ground level instead of yard cranes at stack level, has been proposed by the Italian crane manufacturer Reggiane. This machine, which would be positioned under the backreach of the quay crane, would hold a maximum of three containers one above the other. As a box is taken away from either top or bottom the remaining two boxes can be moved up or down a space. The 100 tonne tare rubber-tyred Liftainer would incorporate eight automatic stabilizers.

The special two-trolley feature offered by a Netherlands company should also at least partially de-couple the quay crane from the back-up transport systems, the aim of all these devices being to get more output and hence postpone the need for new investment. A description of three types of container crane involving the Shifter, Tango and Samba is found on pp. 97–103.

BACK-UP SYSTEMS

Containers are handled in the terminal end using one or more types of equipment, the main items including tractors and trailers, front end loaders (fork lift trucks), straddle carriers, and yard gantry cranes, rail mounted or rubber tyred.

The way this equipment is deployed, either singly or in combination, defines the operating method for the terminal. The several operating methods which are the subject of so much argument and discussion really amount to statements about the sort of handling plant to be used. Practical choices will be restricted by factors such as land availability, size and frequency of vessels to be served, and whether the facilities are controlled by a single user or at the service of many users. At one end of the scale, a port can be operated entirely by tractors and trailers, collecting and delivering directly from the quay crane and parking side by side in single-level storage areas. At the other end, containers can be stacked in solid blocks up to four high accessed by automated rail-mounted gantry linked with the quay cranes and with the inland transport systems. There is no agreement on the best operating method (not surprising since no two ports will face identical conditions of traffic, site, labour and finance), and where realistic alternatives do exist the argument is about flexibility to cope with exceptional demands and events versus the more productive use of land and capital obtained from large machines with computerized planning and control and a minimal labour force. In more concrete terms, should the stacks be built by straddle carriers and/or front end loaders or should they be spanned by yard gantry cranes? One port operator regards the straddle carrier as a machine that has served its purpose in furthering the container revolution but which must now be replaced by systems more reliable, safer, less labour-intensive, more controllable; another is heard to remark that while straddle carriers may injure the workers, gantries injure the shareholders. Successful terminals can be seen using either system.

The popularity of the straddle carrier in a large number of container terminals throughout the world was as much a result of real or perceived disadvantages in the alternatives as of its own freedom from faults. The sideloader was found to be unreliable in a multi-user terminal. The fork lift or front loader required too much land space. The rubber-tyred gantry was cumbersome, the rail-mounted was inflexible and they both required tractor-trailers to supplement them. The straddle carrier was almost the only piece of equipment available which could pick up, transport and set down a container, could stack boxes up to three high, was reasonably economical in land space, and could travel to work anywhere on the terminal (see Diagram XI). It was chosen in the hope that its shortcomings could be overcome, among them its awkwardness to drive, susceptibility to damage, costly maintenance, low availability and its tendency to soak the terminal surface in hydraulic oil. These problems could be ascribed mainly to design or mainly to misuse, depending on one's point of view. Certainly they are being overcome in the newer machines at expanding ports. Shaft drives are replacing chains, diesel-electric operation may replace hydraulics. The modern straddle can lift 35 tonnes under the spreader and stack boxes four high, running on 8 or 10 wheels with rubber suspension. Dual engines with a life of over 15 000 hours and all major components with a design life of over 50 000 hours help to improve reliability and availability, and to reduce planned maintenance down time to 10–15%.

The fork lift truck (FLT) is found in every stage of container operation, from small low-emission machines for container stowing to heavy-duty diesel-powered front end loaders developed specifically for container handling. The earliest and still the easiest technique is to lift directly on the forks, but only for 20 ft (6.10 m) containers fitted with fork entry slots. For containers without slots the FLT can be fitted with attachments to the forks or to the mast, designed to engage the container corner castings. All attachments increase the lifted load, and may also increase the load centre distance. Toplift spreader beams, fixed or telescopic with manual or hydraulic twistlock operation, lift on the top four corners of the container. Sidelift beams, engaging with two or four corners on one side of the container, are widely used for both loaded and empty containers, though not fully endorsed by the standards organizations with work on container racking forces under way. They provide a convenient method for handling empty containers and for stowing laden boxes between decks on Ro/Ro vessels. Because the container is carried broadside on the FLT requires an aisle-width greater than the container length; by using an endlift beam to grip the container at the four corners on one end the travelling width is reduced and empty containers can be stacked end on, pigeon-hole fashion. Such end-on handling operations do not normally take place at maritime container terminals and are usually confined to the handling of empty units at storage depots. FLTs have been produced which specialize in handling and stacking empty containers, a job for which straddle carriers are neither suitable nor economic. One such machine lifts 15 tonnes to a height of 14 m under a hydraulically adjustable toplift attachment and can build a six-high block-stack of empties.

The FLT with container-handling attachments can always revert to handling general cargo. Where this versatility is not required the purpose-designed container handling front end loader may be preferred. Handling techniques are similar to those of the FLT with toplift spreader, but the lift mechanisms are different. Instead of the vertical mast and sliding frame of the lift truck these machines use horizontal pivoting beams and linkages to manipulate the spreader. One Italian design is essentially a mobile crane with an extending boom and a rotatable side shifting spreader in place of the hook; the 'portpacker' uses a shorter fixed-length pivoted boom with a parallel linkage to keep the spreader horizontal throughout the arc of movement. Improved visibility and a wider range of spreader positioning are features of these machines.

All front end loaders carry the load ahead of the front axle, counterbalanced by the machine weight behind the axle. A long wheelbase helps to reduce front axle loads, but impairs manoeuvrability. To reduce bearing pressures on the paved surface up to six tyres are fitted at the front end of the 40-tonne capacity front-loaders.

Surface loads from container-stacking gantries require beam or piled foundations for rail tracks and possibly a running beam for rubber-tyred machines unless multiple wheels are provided at each leg of the gantry. Rail-mounted gantries are electrically powered, usually supplied by reeled cable to permit longitudinal travel; d.c. electric drive systems (Ward Leonard) are robust and reliable, but as the cost of solid state control systems for variable speed a.c. drives continues to fall, their use is likely to decrease. Rubber-tyred machines are self powered, with diesel-hydraulic or diesel-electric drives for hoist, traverse and travel functions. Wheels are individually powered and steered, some recent machines providing 90° steering motion to facilitate lateral movement between separate stacking areas. Modern yard cranes are fitted with anti-sway systems, often by diagonal-reeving techniques, which hold the spreader more or less rigidly beneath the trolley, even in high winds. This is especially necessary if gantry movements are to be automatically controlled.

Within the limited range of basic types of crane there is a wide choice of individual designs; many having been produced to an individual user's specification or from experience at a particular site. This may be viewed as a stage in development towards a number of broadly agreed standard specifications. However, with no expanding market for rail-mounted gantries and the need to take many extraneous factors – such as yard configuration, space availability and throughput requirement – into consideration, it is difficult to see how this would come about.

The potential advantages of the rail gantry crane – high density stacking, fast cycle times, automatic control – will only be fully realized when attendant operations can be planned reliably. A four-high stack planned for a particular sequence of ship arrivals becomes difficult to access if the arrival order is changed. For various reasons containers may arrive at the gantry in a different order from when they left the quay crane or storage stack, modifying the intended sequence of gantry moves. The multi-user terminal will have to cope with a higher level of uncontrollable variation in movements by sea and by land, and single-user ports are probably better placed to develop new systems or new mixes of existing plant to cater for known requirements.

CONTAINER CRANES

Basically there are two types of container crane: those which are rubber tyre mounted and those which are rail mounted. We will now examine three container cranes called Samba, Tango and Shifter, which are used extensively throughout the world and marketed by Sea Containers Ltd.

The Samba – Diagram XII – has a 35.06 m (115 ft) outreach, a 39 ton lifting capacity, and services containerships stowing up to twelve containers across. It has a span of 30.48 m (100 ft), a back reach of 10.67 m (35 ft) with a height under the spreader of 24.39 m (80 ft). Maximum wheel loads are 23.5 tons. The Samba is designed for quick and inexpensive erection. Once the rails have been installed, the crane can be erected in about three weeks. Four

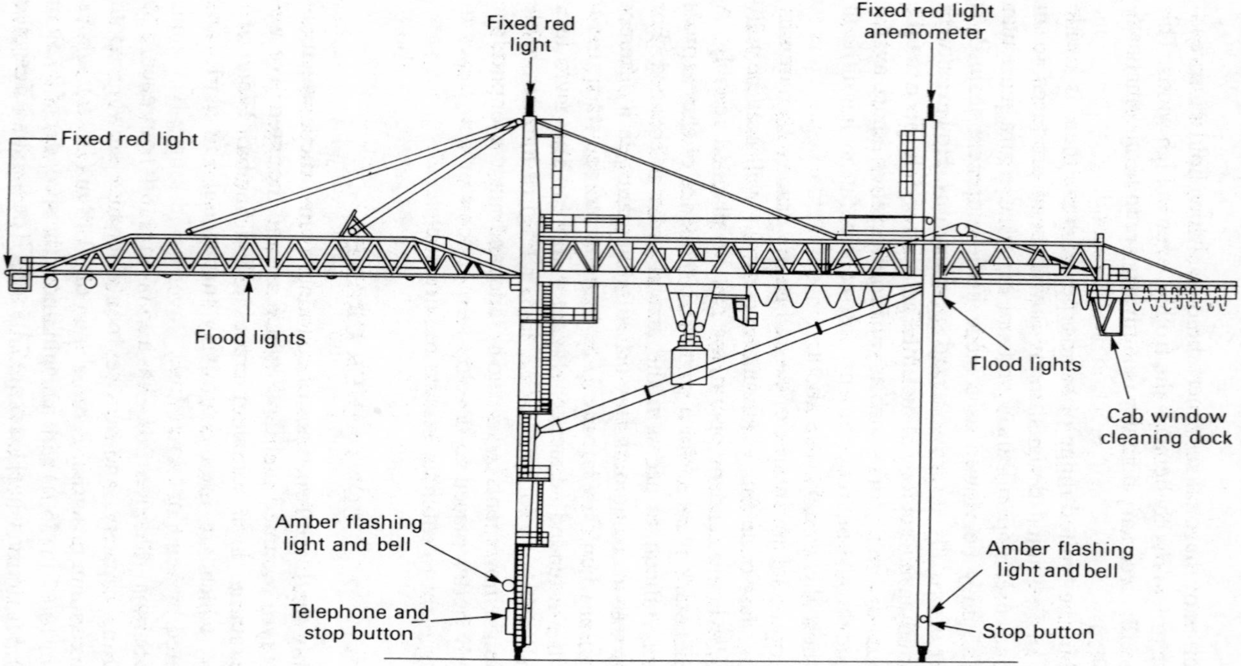

Diagram XII Container crane Samba (reproduced by kind permission of Sea Containers Ltd)

winches and one mobile crane are the only erection equipment needed.

The structural design employs mainly heavy reinforced pin joints, which allows quick self erection and dismantling of the crane without major site welding or the use of large mobile cranes. For example, the Samba can be dismantled and moved either within the port or to another port with great ease. The main beam is a rectangular lattice structure and the legs are welded fabricated box structures mounted on travel bogies. The travel bogies incorporate double-flanged travelling wheels of cast steel which can easily be changed, and four storm anchor points are provided. It is fully tropicalized.

A 385 kW a.c. motor drives three separate d.c. generators to provide power for the d.c. motors of the main crane motions. Stepless speed control is effected by a thyristor-controlled Ward Leonard system.

The steel-frame cabin which is fitted to the trolley, is weatherproof and fully temperature controlled. The large, tinted, safety-glass windows give excellent all-round visibility and are easily cleaned from a special platform provided. All main crane and spreader motions are controlled from the driver's seat and a two-way telephone link to the ground station is provided. Spreader trim and tilt systems are provided to trim the spreader by 4° in the longitudinal axis and 5° in the transverse axis.

The luffable boom is controlled from a weatherproof cabin situated at the docking station from where long travel can also be controlled for driver convenience, and to speed up the operation. The crane surface protection system comprises complete descaling and shot blasting of the steelwork to near white metal; an epoxy weldable primer is applied, followed by a three-coat system of high quality paint to give a minimum dry film thickness of 175 μm.

The modern electrical equipment allows precision of control plus the ability to operate hoist, cross traverse and long travel simultaneously and together. In such situations it enables the operator to achieve a working output of 30–33 moves per hour. The lifting equipment comprises either one telescopic, automatic, spreader for lifting 6.10 m (20 ft) and 12.20 m (40 ft) ISO containers and 10.70 m (35 ft) American Standard (ASA) containers; or two separate automatic, fixed-frame spreaders for lifting 6.10 m (20 ft) and 12.20 m (40 ft) ISO containers, and, as optional extra, a

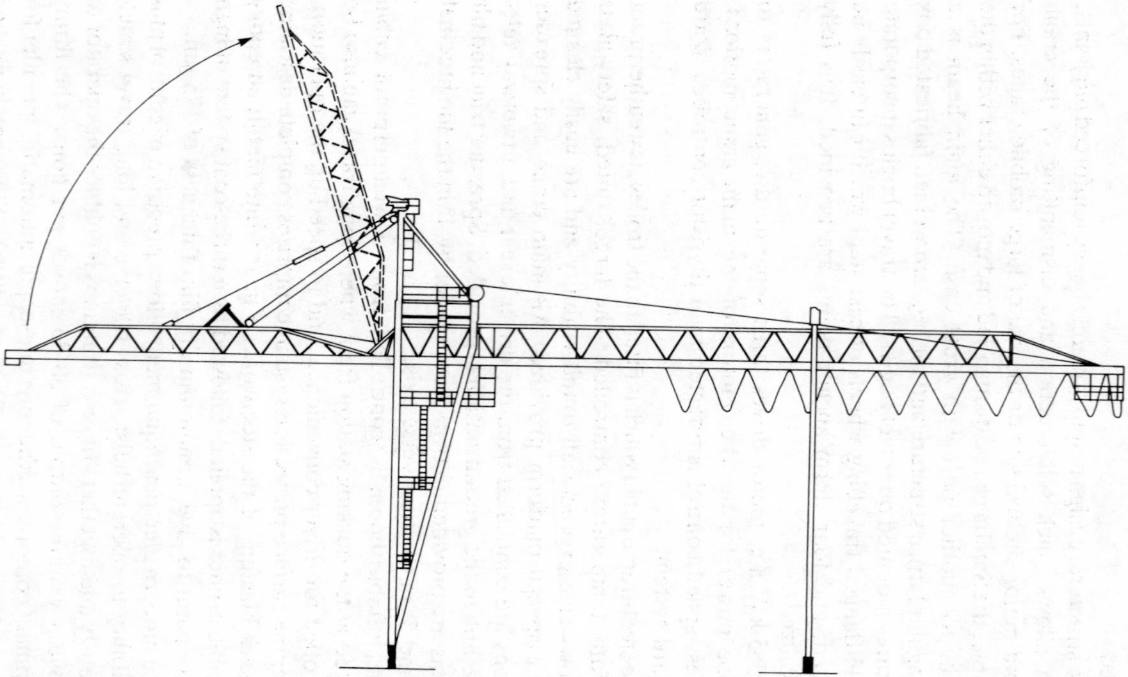

Diagram XIII Container crane Tango (reproduced by kind permission of Sea Containers Ltd)

10.70 m (35 ft) frame spreader for lifting 10.70 m (35 ft) ASA containers. Additionally a 35 ton hook-beam for lifting general cargo is provided.

The Samba has a 30 ton capacity under the spreader, with 35 tons under the heavy lift hook beam. The hoist speed is 120 ft/min under a full load. The trolly speed is 400 ft/min and long travel speed 120 ft/min.

The Tango (Diagram XIII) is a 24.38 m (80 ft) outreach rail-mounted electrically operated container gantry crane with a capacity of 30 tons under the spreader and 35 tons under the hook beam. It has a span of 30.48 m (100 ft), a backreach of 10.67 m (35 ft) and height under the spreader of 21.34 m (70 ft). Maximum wheel loads are 26 tons.

The structural design, using mainly heavy reinforced pin joints, allows quick erection and the dismantling and re-erection of the crane without major site welding. The main beam is a rectangular lattice structure and the legs are CO_2 welded fabricated box structures mounted on travel bogies. The travel bogies incorporate double-flanged travelling wheels of cast steel, one wheel bogey per corner being provided with a rail clamp to fix the crane in position when out of operation. The steel frame cabin is fitted to the trolley.

The 6.10 m (20 ft) and 12.20 m (40 ft) automatic spreaders and the 35 ton hook beam provided with the crane are designed to fit on to the lifting attachment on the crane by pins operated manually by a quick-release lever. Time to change from one to another is 2–3 min. The spreaders are fully automatic and are fitted with eight side flippers. Each pair of flippers at either side or end of the spreader can be operated independently so as to facilitate rapid and accurate positioning of the spreader on to a container. A spreader trim system is provided to trim the spreader by $\pm 5°$ in the longitudinal direction within 30 seconds. Overall the crane is fully tropicalized and can operate in ambient temperatures of up to 50°C.

The Tango can be installed on almost any quay without expensive piling and, like the Samba, the 30.48 m (100 ft) span and 10.67 m (35 ft) backreach utilize space to the maximum for container handling and storage. It is ideal for feeder ports and short sea services where maximum economy is required. Its simplicity of operation and maintenance makes it ideal for ports where highly skilled staff are not available.

The Shifter – Diagram XIV – is a self-propelled, rubber-tyred

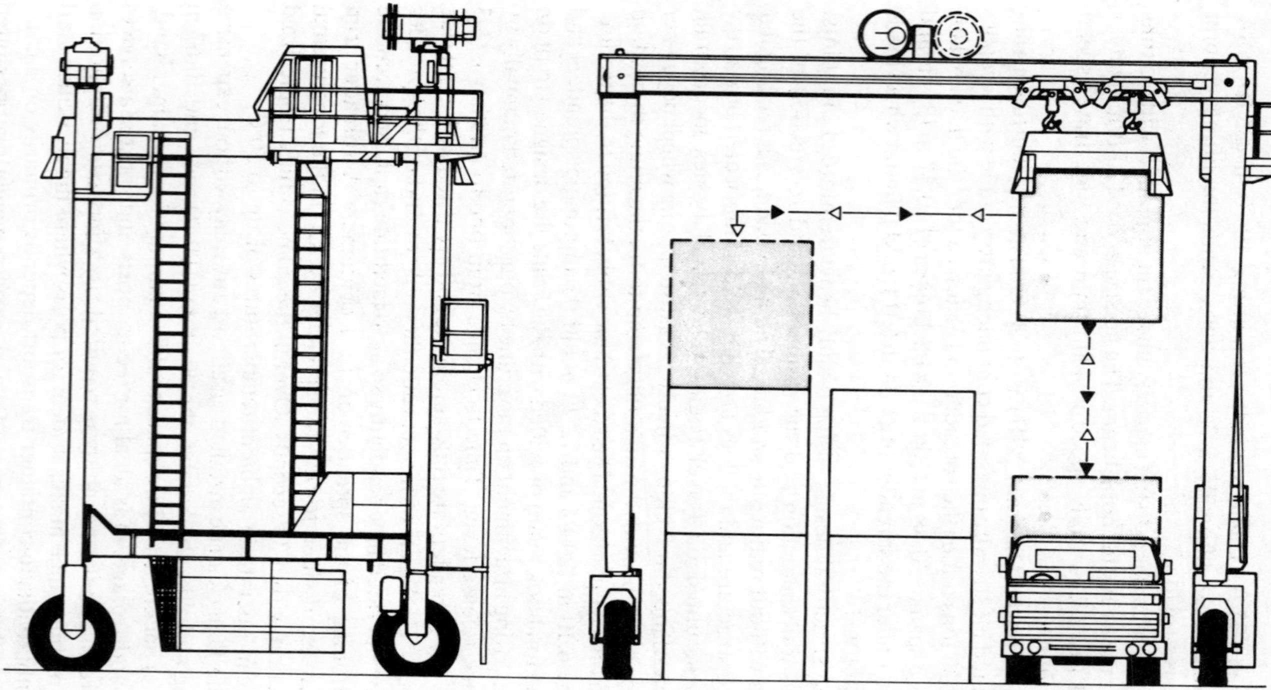

Diagram XIV Container crane Shifter (reproduced by kind permission of Sea Containers Ltd)

diesel hydraulic-powered container crane which can operate anywhere in the world, whether it is 50°C or −40°C. It has a telescopic spreader which can lift 6.10 m (20 ft), 9.15 m (30 ft), 10.70 m (35 ft) or 12.20 m (40 ft) containers up to 30 tons. The crane has a heavy lift capacity under the cargo hook of 38 tons. It can lift, traverse and travel simultaneously, in complete safety through the high mounted cab.

The Shifter has an overall length of 7.7 m (25 ft 5 in), an overall width of 11.33 m (37 ft 2 in) and overall height of 11.89 m (39 ft). The width between the legs is 9.45 m (31 ft) or 12.20 m (40 ft) and height under the spreader is 8.99 m (29 ft 6 in). This permits the crane to span two or three rows of containers plus a vehicle lane or railway line. Container storage space is therefore used to the full, and instead of expensive container-lifting equipment having to move the vehicle, the vehicle can drive to the container crane. It is therefore able to maximize container stacking area utilization better than the fork lift truck and straddle carrier (see Diagram XI).

It is fully tropicalized and can operate in ambient temperatures of up to 50°C. Ground pressure is only 138 lb/in^2 (9.7 kg/cm^2) and the Shifter can travel on ground with a difference in level between wheels of up to one foot, so it can be used on almost any hard standing. It can be erected on the site and operational within a week of delivery.

Overall the Shifter is ideal for dockside, road/rail transfer point, depot or rail head.

STOWAGE WITHIN THE CONTAINER

Our study of cargo-handling equipment would not be complete without consideration of the principles of ISO container stowage, which is an increasingly popular method of international distribution. Moreover, the tendency is for more and more container operators to stuff the container in the transit shed, warehouse/container freight station situated in the port. Additionally, an increasing number of exporters are using the full-container-load consignment and undertaking their own stowage. The principles of container stowage are as follows. Again, it cannot be stressed too strongly that safe container transport depends primarily on a correct and immovable cargo stow and an even weight distribution.

(a) The container must be stowed tightly so that lateral and longitudinal movement of the cargo within is impossible. Tight stowage can be achieved by making the shape and the dimensions of the package an optimum module of the container. Alternatively, if a unit load is being used such as a pallet, the base of it must form a module of the container.

(b) As an alternative to item (a), the cargo must be effectively restrained within the container. This is necessary for a variety of reasons including: (i) to prevent collapse of the stow while packing, unpacking, or during transit, for example, rolls of linoleum on end; (ii) to prevent any movement during transit of part-loads or if there are single heavy items, for example, large pieces of machinery (the heavier the item the more damage it will do if allowed to move); and finally, (iii) to prevent the 'face' of the stow collapsing and leaning against the container doors, that is, to prevent it from falling out when the doors are opened at final destination or for customs inspection.

(c) The consignment must be adequately secured. Details of the various techniques are: (i) *shoring* – bars, struts and spars located in cargo voids to keep the cargo pressed against the walls or other cargo; (ii) *lashing* – rope, wire, chains, strapping or net secured to proper anchoring points within the container and tensioned against the cargo; (iii) *wedging* – wooden distance pieces, pads of synthetic material, inflatable dunnage to fill voids in the cargo and keep it immobile against the container walls; (iv) *locking* – cargo built up to give a three-dimensional brick wall effect.

Basically, there is no simple formula to apply when securing cargo in a container and only experience can aid perfection and solution. Each cargo must be treated on its merits – the type of cargo, the way in which it is stowed, the cargo-handling equipment available and the permanent fittings in the container. The built-in securing points, dunnage brackets, etc. should be used extensively. Any timber dunnage used must be dry and comply with any quarantine regulations. Any shoring which presses against the container wall should have extra timber laid longitudinally between the wall and point of support to spread the weight over two or more side posts. Useful filler pieces for wedging or preventing chafe include old tyres, polyurethane slabs, macerated paper pads, and, for light packages, rolled-up cardboard. Unless an identical stow is anticipated on the return container journey, it is best if the lashing equipment be chosen and considered as expendable. Where synthetic strapping material is used Terylene is preferable to nylon for heavy loads as it is less liable to stretch.

To restrain cargo various techniques exist. Again it depends on the commodity involved. Top-heavy articles should be wedged, shored and lashed to prevent toppling. Heavy weights should be secured to stout ring-bolts (sited in the container floor and side walls) and/or be shored with timber. Chain or wire with bottle screws may be used. Wheeled vehicles should be chocked, and lashed with Spanish windlasses, with the chocks chamfered or padded to protect the tyres. If the floor is of extruded aluminium, portable securing devices must be used. Resilient loads can cause lashings to slacken. This may be overcome by introducing elasticity – for example, rubber rope into the lashing pattern. No securing of pallets is necessary, provided the load is properly secured to the pallet, if the distance between pallets and container walls is 100 mm (4 in) or less. Pallets must not be allowed any longitudinal movement. If securing is necessary, stow pallets against container walls and wedge wood blocks between pallets. It may be necessary to insert sheets of board between pallet loads to protect against chafe and prevent bags, cartons, etc. interweaving and jamming the stow.

In many instances there is a space 400–2400 mm (1–24 in) remaining between the face of the cargo and container doors. Cargo must be prevented from collapsing into this space. It can be achieved in a variety of ways detailed as follows:

(a) Use of suitably positioned lashing points with wire, rope, strapping, etc. woven across.

(b) A simple wooden gate for the wider gaps and heavier cargo.

(c) Use of filler pieces, that is, macerated paper pads, polystyrene, wood wool pads, etc. for the narrower gaps and lighter cargoes – for example, cartons of biscuits.

Care must be taken to ensure that there is no 'fall out' when the container doors are opened. This is particularly relevant to a container which has been completely packed, such as cartons or sacks. Although this can sometimes be achieved by interlocking tiers of packages, it is better to make sure by using any fixing points located in the door posts of the container. Nylon strapping, polypropylene or wire threaded through such points forms an effective barrier.

To ensure that there is adequate and correct overall distribution of cargo within the covered container, the goods must be secure within their packages. Moreover, the pack itself must be as full as possible so as to resist pressures external to it. Packages must be sufficiently rigid to withstand the weight imposed upon them when stacked, usually to a minimum height of 2.10 m (8 ft). If more than one type of cargo is stowed in the container, it is essential that they are all compatible and cannot contaminate or be contaminated. Heavy items and liquids should be placed at the bottom with light and dry ones on the top. Within practical physical limitations of handling, the unit package should be as large as possible since this can reduce costs by up to 20% and increase volumetric efficiency by up to 10%. Consult when practicable the consignee about the proposed method of loading and sequence. This will facilitate discharge at the destination. Where relevant, stowing should be carried out in sequence which will permit rapid checking and stowage operations during and subsequent to unloading. In the event of the consignment being subject to customs pre-entry procedures, it would facilitate customs examination, should this occur and obviate unloading, if such cargo was stowed at the door end of the container. Shippers should avoid having a gap in the stow along the centre line of the container or at the sides as this will generate cargo movement in the transit and possible cargo damage.

Undoubtedly much of the foregoing cargo stowage principles relative to ISO covered containers can likewise be applied in many areas to stowage in other transport modes, particularly train ferry wagon and the Transport Internationale Routier (TIR) international road haulage unit conveying consolidated/groupage cargo in a covered enclosed transport unit.

CHAPTER 6

Free ports/free trade zones

Our study of ports would not be complete without consideration of the free port or, as it is often called, free trade zone. It is potentially a growth area in the next few years in many countries as governments and industry realize the benefits which flow from the free-port concept especially in economic, political and job creation terms.

A free trade zone has been defined as a specified area where trade is based upon the unrestricted international exchange of goods, with customs tariffs used only as a source of revenue and not as an impediment to trade development. Free ports are thus onshore enclaves treated as customs-free zones – or technically as foreign territory for tax purposes. They are designed to attract overseas traders and manufacturers to set up businesses. Duty is payable only when goods move into the host country.

Goods which are imported from abroad are not subjected to any domestic tariffs, duties or regulations until they actually leave the free port. If their destination is another foreign country, they are permitted to leave the free port without the burden of the customs dues which they would have incurred at any point. If the imported goods leave the free port for a destination in the same country, they are taxed on leaving the free port as if they had just arrived from abroad.

The concept of the free port is that of a focus to attract investment which will stimulate the domestic economy. It is intended to attract foreign goods to receiving centres located within it, at which inspection, packaging, sorting, labelling and reshipment will take place. The free port thus aims to become an entrepot.

The Phoenicians started the idea about 2000 BC and the merchants of the Hanseatic League grew rich carving free ports out of the feudal hinterland in the Middle Ages. Today's free ports had their birth about 100 years ago in Hamburg and have been taken to impressive degrees of success in the USA and the Far East.

Moreover, they are becoming more popular in the Middle East, and the UK within the EEC is the latest to approve of six free ports.

Existing worldwide situated free ports include Shannon in the Republic of Ireland, Hong Kong, Taiwan and Singapore. Further free ports are planned in South Korea, Malaysia, the Philippines and Sri Lanka. Overall there are some 400 free ports with over two-thirds in the developing countries. Some 63 free ports are in South America, with some 40 in the USA and a further 20 planned.

Free ports also exist at Hamburg, Stockholm and Copenhagen. Stockholm is entirely concerned with warehousing facilities, while Copenhagen gives no great tax concessions. Hamburg, which is Europe's most successful free port, handles an annual trade of £15 000 million and has a work force of 20 000 engaged in manufacturing and entrepot employment.

A special advantage of the free port of Hamburg lies in the fact that, although within the EEC customs area, it does not belong to the German customs territory. All shipping and goods traffic within the free port is free of customs and other duties, there being no formalities to restrict and hamper the flow of goods. Cargo can be loaded and unloaded, transported, stored in unlimited quantities for an unrestricted period of time, inspected, sampled and subjected to certain types of treatment during storage without any customs clearance or provision of security. Only when goods deemed to come from beyond the Community customs area leave the free port and enter national territory, do they require customs clearance.

Some 9% of world international trade passes through free ports, generating six million jobs. Successful free ports require effective zone management. Moreover, they must keep abreast of new developments, both in the facilities which they can offer and in the tax exemptions and deregulations which affect their competitiveness.

The potential of free ports in terms of trade volume worldwide varies. However, in 1984 a Dr Madsen Pirie, president of the Adam Smith Institute and a longtime proponent of free ports, believes the entire US automotive industry including Detroit will be housed within free ports within 18 months. About 20% of international trade is expected to flow through free ports in 1985.

In early 1984 the UK Government approved the provision of some six free ports: Southampton, Liverpool, Prestwick, Cardiff,

Belfast and Birmingham. The Isle of Man plans to have a free port at Ronaldsway. All the foregoing seven free ports are likely to be operational by 1986.

An interesting development is the free port of Southampton. As with all the UK free ports, its success will depend to a great extent on the types of industry it can attract. Southampton is likely to attract a high level of interest from Far Eastern and to a lesser extent North American companies, some of them new to the UK. The industries are mainly high technology, clothing and agricultural commodities.

FEATURES OF FREE PORTS/FREE TRADE ZONES

A free trade zone is usually situated adjacent to a port or inland in an industrial area which generates a significant volume of international trade. A typical free trade zone would have an area of between 2 and 6 million m^2 with the larger area usually found in the inland zone. It would include transit sheds; open storage areas; storage warehouses and suitable sites for manufacturing enterprises; and for mixing, blending or packing operations for distributing the products to buyers in the domestic and international markets.

Imported stocks and manufacturing of goods located in the free zone become available for prompt supply to both the domestic and international markets. Such free zone areas are particularly advantageous to countries with a limited export base, as they can import products/materials and by processing them meet local national needs and international markets under the most favourable industrial production circumstances. This helps to develop a country's overseas trade balance.

An interesting small free trade zone exists in Jordan. Two such free trade zones exist, one in the Port of Aqaba, and one in the Zarqua region. Details of their facilities are given below:

A wide range of facilities is provided including transit sheds, open storage areas, modern cold stores, storage yards and manufacturing units, together with good communications by road, air and sea transport services through the port of Aqaba.

A modern 6000 ton capacity cold store is provided for meat, fish, poultry and all kinds of food-stuffs and perishable goods for despatch to Saudi Arabia, the Gulf States, Iraq, Syria and further east to Iran, plus the Jordan market. It is designed primarily for maritime containerized shipments.

Trading companies complying with the requisite regulations may use the free zone storage yards, sheds or warehouses, or construct their own facilities. Rental rates are reasonable and the first year rental dues are waived in favour of companies hiring sites for not less than a 10 year period.

A wide range of free trade zone exemptions exist and these are detailed below:

(a) Trading activities including import, export and transit shed facilities enjoy the following incentives:
  (i) Relief from rental dues on leased sites for a period of one year.
  (ii) Exemption from taxes and other fees on all buildings and structures erected by investors.
  (iii) Exemption of goods entering the free zone from customs duties, taxes and fees.
  (iv) Special banking facilities are granted by the Jordan Central Bank in respect of imports, exports and transfer of capital and profits.
  (v) Facilities are accorded for part shipment of goods, mixing and blending and packing without restriction.
  (vi) Exemption from income tax for 12 years.
(b) Industrial companies are accorded generous facilities and tax incentives including the following:
  (i) Income tax exemption for a period of 12 years.
  (ii) Full repatriation of foreign exchange of all profits and capital without restriction.
  (iii) Relief for two years from rental dues.
  (iv) Existing laws and regulations specially support the inviolability of the private sector and thereby favour private ownership and rule out all possibilities of nationalization.

No limitations on trade exist with oil-producing countries and it favours dealings with the Arab petro-dollar markets.

The free zone at Aqaba is served by modern overland routes forming the hub of the crossroads of the Middle East and the three continents of Africa, Asia and Europe. It is served by a modern natural deep-water port at Aqaba and an airport at Aqaba used by 25 international airline companies.

Communications are good, including direct satellite telephone lines to Europe and the USA.

Labour resources are adequate, skilled and low cost. Many are bilingual.

Economic stability and growth obtains throughout Jordan, which is the ideal environment for the foreign investor coupled with the wide range of tax and other concessions described earlier.

Some fifteen categories of industry exist in the free trade zone including printing and publishing; education; steel; machinery and transport equipment; electrical; electronics; plastic; food and pharmaceutical; woodwork; toys; textile, garment and travel goods; ship and aircraft services; chemical; and defence.

Obviously the range of facilities provided in the free trade zone will vary by country. Likewise the incentives and financial environment will be different. Nevertheless, the importance of the free trade zone will grow, especially in a country keen to develop its economic base and improve its balance of trade.

In contrast to the Jordanian free trade zones, established but much larger ones exist in the Far East at the Port of Singapore port authority. It has six free trade zone areas as detailed below:

Zones	*Date of establishment*	*Type of traffic*
Keppel Wharves	1 September 1969	Conventional traffic
Container Terminal	1 September 1969	Container traffic
Telok Ayer Wharves	1 September 1969	Coastal and lighter traffic
Jurong Port	1 September 1969	Dry bulk and conventional traffic
Sembawang Wharves	1 November 1974	Timber, container and other high-volume, low-value traffic
Pasir Panjang Wharves	25 January 1975	Conventional, coastal, LASH (lighter-aboard-ship) and lighter traffic

In the second half of 1981, a 78 ha cargo complex at the northern end of the Changi Airport also became a free trade zone. This new zone is accessible by road via two new motorways, the East Coast Parkway and the Pan Island Expressway.

The zone is served by two ground-handling companies with capacities as detailed below:

Singapore Airport Terminal Services	300 000 tonnes/annum
Changi International Airport Services	130 000 tonnes/annum

In the zone, 68 units of warehouse/office accommodation are available for cargo forwarding agents.

The zone is also served by a customs office and warehouse; an imports and exports office, and an airmail transit office.

In 1984 the six free zones handled some 30 million tons of traffic. The container volume totalled over 1 million TEUs. It is a continuing growth area. Total storage space is 1.4 million m^2 of which 400 000 m^2 is covered accommodation. About 85% and 95% of the covered and open storage areas respectively are operated on a common user basis. Modern warehouses are five and ten storey. Expansive plans are under way for a larger container freight station and multi-purpose warehouse complex on some 22 ha of land. It will link Keppel Wharves, Container Terminal and Telok Ayer Wharves. This is scheduled for completion in the late 1980s. Overall three deep-water berths exist capable of working conventional ships up to 10 m draught.

The principal features of the zones for sea-borne cargo are given below:

(a) A 72-hour storage for import/export conventional cargo and import containerized cargo. Free within the time period specified.

(b) A 7-day storage for export containerized cargo. Free within the time period specified.

(c) A 28-day storage for transhipment/re-export cargo. Free within the time period specified.

(d) Free of customs duty and customs control documentation while goods remain in the zones.

(e) Extended storage of goods until market conditions are favourable for re-export or local use.

(f) Goods may be exhibited or sampled.

(g) Sales may be effected at the zones.

(h) Goods may be stored, bulk-broken, graded, repacked or remarked for the local or export markets.

(i) Goods may be exported by parcel post from the Parcel Acceptance Office run by the Postal Department at Godown 154.

(j) Dutiable ship stores of liquor, cigarettes and tobacco may be supplied direct to vessels from Godown 154.

(k) It is well maintained, with sufficient modern equipment and experienced personnel to handle vessels and goods.

(l) It has strategically located warehouses close to the wharves as well as the commercial and industrial areas, resulting in minimum transportation and costs.

(m) Adequate covered and open areas for storage.

(n) A common-user repacking area at Godown 154 for the reconditioning and consolidation of cargo meant for export.

(o) Entrepot cabinets at Godowns 153 and 154 for lease to entrepot traders for storage, repacking and re-export activities. A cabinet at Godown 154 is air conditioned for the storage of confectionery and other commodities that require low temperature.

(p) Maximum round-the-clock security for goods stored.

(q) Economical ordinary warehousing (i.e. not connected with import/export, re-export or transhipment) storage rentals.

(r) Reasonable removal charges and equipment hire rates.

Undoubtedly the Singapore free trade zone will continue to grow and is playing a decisive role in the Far East markets.

ADVANTAGES OF FREE PORTS/FREE TRADE ZONES

Our study of the free trade zone would not be complete without examining its advantages, which are detailed below.

It brings to a particular area/region/country improved job opportunities and economic activities.

It develops the economic resources of a particular area and its infrastructure. This includes particularly communications and transport, viz. road, rail, air and sea, so essential to the well-being of an economy.

It helps to improve a country's balance of trade.

It encourages the economies of scale and in so doing facilitates bulk purchasing arrangements. This in turn enables local industry to be served at more competitive prices rather than rely on direct imports in small quantities at higher prices.

It permits countries without an export manufacturing base to develop a semi-manufacturing base and likewise serve neighbouring countries. Examples are Jordan and Singapore.

It helps to develop trading centres with all its competitive advantages especially in price. Singapore is a good example.

It encourages the inflow of foreign capital. This is particularly advantageous in countries which are short of capital resources.

The development/attraction of foreign investors tends to bring with it the most modern foreign management skills/techniques and technology. This is very advantageous to a country as it sets new standards.

It encourages greater economic and political stability in a particular country.

It develops a particular country's international shipping and air services. Again Singapore is an example.

It stimulates the domestic economy through the attraction of foreign investment.

Foreign investment creates confidence in a country's economy.

There are no customs duties on imports and goods due for re-export.

There is 24-hour per day protection/security for the goods.

Storage is duty free while awaiting better market conditions.

There is no duty on loss caused by shrinkage, seepage, evaporation, damage, etc. or on discarded, substandard goods.

Opportunity exists to employ operating capital for a longer period without having it tied up in duty-paid goods.

There is avoidance of fines and penalties for incorrectly-labelled goods by correcting errors in the zone.

Exhibition facilities are provided by the zone authorities to help businesses to sell/promote goods in the zone.

Goods may be auctioned or sold while still within the zone, and before duty or taxes need to be paid.

To conclude our examination of the free-port, one cannot stress too strongly that it is a growth market due not only to tax advantages, but also to the economies of scale which flow therefrom. Overall it seeks to attract foreign investment, to capitalize on its position as a transit centre for imported goods, and to grow, within its free trade and deregulated boundaries, manufacturing industry which would not otherwise have developed in the country at all. Good management plays a decisive role in its success.

CHAPTER 7

Port investment criteria

As we progress through the 1980s and beyond there is no doubt that the importance of sea ports will increase to the extent that more emphasis will be placed on their efficiency as an aid to develop international trade. Further, the concept of the combined transport operation (see Chapter 9 of *Economics of Shipping Practice and Management*) will continue to develop, placing paramount importance on fast port turn-round of the vessel (see pp. 129–130) and no impediment to the smooth flow of goods through the port.

The foregoing development, especially in the areas of containerization, Ro/Ro services, multi-purpose vessels and specialized bulk-cargo ships, will call for continuing investment in ports. It is likely to result in fewer ports that are more capital intensive in their operations and have greatly improved dock labour efficiency. The bulk of the investment will be undertaken by the port authority, but there will be areas where the shipowner contractually using the port facilities will become involved. An example arises through a leased berth whereby the shipowner or consortia of shipowners provide all the warehouse/transit shed facilities together with cargo-handling equipment.

It is against the foregoing background that we examine the important area of port investment criteria within the context of port management.

ECONOMICS OF NEW AND SECOND-HAND PORT EQUIPMENT

During the past few years there has been an increasing tendency at many ports to consider and in many cases buy second-hand equipment. It may be cargo-handling equipment, a pontoon, gangways, straddle carriers, stevedoring equipment, computers, road vehicles, and so on.

The following factors are involved in any such second-hand purchase evaluation.

A detailed examination should be made of the general condition of the equipment, and the availability and cost of the spares.

An assessment should be made of the future annual maintenance and certification cost: lifting apparatus and other such equipment are subject to an annual inspection and tests in regard to their safe working proficiency. The cost tends to increase each year in real terms as the examination becomes more severe on the ageing asset.

The compatibility of the equipment with similar resources within the port must be considered, for example if additional vehicles are being sought; it may be desirable to have all from the same vehicle manufacture.

There is a requirement for an assessment to be made of the impact in labour resources/efficiency within the port. Part of the justification for the second-hand purchase may be to eliminate labour-intensive cargo-handling techniques and introduce more productive labour methods.

Second-hand equipment would be much cheaper than new equipment. Nevertheless there is a requirement for the discounted cash-flow evaluation technique (see p. 119) to be applied and full cognizance taken of depreciation, amortization and resale/scrap value.

Second-hand equipment can be an attractive proposition to a port authority with limited financial resources anxious to modernize its port operation to attract new business and more modern tonnage. This is particularly so in developing countries when capital availability is scarce and the need to keep pace with modern technology paramount in the interest of developing international trade. It is a means of introducing such facilities on a low-risk capital basis and thereby enables the market prospects to be tested and developed. If the project fails the financial loss is less severe.

A major advantage is that the equipment/facility following completion of the purchase becomes available immediately. This enables it to be introduced usually much sooner when compared with new equipment with a lengthy delivery date. Conversely, one must be conscious of the risk of obsolescence with its attendant replacement parts availability problems.

There is a requirement for an assessment to be undertaken of the modifications necessary, together with the time scale to adapt it for efficient use within the port and to meet local port operating needs.

Any tax concession or government grant requires to be explored.

The operating expenses to operate/man the equipment should be determined. This should take account of any regular/routine maintenance schedules which may be more frequent than for more modern equipment in the port. This applies especially to cargo-handling equipment.

The equipment may require modification to comply with national statutory obligations and the practicality of such modification should be closely examined and costed with a time scale. This is additional to any modifications necessary to meet operating or other port needs detailed in the paragraph last but two preceding.

Transportation cost to convey the goods from the place of sale to the port must be taken into account together with assembly/installation expenses.

How does the equipment fit into the port authority's five year business plan?

The cost of training personnel both to operate and maintain the equipment requires evaluation.

A detailed survey is needed of the port to determine any modifications/alterations necessary to accommodate the second-hand equipment. This should be treated as part of the project cost.

The method of financing the second-hand equipment may involve funds within the port authority liquidating reserve capital, loan capital obtained on the open market, or government grant/subsidy. Overall, it could be a mixture of the foregoing.

The case history of the equipment should be determined, and all the documentation involved, especially annual inspection certificates and related reports, examined.

The market for second-hand port equipment has tended to increase in Third World countries which are anxious to attract modern tonnage to their ports and introduce more productive work practices. A professional assessment should be undertaken before any purchase is made and special emphasis should be placed on the compatibility of the equipment and likely operating and maintenance cost together with spares availability. The major advantage rests with its almost immediate availability following sale completion.

Finally, as an alternative and valid comparison, the purchase of new equipment outright or leasing should be examined. One must bear in mind that new equipment will be more expensive, but be more reliable, have longer life, lower maintenance costs, reflect current modern technology in design, operating and maintenance techniques; and provide higher standards of efficiency. This will ensure that the most favourable decision is taken having regard to all the facts, both in the short and long term.

METHODS OF FINANCE

Port equipment may be financed from three main sources detailed below:

(a) The port authority own funds raised through the liquidation of reserve capital and possibly the sale of assets such as redundant port equipment, land sale, and so on.

(b) Government grants and subsidies. This may be central government funds or local/federal government finance. Such finance is usually conditional and can involve a government-appointed director on the port authority board of directors.

(c) Loan capital obtained on the open market including bank mortgages, which may be provided at very low interest rates.

Port authorities are often unable to finance schemes entirely from their own resources owing primarily to the low capital return on existing port operations and high rate of inflation in new equipment/modernization cost. Many port authorities supply up to one-third of the capital for a new project from their own funds and raise the residue externally. Such external finance may take several forms as detailed below:

(a) Subsidies provided by governments or government agencies to port authorities. Such subsidies would be repayable only in exceptional circumstances.

(b) Domestic loans granted by governments or government agencies for the provision of port projects. It may be land reclamation for a port extension, new berths, cranage equipment, dredging, and so on.

(c) Grants provided by governments or government agencies in the form of subsidies, incentive grants, or loans for the modernization and/or expansion of ports and their installations.

(d) Bank loans. In the 1980s banks and other financial institutions will probably become involved on an increasing scale in the development of the non-state-owned port or port installation. This could be the iron-ore terminal serving a steel plant or oil jetty serving an oil refinery.

(e) Leasing or sale/leaseback arrangements over 15 years or longer with commercial banks. These are attractive to port authorities as they release financial resources but allow them to retain the use of the asset concerned. Tax incentives are available in some countries. Sale/leaseback provisions may be incorporated into package deals, especially where the circumstances are particularly favourable. This can arise in the provision of cargo-handling equipment with a contractual commitment from a shipping line for a long-term contract.

(f) Loans from specialized institutions such as commercial banks specializing in port/shipping investment, which raise the necessary long-term funds by means of private placings or the sale of bonds.

(g) Long-term loans provided by insurance companies, pension funds and certain private lenders for first-class borrowers.

In many countries the port authority is State owned and controlled. Hence credit provided or guaranteed by government will dominate the scene in many countries relative to the finance of port modernization/development. Conversely, in countries operating on a mixed economy basis, with ports operating in the private sector, commercial institutions will play their role.

The need to fund port modernization/development on a sound basis cannot be overstressed. So doing will facilitate the development of international trade and thereby foster the expansion of a country's resources.

FACTORS DETERMINING PORT INVESTMENT CRITERIA

The following factors must be borne in mind as criteria for investment in new equipment, provision of a new berth or modernization of an existing one, or the purchase of second-hand equipment. It must be stressed at the outset that the importance and significance of each item will vary with individual circumstances, especially the type of port, the form of ownership, and the country of location – the latter reflecting any government policies relative to investment especially with regard to the availability of funds and its terms.

(a) The actual market prospects of the port both short and long term; in particular the trade related to the investment. This may be the provision of new cargo-handling equipment; modernization of berth, or navigational equipment. Trade prospects are most difficult to forecast, as international trade is unpredictable by nature and susceptible not least to political climate, which can change the whole pattern of events within the time scale of the project. The market can be assessed by means of commercial research in the widest sphere possible: trade statistics published by governments and international organizations should be studied and contact made with trade associations, chambers of commerce, port councils/associations, shippers' councils and international organizations such as the International Cargo Handling Co-ordination Association (ICHCA), the United Nations Conference on Trade and Development (UNCTAD) and the Organization for Economic Co-operation and Development (OECD). Consultants may be engaged for the purpose; the fee involved may be high but it is small in relation to the capital cost of the project.

(b) Commercial factors in the context of maintaining or increasing the port market share in the trade/area/region. This is particularly relevant on seaboards where a group of ports exist perhaps in different countries, all competing for the same traffic which is destined for landlocked countries. An example arises in Western Europe involving Dunkerque, Antwerp and Rotterdam. Many factors arise including tariff levels, distribution arrangements such as rail, canal networks, transit time, industrial relations record, and so on. Usually modern facilities – especially those of a capital intensive nature and competitive tariffs – attracting modern tonnage, contribute significantly to secure an increased market share.

(c) An analysis of the existing equipment/berth resource covering the general condition for both current trade and expected short- and long-term trade developments; maintenance costs; any possible resale value or redeployment within the port area; and finally the residual life of the asset as an economic unit. Such an analysis will involve the departments of the chief engineer, commercial manager, port accountant and operations manager.

(d) An assessment of present and future competition in the widest sense of the term. It should cover direct competition from other ports as expressed in tariff levels; turn-round time of vessels, efficiency of dock labour, range of port facilities; overall port operating efficiency; distribution arrangements embracing rail, canal/inland waterways, road, cargo clearance, the extent to which computers feature in customs clearance, cargo manifest, etc; the period of credit afforded to shippers/shipowners with regard to the payment of accounts; any subversive competition such as national flag tonnage being afforded priority in berth allocation; and more favourable port tariff levels, which is generally termed 'flag discrimination (see Chapter 14 of *Economics of Shipping and Management*).

(e) Any credit facilities granted or tax concessions offered by government. An increasing number of major ports worldwide are completely or partially financed by government and accordingly provide capital within certain criteria for investment.

(f) Capital availability and methods of finance. The cost of the capital ultimately sought must be closely evaluated. The technique generally used is that of discounted cash flow, generated annually by the new equipment/berth, etc. compared with the situation that would prevail if no investment were undertaken: initially there may be a loss, with profit appearing in later years.

(g) The economics of the new investment, i.e. equipment, berth (see pp. 115–118).

(h) Available industrial capacity and the time scale of the project. Tentative enquiries are made of suitable contractors/companies likely to tender for a such a project and the time scale each would recommend having regard to existing commitments. Many major port projects involve the prime contractor relying on subcontractors to undertake certain work.

(i) An assessment needs to be made on the impact the construction work will have on the day-to-day operations of the port. The provision of a new berth, reclamation of land, installation of new cargo-handling equipment, provision of a Ro/Ro ramp, provision of a new warehouse, realignment of roadway, provision of a container stacking/parking area, provision of a bonded area, provision of an enclosure to house dangerous classified cargo consignments, provision of immigration facilities, and so on. All will require a works construction programme to be devised. This will ensure that the work on the site causes the least disruption to the day-to-day running of the port and thereby maintains quality of service to port users. Such construction can extend from a few months to several years.

(j) The manner in which the new investment fits into the company's five year business plan, if any.

(k) Any effect the new investment will have on other services/ports within a company controlling a group of ports, such as Associated British Ports or Sea Containers Ltd. For example, it may be decided to centralize container resources on two ports rather than five. Similar remarks apply to rationalizing facilities of a like nature at a port. Overall such rationalization of facilities could likewise result in tariff adjustments and streamlining of tariff structure.

(l) Policies laid down by IMF, the World Bank, OECD, particularly credit terms with which a particular government may be associated.

(m) The invisible export earning of a particular port. This also applies to an entrepot involving transhipment traffic such as is found in Singapore.

(n) Depreciation of the asset over its estimated useful life. This will involve offshore equipment and landward assets, both of which will have a varying depreciable life expectancy.

(o) The need for new investment may arise through statutory or safety considerations. These require careful evaluation. For example, it may involve a new method of processing inwards passengers through immigration, or replacement of cargo-handling equipment which failed to pass its annual safety inspection.

(p) An increasing number of berths are leased to a shipping company or consortia of shipping companies. Accordingly, any investment in such circumstances could be recovered long term in the leasehold package arrangements. This needs to be reflected in any investment submission. A similar situation could arise through the port authority introducing some computerized cargo control/clearance system involving the agents contributing to the investment on an annual rental basis. A good example is the direct trader input system (DTI). See Chapter 7 of *Elements of Export Practice*.

To conclude our review of the factors influencing investment, it is important to bear in mind that the sums are usually substantial. As we have seen in the past, the successful port operator is one who anticipates and adapts to change. The current decade will see the emergence of changes in the pattern of international trade, but equally it will present a multitude of opportunities to the investor and good entrepreneur and manager.

CHAPTER 8

Port traffic control

PORT OPERATIONS AND COMMUNICATIONS CENTRE

In our study of port traffic control, an important area to examine in a modern major port is the port operations and communications centre. Such a facility is operated for example by the Maritime Services Board of New South Wales, Australia which we will now consider. It has the following responsibilities:

(a) Provision of port traffic management systems to assist in the safe and efficient flow of vessel traffic in Sydney and Botany Bay.

(b) Operating and information services such as acceptance of bookings for pilots, and recorded telephone advice of shipping movements and berths.

(c) A radio service (the Navigation Information Service) dealing with the movement and safety of ships outside port limits.

(d) Domestic communications service – which handles all the board's internal communications needs through its telephone and radio networks.

The Centre is manned continuously throughout the year. Each watch is under the control of a Port Operations Officer – a qualified master mariner – who is assisted by two Communications Attendants. The Port Operations Officer controls the port traffic management system, maintaining constant watch on vessel movements and giving approval for ships to enter the port or leave a berth.

The communications centre has the following role:

(a) Operates the port traffic management system and regulates shipping movements so that traffic can flow safely and efficiently.

(b) Keeps watch over the port area and alerts appropriate personnel so that prompt action can be taken to deal with incidents such as oil spillages, smoke pollution, fires on wharves or ships breaking adrift in high winds, etc.

(c) Provides information required by pilots and ship masters for safe navigation inside port limits, e.g. traffic information, state of tide and weather forecasts.

(d) Keeps continuous radio watch for distress and emergency calls.

(e) Operates the Maritime VHF Radio Service covering the coast stations network. This service deals with the movement and safety of ships outside port limits. For example, messages may be required for berthing, anchoring, tug requirements, local navigational warnings, port radar services, tidal conditions, depth of water in channels, shipping movements and emergencies.

(f) Serves the board's internal communications needs through its telephone and radio networks. In this respect the centre provides all-hours contact with personnel, launches, floating plant, trucks, cars, wharf patrols, etc.

(g) Operates direct links with South Head Signal Station, police, fire brigade and other emergency services.

(h) Provides the public with information about shipping movements, berths, arrivals and departures.

The port operations and communications centre is situated on the waterfront in a control tower some 87 m above sea level and thereby has the operating advantage of full visual control of the harbour. This has greatly improved the centre's ability to manage vessel traffic in Australia's busiest port.

PORT TRAFFIC MANAGEMENT

Port traffic management is very important in the operation of large ports and it is given much attention by port and navigation authorities throughout the world. As international trade expands, it results in a greater concentration of shipping in ports and their approaches. In addition to actual numbers, there is a continual increase in the size of vessels especially in the case of tankers, bulk carriers and container ships.

An important function of a port traffic management system is to assist in preventing loss of life, damage to property and harm to the environment by improving the safety of navigation in congested waters. Ships colliding or running aground can cause costly damage to property and even loss of life. But environmental and economic effects can magnify the damage and cost to the community enormously. Disruption of normal trade and port operations caused by a grounded ship blocking a busy channel would naturally have adverse effects on the economy of the port and the community it serves. The environmental impact is obvious if a tanker or bulk carrier with a cargo of oil or dangerous chemicals is involved in a collision. This is even more important where the port is situated in a densely populated area.

Another purpose is to make shipping movements more efficient. Modern vessels can cost over £20 000 a day to operate and shipping economics demand that a ship spends as little time as possible in port. Container ships – which spend 15% of their time in port as compared with 60% for conventional vessels – are a result of the continuing efforts to reduce turn-round time. Port traffic management plays its part by organizing customs entries, ship departures and movements in the port to minimize delays caused by congestion, unexpected ship movements or other hazards.

In Sydney and Botany Bay all sea-going vessels are required to participate in the port traffic management system. They must not enter the port area or leave a berth until the port operations and communications centre advises that the manoeuvre can be made safely. When authorizing movement the centre also provides information of the current traffic situation.

The centre monitors the progress of each vessel and requires that it report its position at certain control points. This allows the centre to advise on the traffic situation or potential hazards at any stage of the vessel's progress.

An instruction from the centre does not override the ship master's responsibility for the safety of his ship. If he feels that obeying the instruction will put his ship in danger he can advise the centre and request further information or indicate what action he intends to take to maintain the safety of his ship.

The Maritime Services Board ensures that navigation in the ports of New South Wales stays as safe as modern technology allows. As the pace of shipping activity quickens so does the need for increased safety and efficiency in port operations and the board continually updates its port traffic management.

The building of a modern control tower to house the port

operations and communications centre is an example of the constant improvement necessary. The tower commands an overall view of most of the port – particularly the major wharfage area and the waterways used by commercial vessels outside the marked channels.

Although operating staff have had a direct intercom link with South Head Signal Station, which in turn provides visual and radar surveillance of the port entrance, until now the centre's only direct contact with vessels has been by radio.

Without direct visual control, traffic surveillance was by vessel position reporting only. Vessel tracking was by dead reckoning, updated only as vessels reported. The difficulties of operating under these conditions are obvious. Vessels such as pleasure craft, not in radio contact, can become unknown hazards and traffic management is limited to time spacing of ships through port areas to ensure safe operation.

The tower enables the positions of vessels moving or stationary in critical areas to be seen at a glance.

All vessels under observation can be seen and allowed for whether they are in radio contact or not. Communications between the mariner and the port operations and communications centre will have an added meaning as the centre can now provide an accurate word picture of the traffic situation, based on actual observation.

A wider range of potential hazards can be visually identified and acted on. The time between movements to ensure safety can be reduced – saving valuable time for the shipping industry. In short, a far more positive approach can be adopted to assist shipping in the most vulnerable areas.

A similar system but involving radar operates in the Port of Rotterdam. It is called the Vessel Traffic Management System which covers the Euro Channel and the Hook of Holland roadstead, the Rotterdam Waterway and Nieuwe Maas River up to 3 km upstream from the Van Brienenoord Bridge, Koningshaven, the Oude Maas River up to 5 km upstream from the Spijkenisse Bridge, the Beer Canal, Caland Canal and Hartel Canal, including the dock basin bordering on these waterways.

The new Vessel Traffic Management System comprises: a main traffic centre, the harbour co-ordination centre (HCC); three regional traffic centres linked to two local traffic centres; 26 unmanned radar stations; a multiradar tracking system; a number of locations for a closed-circuit television network; a Radio Direction Finder system; devices to measure visibility, water level, wind direction and speed; an extensive data handling system; and a communications system.

The regional traffic centre is located at Hook of Holland, in the Botlek area and opposite the Waalhaven basin. The latter covers the city area from Eemhaven to Van Brienenoordbrug. The regional traffic centres are supported by two local traffic centres, which are also situated at vital points in the harbour area. The regional traffic centre at Botlek for instance is connected with a local traffic centre at the entrance to the Hartel Canal. From this centre the watchmen have a good view of the busy crossing on the Oude Maas. The local traffic centre at Maasboulevard, as a part of the city area, offers a good view of the Koningshaven and Maas bridges.

The regional centres collect data from the surrounding radar towers. These are simple masts, supporting the radar scanners and containing an automatic tracking system. Microwave links transmit the video to the regional centres while track data are carried to the centres by standard telephone line. Fed in this way, they carry out their traffic management activities.

These are localized functions, but very important ones because they enable the centres to give traffic information and advice directly to sea-going and inland vessels within their regions.

Additionally, there is a constant exchange of information between the regional centres and the HCC in charge of overall traffic management. The duties of the HCC include the central traffic control and activities such as preparing the clearance of incoming sea-going vessels, directing operations in case of catastrophes, and supervising transport of dangerous goods.

In developing the system the limits of the possibilities afforded by modern technology had to be determined. Can a computer process raw radar signals obtained in a 'problem area' such as the Port of Rotterdam, which is crammed with towering cranes, chimney stacks, buildings and other tall structures?

That this is technically feasible, is one of the most important conclusions from the preparation phases.

Automatic feeding of a computer with radar signals, from which location, speed, overall measurements and other relevant information on incoming and outgoing vessels can be derived, is called target extraction. All this information – coded in figures – is processed, stored and made available in systematic form by the computer. By using several computers the main centre may obtain a complete and reliable picture of the traffic as it is throughout the 40 km operational area of the port of Rotterdam from minute to minute, with predictions of what is going to happen in the next few minutes. This is a highly attractive prospect.

Exact and automatic tracking and registration of shipping movements by a computer greatly facilitate the task of the watchstanders. Watching and interpreting a radar image is fatiguing and imposes a strain on the operator. This may become unacceptable in some circumstances, say, when traffic is busy at a time of reduced visibility.

Even in the preparatory phase questions were raised, such as: what is the average time for a radar operator to remain fully concentrated on his job? And: is it possible to automate the fatiguing part of an operator's duties?

Target extraction gives the redeeming answer, as research showed. Routine operations will be executed by the computer. The operator is able to spend his time on actual traffic management work: reflecting, evaluating and deciding. This is the whole point of the new system.

An ingenious shore-based radar system is of eminent importance, of course, but it remains only part of the overall Vessel Traffic Management System as now constructed.

The foregoing commentary on the similar systems operative in New South Wales and Rotterdam demonstrates the importance of the subject in port management.

SHIP TURN-ROUND TIME IN PORT

The objective of Port management is to maximize the throughput of business through its port. An important area in this realization is the aim to minimize the time a vessel spends in port, thereby making the best use of the berth and associated equipment, and permitting the maximum throughput at the berth.

In examining ship turn-round time in port, let us consider the benefits which accrue from maximizing throughput at the berth.

It maximizes utilization of berth resources including cargo-handling equipment, dock labour, transport resources, and so on.

Good utilization of port resources enables the optimum number of berths and equipment to be provided. This in turn reduces the capital investment level to a minimum and facilitates the most favourable profit margins to be made.

Maximum utilization of port resources enables cost to be contained at a low level and thereby permits the most competitive rates to be devised. It enables lower unit cost to be incurred as the greater the tonnage throughput, the lower the cost per ton. A port with an overprovision of berths and equipment/labour is faced with the situation of much idle time of the equipment and/or berth(s). Hence a ship which is only worked 8 to 10 hours a day at a berth is likely to prove more expensive to the port authority to discharge her cargo than one where the berth is operational 24 hours per day. Moreover, the cost to the shipowner is more expensive as the vessel being discharged continuously will spend less time in port and more time operational at sea.

Reduced port turn-round time enables the shipowner to convey the same volume of cargo with fewer ships. A good example is the container vessel which has displaced up to eight 'tween-deck ships. Such tonnage spent half of their time in port compared with the modern container ship which spends about 10% of a schedule transhipping cargo in port.

Reduced port turn-round through much improved port efficiency involving good utilization of berths and allocated resources, facilitates more competitive rates being devised as the basic cost is lower. This in turn encourages trade and improves the competitiveness of the port. Overall the lower the distribution cost which includes port charges, the greater the prospect of maximizing the level of traffic through a port.

A high level of berth utilization enables the minimum number of ports to be provided to serve a country/region/area.

Good berth utilization attracts business to the port, which, overall, raises the quality of service provided and the range of port facilities. This includes rail and road distribution facilities, warehouse accommodation, ship repair/survey and container survey/repair facilities, and so on.

Port turn-round time is an area of increasing importance in port management. It has become an efficiency measure for comparison with other ports.

PROCESSING THE CONSIGNMENT THROUGH THE PORT

An area of much importance to port management is the efficiency by which the consignment inwards (import) or outwards (export) is processed through the port. It depends on many factors and efficiency is only realized through adequate operational pre-planning which is examined on pp. 139–143. It is very much related to customs procedure and readers are urged to read Chapters 7 and 13 of *Elements of Export Practice*. However, it is appropriate to consider the various stages through which a consignment is processed, which can vary by transport mode and port organizational structure. We will confine our analysis to the processing of the consignment and exclude the detailed procedure of inward and outward customs clearance of the vessel, which is dealt with in Chapter 6 of *Elements of Shipping*.

The import (inwards) consignment

Given below is a summary of the sequence of events relative to inwards (import) consignment which may be a bulk shipment of iron ore, containers, Ro/Ro units, loose cargo, and so on.

On arrival at the port the master and/or his agent will require the vessel to be 'entered in' with customs. Subject to customs being satisfied that the ship's crew and any passengers are free of any contagious disease, authority is issued for the vessel to enter port and proceed to her allocated berth. The next stage is for the master to present to customs the requisite document and a general declaration of the ship's arrival. This includes where applicable pilotage slip; custom house report form; deck cargo certificate; grain cargo certificate; passenger return; and tonnage dues slip. On the basis of the documents being 'in order' cargo discharge may commence. This procedure applies to all deep-sea vessels wishing to discharge cargo at a port, but in the case of ferry vessels operating a frequent service between two seaboards, the procedure of entering in and clearance of documents before discharge may commence is very much quicker. For example, for a service between the UK and Europe involving Dover to Calais route of a 90 minute voyage and a frequency of one sailing every hour, the vessel proceeds direct to her berth and immediately on arrival discharge commences. Simultaneously the vessel is 'entered in' and customs officers board the ship to examine and clear the documents.

The task of discharging the vessels involves close liaison between the shipowner and the stevedore/cargo superintendent responsible for the dock handling resources. This may be cranage, cargo handling labour and so on. An important area for the importer's agent is to have adequate tallying (checking) resources available to record the quantity of cargo discharged and ensure it agrees with the bill of lading. This applies to all cargo and, in so far as the loose break bulk consignment is concerned, it results in tally clerks being on the quay recording each consignment discharged from the ship.

Prior to the arrival of the vessel at the port, the agent acting on behalf of the shipowner will have received an estimated arrival time. Accordingly, the ship's agent will inform the importer or his agent to ensure that all the requisite documentation is available to lodge with customs for import customs clearance purposes. In many ports the agent receives by telex or by airmail the computerized cargo manifest of the specified vessel. This gives full details of the consignments to be discharged at the port together with other relevant information for customs purposes. The foregoing arrangements apply to deep-sea tonnage, but for the short sea ferry operator the cargo manifest is telexed and the scale of the documentation needs is much less. Moreover, the financial arrangements tend to be more on the 'open account' basis with few operating under a letter of credit procedure (see pp. 165–166).

The next stage is for the goods/consignment on arrival and discharge from the vessel into a transit shed/warehouse/quayside to be presented/lodged with customs for clearance. This involves the customs documentation specifying the cargo, its value, name of consignor and consignee, description of cargo, cargo markings, and so on. Customs will require accompanying/supporting documentation which will depend on the country of origin of cargo, the country importing the consignment, cargo specification, and so on. Other documents may include bill of lading, certificate of origin or consular invoice, import licence, and so on. Readers are urged to study Chapters 12 of both *Elements of Shipping* and *Elements of Export Practice* which examine documentation. The goods may be loose, in a container, on a trailer/road vehicle, in a train ferry wagon or in a barge. In an increasing number of ports, the details are fed into the customs computer by the agent at the port. In the UK the system is called direct trade input (see *Elements of Export Practice*, pp. 147–148).

Customs on receipt of the imported consignment details will decide on the documentary evidence and other relevant considerations, including tariff regulations, whether or not to clear the cargo through customs and release it to the importer. A number of options arise:

(a) The goods may attract a customs duty based on a percentage of the declared value of the consignment and payable at the time of importation or within a specified period shortly after the release of cargo.

(b) The customs may decide to examine the goods to satisfy themselves that the specification accords with the actual goods as found in the container, trailer, etc. Such an examination is undertaken in a specially designated area usually called the customs examination shed/warehouse.

(c) Customs may reject the documentation as being inadequate owing to its being incorrectly completed. Furthermore, some of the documents may have lapsed in their authenticity, such as the import licence expiry date and an extension being required.

Situations do arise where cargo is detained at the port awaiting documentation. This attracts demurrage and results in port congestion. It also arises from item (c) above.

Specialized cargoes, especially livestock and dangerous classified consignments, tend to receive accelerated dispatch from the port in many countries. Both are usually handled in purpose-built designated areas of the port but are subject to very rigorous regulations which must be strictly observed.

An increasing volume of cargo is now conveyed under customs bond such as a TIR vehicle or container (see *Element of Export Practice*, pp. 122–126). In such situations the cargo passes through the port without any customs examination and could be examined and cleared by customs at an Inland Clearance Depot. Alternatively, the goods may be passing through a transit country.

When the cargo has been cleared through customs, the consignment may proceed to its destination. This will involve the importer or his agent making the transport arrangements by road, rail or inland waterway.

It is important to bear in mind the role of Incoterms 1980 (see

Chapter 8 of *Elements of Export Marketing and Management*). Under Incoterms 1980 the responsibility of the seller and buyer are clearly defined which includes the cargo discharge arrangements, customs clearance and effecting payment for the goods.

Every effort must be made to dispatch the goods from the port when they have cleared customs otherwise port congestion will arise and efficiency be impaired.

The export (outwards) consignment

We will now examine the sequence of events relative to the outwards (export) consignment which may be a container, Ro/Ro unit, loose cargo, shipload of phosphate, and so on.

In the case of general cargo shipments operating under liner cargo arrangements involving a container operator or agent promoting a shipping line, a monthly or weekly sailing list will be issued to potential clients/shippers. This will give the receiving and closing dates on which the container operator or agent will accept cargo for the specified sailing, usually at his warehouse where the cargo is assembled/stuffed into a container. This is usually situated in an industrial area outside the port although an increasing number of container operators' depots are sited close to the port. In many countries inland clearance depots are provided where customs facilities clear the cargo for export, thereby enabling the consignment to travel to the port under bond.

Alternatively, the cargo can be assembled in the port in close proximity to the berth. This situation is distinct from the cargo assembly area detailed above. The nature and range of facilities provided will vary with the commodity handled, the volume of cargo and transport mode. For loose cargo it is a transit shed; for containerized cargo, it is assembled/stuffed in the container shed operated by the agent or container operator. Often such accommodation is designated import and export sheds.

Cargo requiring customs clearance at the port – as distinct from the consignment travelling through the port under bond from an inland clearance depot – would be presented to customs with the requisite documentation. This will include the customs specification of the consignment including its value; and any associated documents such as an export licence. In an increasing number of ports, such information is presented by computer as found in the direct trader input system. The customs have the right to examine the goods being processed for export. Stringent customs regulations exist in many countries regarding the export of arms and art treasures.

When the cargo has been cleared by customs, the goods are available for shipboard loading. It may be loose cargo, a container, or road trailer. This involves stevedores, cargo-handling equipment and good liaison among all concerned. This includes marshalling/assembling the cargo; the actual loading of the cargo and its tallying, shipboard stowage and so on. The shipowner representative would have a stowage plan which will identify the location of the consignments to be stowed on the vessel. Good liaison is essential amongst port authorities, stevedores, agents, customs, and so on.

On completion of the shipboard loading the master or his agent will present the requisite documents to customs to enable the vessel to clear customs prior to the ship's departure. Documents involved are ship's stores, loadline certificate, ship's certificate of registry, wireless certificate, light dues certificate, safety equipment certificate, passenger certificate, cargo manifest. Further details can be found in Chapter 6 of *Elements of Shipping*.

A fundamental aspect relating to the process of discharging and/or loading of a vessel is the need for adequate preplanning of the operation to ensure optimization of all available resources (see pp. 139–143). We will now examine the various transport modes and their particular features regarding the process of discharging/loading cargo or passengers on to the vessel.

Loose cargo

This category is a very labour-intensive system, requiring the goods to be manhandled throughout the cargo transhipment operation. The quays are general cargo berths equipped with cranage and transit sheds and are road and rail served. The unloading sequence involves the manhandling of the goods in the ship's hold and requires extensive use of the sling or strap for handling wooden cases or bagged cargo or the snotter or canvas sling for bagged cargo (see pp. 60–67). A gang of up to six men would be in the ship's hold loading the cargo on to the ship's derrick or shore-based crane. A similar number of men would be on the quayside to receive/stack the cargo. A tally clerk would be on the berth to record each consignment unloaded. Fork lift trucks and other mechanized cargo-handling equipment would be used. A gang foreman would be in charge supervising the shipboard and shore-based operation in consultation with the crane driver. Cargo would be placed in a transit shed or warehouse. Usually loose cargo is cleared through customs at the time of transhipment. A similar operation would obtain for the export consignment except that the stevedoring superintendent would indicate to each gang foreman the location of each commodity in the ship in accordance with the cargo stowage plan supplied by the shipowner's representative to the master. A substantial proportion of such cargo is now loaded or discharged from lighters/barges, which involves a similar operation but is largely reliant on the ship's derricks. The volume of loose cargo shipments primarily involving 'tween-deck tonnage is very much on the decline as it is displaced by containerization.

Bulk cargo shipment
This represents over 40% of world trade volume embracing oil, ore, chemicals, fertilizers, coal, timber, stone, grain, cement, and so on. Many of the berths are purpose built to enable fast loading or discharge involving a capital-intensive operation, achieving fast port turn-round time. For liquid cargoes and certain dry commodities like cement or grain, transhipment is by means of pipeline involving a shore-based storage plant. Alternatively, for coal, ore, timber, stone, fertilizer, and so on the distribution is by rail and less frequently by road. The berths are usually under lease or privately owned by the shipper. The berth is managed and operated by the shipper. It may be part of the port complex or in the case of many oil and ore terminals, situated close to oil fields or ore mines. With regard to the oil terminal, with the development of ULCCs and VLCCs (see *Elements of Shipping*, pp. 45 and 55–6) involving vessels offering a draft of 22 m and 400 000 d.w.t. a jetty is often provided to give safe anchorage during transhipment. Bulk cargoes are usually cleared through customs at the port at the time of transhipment.

Containerization
The growth of containerization continues worldwide and likewise the range of container types. It embraces an ever-increasing range of commodities covering consumer goods; bulk cargo containerized shipments such as cement, wine and fertilizers; groupage consoli-

dated consignments (see *Elements of Shipping*, Chapter 16), and so on. The berths are purpose built with specialized cargo-handling equipment (see p. 37). Adequate standage areas must be provided permitting container stacking up to three tiers high. Many berths are rail served to an inland clearance depot/container freight station, or inland industrial areas. Road features prominently in the distribution arrangements in many ports. A significant proportion of the containers travel under bond through the port. Container transhipment is a capital-intensive operation involving extensive pre-planning and growing use of computers which plan the shipboard cargo stowage arrangements. A key factor is the need to minimize port turn-round time and ensure an unimpeded flow of container transhipment arrangements. An increasing number of container shipowners lease and manage their own berth and provide a freight consolidation service from the port.

Dangerous classified cargo
Stringent regulations apply to the shipment of dangerous classified cargo (see *Elements of Export Practice*, pp. 100–105). It may be the oil tanker shipment, the container consignment, the road vehicle conveying the dangerous classified liquid consignment, or the loose cargo consignment. Port regulations are very severe and in most ports such cargoes must be isolated from the general cargo consignments. Moreover, particular emphasis is given to ensuring that the cargo passes through the port quickly, thereby minimizing the risk of any hazard. Usually such cargoes are cleared through customs at the port.

International road haulage (Ro/Ro)
The growth of the Ro/Ro business in many trades has been dramatic during the past few years and today many vessels are equipped to handle wheeled consignments on a trailer, or slave trailer. In such circumstances the trailer is driven on/off the vessel by means of the ship's ramp on to the vehicle deck/quayside. An important port dealing with such traffic is Dover, which handles some 3000 road vehicle movements daily. It provides vehicular ferry services to Europe. A feature of the scheme is the fast customs clearance for both export and import consignments. Usually a vehicle would be cleared within 2 to 6 hours of arrival at Dover. The vehicles may be unaccompanied or accompanied on the Ro/Ro vessel (see *Elements*

of Shipping, pp. 52–6), with the latter involving the driver travelling with the vehicle on the ship. Vehicles on arrival are processed through the port by the shipowner relative to the documentation and customs arrangements or by agents. The vehicles are marshalled into their correct allocated areas pending shipment. Parking/standage areas are specially designated for import and export consignments. The vehicles are called forward into their respective designated areas for shipment on specified sailings. A similar arrangement applies to the imported consignment. The Ro/Ro consignment in the deep-sea market operates under similar arrangements and usually involves the combi-carrier type of vessel (see *Elements of Shipping*, pp. 47–50), involving a variety of cargo shipment types such as containers, heavy lifts, loose cargo, and so on. A feature of the Ro/Ro traffic is that the unaccompanied trailer movement involving the services of a tug master tends to slow up the transhipment arrangements compared with the accompanied road vehicle.

Indivisible load
An increasing number of indivisible load consignments are now being shipped. Such consignments require special arrangements at the port. It may be a transformer, a railway locomotive, or some other consignment of excessive width, height or weight. This requires special arrangements at the port, embracing heavy lifting equipment, marshalling of the consignment, transportation arrangements, and so on. It requires much pre-planning, with regard not only to the shipment arrangements, but also to the transportation arrangements to/from the port, which may be by rail, road or lighterage. Special stowage arrangements must be undertaken on the ship. Customs clearance is usually undertaken at the port.

Passenger traffic passing through a port is subject not only to customs examination of accompanying luggage, but also to immigration, involving passport examination and related documents including visas, health certificate, and so on. The purpose of immigration is to exercise control over people entering a country. Customs examination is undertaken to limit the quantity of free dutiable goods accompanying an adult entering a country such as cigarettes, tobacco, wine, spirits and perfumes and gifts such as watches, jewellery, etc. and apply other restrictions such as on the importation of drugs. For passengers entering a country the first control is the immigration, to be followed by customs examination. The same procedure applies for a person leaving a country. Basically, three types of passenger traffic exist at a port:

(a) Foot passengers are those passengers passing through a port on foot. For passengers leaving the country they may have arrived by rail, coach or car. Many such passengers may be going on a cruise or short ferry crossing of up to 8 hours.

(b) Motorist traffic involves the driver and passengers travelling with his/her car on the vessel. To cater for this traffic a car examination hall would be provided at the port.

(c) Coach traffic concerns the driver and passengers, which may number up to 70 on a double-decker coach. A coach examination hall is provided at the port to examine passenger baggage.

To conclude our study of processing the consignment through the port one must bear in mind that the arrangements will vary with the individual port. The central theme must be to ensure prompt throughput of the cargo at the port at all times, which involves co-operation and liaison among all the interested parties.

PORT OPERATIONAL PLANNING

An important management function in port operation and traffic control is operational planning. This depends on the nature of the traffic and the type of port: a multi-purpose port, for example, would have a complex organizational structure which would be grouped into four main areas as detailed below:

(a) Ship control and handling. This includes harbour master's, port conservancy, port control, pilotage, engineers, maintenance, and so on.

(b) Cargo control and handling. Such a group includes stevedoring, transit sheds and warehousing, forwarding agencies, transport, etc.

(c) Statutory controls. These include customs, immigration, police, health, and so on.

(d) Management control. This group includes day-to-day superintending, marketing, the hinterland served, trading, and so on.

Port operational planning falls into two distinct categories: the process of handling/distributing inwards (import) cargo, and conversely the process of assembling/handling outwards (export) cargo.

We will now examine each function.

Inwards cargo planning involves the ship arrival and discharge arrangements in the most efficient way practical. It will involve an evaluation of the following factors:

(a) The nature of the cargo. It may be a bulk cargo of coal, ore, consolidated cargo in containers or dangerous classified cargo which requires special resources/arrangements.

(b) The type of vessel. The ship may be a parcel tanker, ore carrier, combi-carrier, Ro/Ro vessel, cellular ship, and so on.

(c) The type of berth required is primarily dependent on the type of vessel and commodity.

(d) Customs/immigration requirements. Passengers require both immigration and customs examination. Cargo needs to be processed through customs examination, the extent of which will vary with country and port. See item (e).

(e) The country of origin relative to the cargo or nationality of the passenger. This will have a profound effect on the process of customs examination and immigration regulations. Traffic which moves within a free trade area requires less customs documentation, as for example within the EEC, compared with goods imported outside the free trade area. Additionally, cargo classified as coastal requires limited customs examination and only nominal documentation needs. Coastal traffic arises within a country's seaboard, such as the movement of cargo from Dieppe to Dunkerque within the French seaboard.

(f) The port resources required and their availability – a major consideration. This includes type of berth, cargo-handling equipment, dock labour, lighterage, warehouse/transit shed accommodation and/or standage area required, as found in Ro/Ro traffic and the container stacking area; customs resources; availability of transport to distribute the cargo/passengers which may be rail, road, canal/inland waterways or transhipment to another vessel for onward shipment such as container ship feeder service; security resources available, including both river and shore-based police personnel.

(g) As detailed in item (f), the type of cargo-handling equipment required will be determined by the nature of the cargo and the type of ship. This is an important factor and is critical in the efficient flow of cargo from ship to shore. It is paramount in the fast turn-round of vessels.

(h) Weather conditions and the date of the ship arrival. This involves tidal variations, fog conditions and sea conditions. Ports which are classified as open ports with no protecting arm/ breakwater, etc. are vulnerable to interruption to the process of cargo discharge due to swell conditions within the harbour. Ports operative within an enclosed dock system are virtually immune to adverse weather conditions.

(i) Availability of tugs. This arises, for example, in ports subject to adverse weather conditions, or in circumstances where the sheer size of the vessel, such as an ULCC or VLCC, warrants tug assistance to enable the ship to berth safely.

(j) The cost of the cargo transhipment constituents. This includes tugs, cargo handling, customs, dock labour, and so on. In the ideal port operation system one must strive to have the ship berthed and discharged of her cargo as quickly as possible. Delays may be encountered to the achievement of this objective. This may be due to bad weather preventing the vessel docking or interrupting the continuous process of cargo discharge; non-availability of a suitable berth due to a build-up of traffic resulting in the vessel having to lay anchor until such time as a suitable berth becomes available; slow clearance of cargo through customs due to non-availability of requisite documentation thereby creating port congestion and attracting demurrage; poor distribution arrangements resulting in a build-up of cargo on the quayside and in the transit shed, which in turn creates cargo congestion and creates an impediment in the smooth flow of cargo discharge; and the high cost of dock labour which tends to discourage working on Sunday. It is most important to bear in mind that a vessel is only earning income while at sea carrying cargo, and every effort must be made to minimize port delays and to strive to achieve a minimum port turn-round time.

To conclude our examination of inwards cargo transhipment, it is usual in modern ports to devise a berthing plan identifying the period each vessel is scheduled to be in port. It is published monthly or in more busy ports weekly to reflect recent alterations of predicted ship arrivals/departures. Such a berthing plan enables all the related resources to be available including customs, cargo-handling equipment, dock labour, transport distribution, ship husbandry, agents, and so on.

We will now examine the outwards (export) cargo planning operation involving the trading of the vessel and her departure from the port. It involves the following factors, a number of which are also found in the inwards (import) cargo planning operation evaluation.

(a) The nature of the cargo.

(b) Customs and immigration. Export cargo customs procedures tend to be quicker than for the imported cargo consignment. Nevertheless, adequate pre-planning is required in terms of the availability of customs officers and required customs documentation including export licences.

(c) The type of berth required.

(d) The destination country of the cargo. This factor, coupled with the nature of the cargo, will determine the degree of customs examination/documentation. For example, an export licence may be required to limit/control the volume of such cargo to a specific country.

(e) The type of vessel – an all-important factor which will determine the required port resources. This may impose constraints due to the dimensions of the vessel and the availability of a suitable berth.

(f) Port resources required and their availability.

(g) The extent to which cargo can be called forward for shipment. For example, with general cargo shipments this will depend on the adequacy of the cargo assembly area and its proximity to the berth. A cargo assembly area situated adjacent to the berth and of sufficient capacity to accommodate all the cargo for shipment on the specified sailing will produce the quickest and most efficient cargo-handling operation. Cargo awaiting shipment some distance from the berth tends to extend the period of cargo loading.

(h) Weather conditions.

(i) Availability of tugs.

(j) The general efficiency of feeder transport services such as lighterage, rail or road. It is essential that such services are co-ordinated to ensure that the cargo is called forward and is available for shipment in adequate time to enable unimpeded loading. Under the combined transport operation conveyed under customs bond, both import and export cargoes are virtually immune from any customs examination at the port, thereby speeding up the flow of cargo through the port and contributing to fast port turn-round time (see *Elements of Export Practice*, pp. 153–156).

(k) The cost of the constituents of the cargo transhipments.

To conclude our review of operational port planning, one cannot stress too strongly the need for adequate and continuous liaison/co-operation among all the parties involved to ensure optimum performance and the fastest port turn-round practicable/possible. This includes the shipowner, port authority, receiver, shipbroker, agent, stevedores, railway company, road operator, lighterage company, customs, ship's husband, shipper, and so on. Our evaluation has been confined to the general cargo vessel dealing with a wide variety of cargoes which may be conveyed on a container vessel, combi-carrier, 'tween-deck ship, Ro/Ro vessel, and so on. Such tonnage usually offers regular services while in contrast the bulk cargo vessel may be chartered, sometimes requiring a one-off arrangement. The advantage of the bulk cargo shipment is that it lends itself to a smoother transhipment pattern and less complex customs procedure, dealing with one complete shipload compared with some 2000 consignments on a general cargo vessel. In particular, the distribution arrangements are more favourable and easier to plan subject to the adequacy of available resources. This may be by pipeline for oil, as in Rotterdam, rail for iron ore in Dunkerque or phosphate in Aqaba. Such tonnage requires purpose-built berths – which maximizes efficiency. In such situations the shipments are regular. Computerization is becoming more prominent in the pre-planning arrangements.

CHAPTER 9

Port tariffs

THEORY OF PORT TARIFFS

A port tariff is the reward payable to the port authority for the rendering of a service. It may be a 'turn out' of a container, or the discharge of cargo from a vessel to the quayside.

The pricing of port services, like all pricing, is dependent on the forces of supply and demand but the factors affecting both supply and demand are perhaps more complicated than in the case of most other industries and services. As with all forms of transport, the demand for shipping and associated port facilities is derived from the demand for the commodities carried, and is, therefore, affected by the elasticity of demand for these commodities.

The demand for sea transport and associated port facilities is affected both by direct competition between carriers and port authorities, and, because it is a derived demand, by the competition of substitutes or alternatives for the particular commodity carried. On any particular route involving a particular port, the shipowner and port authority are subject to competition from carriers and associated port operators on the same route and also from carriers operating from alternative supply areas. The commodities carried by the latter may be competitive with the commodities from his own supply area and, to that extent, may affect the demand for his services. On some routes there is also competition from air transport, and in the coasting trade there is also competition from inland transport. Such situations affect the trade volume passing through a port and its associated demand.

The elasticity of demand for shipping services and associated ports varies from one commodity to another. In normal times an important factor affecting elasticity of demand for sea transport services and associated ports is the cost of transport in relation to the market price of the goods carried. Although it can be negligible, the cost of port charges is also a significant element in the final market price of many commodities. It may be between 2% and 5% according to the trade. The sea transport cost including port expenses is between 8% and 15%.

The price eventually fixed depends largely on the relationship between buyers and sellers. When both groups are numerous and have equal bargaining power, and where demand is fairly elastic, conditions of relatively perfect competition prevail. Under these circumstances, prices are fixed by the 'haggling of the market' and are known as contract prices. The market for tramp charters operates under such conditions and the contract is drawn up as an agreement known as a charter party. The tramp companies are usually medium-sized concerns, and the merchants who deal in the commodities carried by them usually possess equal bargaining power. Port charges may or may not be included in the fixture rate of the chartered vessel. See Chapter 6 of *Economics of Shipping Practice and Management*.

The contract may be for a single voyage at so much per ton of the commodity carried, or it may be for a period at a stipulated rate of hire, usually so much per ton of the ship's deadweight carrying capacity. The charter rates are quoted on a competitive basis, in various exchanges throughout the world. Choice of port used is very much dependent on the range of port facilities, the tariff and the overland arrangements required by the importer/exporter.

Under these conditions the rate structure for tramps and associated ports is a very simple product and emerges from competitive interplay of supply and demand. From the economist's point of view, rates made in this way represent the most efficient methods of pricing, for where price is determined under conditions of perfect competition, production is encouraged to follow consumers' wishes, and price itself does not deviate to any great extent from average total cost. In this way the customer is satisfied and production capacity most usefully employed.

In the liner trades, the shipowners control fairly large concerns, and although some of their shippers may be very large firms, the bulk of their traffic comes from numerous overall shippers. In these conditions, it is more convenient for the shipowner to estimate how much his customers are prepared to pay and to fix his own rate. Such prices are known as tariff prices.

Liner rates are based partly on cost and partly on value. Many freight rates are quoted on a basis of weight or measurement at ship's option. This means that the rate quoted will be applied either by per metric ton of 1000 kg (2205 lb) or per tonne of 1.133 m^3, whichever will produce the greater revenue. Port dues incurred by the shipowner are usually included in the rate, but cargo-handling expenses are raised separately for payment by the shipper. Again, the shipper's choice of port will depend much on the importer's wishes and the general competitiveness/adequacy of the port and quality of service. The distribution arrangement and speed of customs clearance are important factors in the shipper's choice of port. It will also be influenced by the cargo delivery terms such as CIF, FOB as agreed between exporter (seller) and importer (buyer). See Chapter 8 of *Elements of Export Marketing and Management*.

To conclude our examination of the theory of port tariffs, it is apparent that they are very much integrated with the sea transport tariff. Hence they are subjected to the same economic analysis as described earlier. In the long term the port tariff could become more consolidated with the sea transport tariff as it obtains today. This applies particularly to the container market.

FACTORS INFLUENCING THE LEVEL OF PORT TARIFFS

We shall now examine the main factors that influence the level of port tariffs.

Competition in its many forms

Ports which are situated in close proximity to each other and are capable of competing in the same markets tend to compete with one another in service of quality and ancillary services. Competition undoubtedly has a profound effect on rates and can result in manipulation of the discounted rates usually aligned to traffic volume. Port authorities must constantly bear in mind all aspects of competition to ensure that they can maximize their traffic throughput.

The nature of the product

It may be ship's dues, lighterage dues, stevedoring charges, cargo dues, and so on. In the case of loose cargo it will depend on the nature of the commodity, its quantity, overall cubic measurements, dimensions, value and period of shipments. Cargo which is dangerous or exceptionally dirty/obnoxious usually attracts a higher rate, which may be negotiated on a per individual shipload basis. Likewise livestock, awkwardly shaped, heavy indivisible consignments, containerized consignments, road haulage vehicle shipments and palletized shipments all attract a special scale of rate.

The trade in which the cargo originates
It may be coastal, deep sea or short sea. Generally, deep sea cargoes tend to attract a higher tariff than the coastal or short-sea trades. The prime reason for this is that the total sea freight for the coastal or short sea voyage tend to be overall lower than the deep-sea consignment. Hence the rate is often based on the 'what the traffic will bear' concept with the longer voyage better able commercially to accept the higher port tariff. See page 164.

Port cost
This is a major factor. The port authority must determine the cost of the service provided and formulate a tariff accordingly based on both direct and indirect cost plus an element for profit. Direct cost would embrace dock labour, electricity/fuel consumption and day-to-day maintenance, while indirect cost includes depreciation, loan interest, administration, and so on. Some ports operate on a cross-subsidization basis whereby the profitable revenue from one berth would subsidize the deficit income on another berth. However, this practice is tending to become less common as each cost centre such as a berth must be sufficiently profitable to enable it to fund new technology and thereby attain continuing improved efficiency standards. It is most important that profitability levels are adequate to fund new technology and thereby improve the competitiveness of the port to the benefit of its users and the hinterland that it serves.

Special facilities to handle the commodity
The range of facilities provided to handle the cargo/passenger will influence the cost and ultimate tariff. Heavy-lift cargoes, usually involving an indivisible load such as a transformer or locomotive, require a heavy-lift crane of up to 200 tons. Likewise, modern passenger ports such as Dover, Harwich, New York, Sydney and Rotterdam have invested heavily in the range of passenger

amenities and accordingly their investment cost, maintenance, etc. must be reflected in the passenger dues.

Transport mode
The mode of transport which may be a container, international operated road vehicle, train ferry wagon or loose cargo will determine the port handling arrangements. In recent years loose or break-bulk cargo consignments have become less and less as they are expensive to handle in dock labour terms. The development of the combined transport operation, especially the container, and, on the short voyage, the international road haulage vehicle, has modernized and quickened the movement of cargo through the port. Accordingly, this permits a lower handling cost per tonne compared with the loose cargo consignment.

Exchange rate variations
In situations where there is a range of ports situated in different countries and able to compete for the same traffic the exchange rate can have an effect on the competitiveness of the port. Exchange rates which are weak can attract traffic against those which are strong. Hence the port authority with a strong currency may wish to reflect on such a factor in the formulation of the tariff to remain competitive or offer discounted rates for volume business.

Agreement with other port authorities
Circumstances do arise in some countries or group of ports to pitch the tariff at a particular level to ensure that it lessens the competitiveness of individual ports within the group of ports and thereby avoid rate dilution which could result in an uneconomic tariff structure.

Statutory controls
Many countries have State-owned ports and thereby government controls the level of charges.

Relations with shippers' councils and trade associations
An increasing number of ports throughout the world have strong ties with shippers' councils and trade associations which represent the users of the ports. An area of regular discussion is the level of tariffs and port efficiency.

Subsidies
A number of ports receive conditional State subsidies for a variety of reasons. A major one is to ensure the tariff remains competitive and thereby help to attract the maximum volume of business through the port.

Flag discrimination
This technique is widely practised worldwide and involves the national flag operator having a more favourable tariff than foreign tonnage. Also, the national flag takes preference over the foreign flag in berth access. Its aim is to encourage shippers to support the national flag and thereby maintain a national fleet. See Chapter 14 of *Economics of Shipping Practice and Management*.

Marketing
Port authorities have tended to become in recent years more conscious of the need to market their product and thereby encourage more shipping lines to use their port and stimulate existing users to expand their business. This tends to encourage negotiated rates based on business volume and commitment/loyalty to the port, coupled with investment in port facilities by the shipowner under a leased berth arrangement. It results in lower rates. The task of cargo handling and processing of cargo through customs and related distribution arrangements is usually all undertaken by the shipowner.

Value of the goods
Cargo of high value requiring extra security and handling precautions attracts a higher port tariff.

Compliance with customs requirements
This involves 'turn out' of cargo for customs examination and presentation/lodgement of requisite documents.

General fragility or awkwardly shaped cargo
Merchandise which is fragile or awkwardly shaped, requiring additional handling facilities, tends to attract a special tariff.

Palletized cargo
Palletized consignments aid cargo-handling efficiency and in many

ports concessionary tariffs exist to encourage such traffic.

Ease of handling and stowage
Merchandise which is easy to handle and stow is a significant factor when any negotiated rates for cargo handling/stowage are undertaken.

The foregoing factors must not be regarded as exhaustive but merely the major factors. Overall, the port tariff should be so devised as to generate the maximum income on a viable basis and thereby enable the port authority to develop the port on a cost efficiency level.

MARKET PRICING

An increasing number of major port authorities are now using the technique of market pricing which is essentially the practice of correlating the port tariffs to potential market demand and sensitivity in order primarily to maximize cash flow, attain good utilization of dock resources, counter competition, stimulate market growth and improve profitability. Examples of market pricing include discounted tariff for volume commitment from a shipowner, such as 10% discount on published tariff on 100 000 tons annually; or lower tariffs in the less busy periods to spread the traffic flow through the port (see p. 147).

In adopting a market pricing policy, care must be taken to ensure that the full rate traffic is not diverted to the lower rate in endeavouring to generate a higher volume of business. Moreover, whereas the basic tariff must cover direct costs and make a major contribution to indirect costs, the reduced tariffs should at least cover direct costs if possible. The formulation of graduated tariffs requires careful evaluation of existing tariff levels, costs, competition, agreements with shipowners and, above all, market sensitivity. For example, there is nothing to be gained by offering a 40% 'off season' discount for particular traffic if the market is insensitive to price; the slightly higher throughput that would ensure, say 5% higher, would produce less revenue overall, so that in accordance with the principle of profit maximization the tariff should remain unchanged. Finally, market pricing policies that lead to a tariff war should be avoided. They may generate additional traffic, but the average rate will fall and there may be little prospect of increasing revenue.

PORT TARIFFS

When levying any charges for services in the port there are two important principles which should be adhered to:

(a) Revenue should be adequate not only to cover the cost of providing the facility/service embracing both direct and indirect cost but also for provision to be made for future investment to sustain the quality of service and improve efficiency. Direct cost usually embraces all those expenses involved to provide the service such as dock labour, maintenance and fuel, but indirect cost includes amortization depreciation and interest on loan capital.

(b) Charges should be shared equitably by all users of the port. This does not obtain in all ports, especially those which practise flag discrimination and in so doing discriminate against the foreign flag tonnage, thereby favouring the national flag fleet operator.

The charges levied by the port are generally divided according to the facilities made available to the customer. In general terms there are broad headings: ship's dues; cargo handling; cranes and plant; warehousing and storage; sundry services and facilities; rents; and other revenue. Each category will now be examined. Overall the charges raised may be by the port authority or the tenants leasing the property such as quay, warehouse, etc.

Ship's dues

Revenue from dues on ships, consisting of harbour, dock, quay or river conservancy dues, or some combination of these, is applied to cover the cost of services such as dredging, lighting and buoying the channel, and the maintenance of the quay berths and locks. The ship's dues are charged to shipowners or charterers on the basis of either the gross or net registered tonnage of the vessel and are usually varied in accordance with the nature of the voyage, foreign-going ships being charged at a higher rate than coasters.

An increasing number of port authorities also operate a 'part cargo rate' which levies charges according to the amount of cargo being carried on the ship if this is lower than the Net Registered Tonnage (NRT). This practice has helped to encourage ships with small UK parcels to call in at a particular port direct rather than go to another port and tranship the cargo to a feeder vessel service. The dues normally allow the ship to remain for a specified period, e.g. 30 days, but in some ports this can be extended to 60 days. A daily charge is raised on expiry of the specified period. Vessels below 75 Gross Registered Tonnage (GRT) in many ports are excluded, together with warships and hospital ships. A ship engaged on regular liner services calling at the port regularly such as once per week would be granted a discounted rate of up to 35% depending on the service frequency and volume of overall business. Likewise, vessels calling only to bunker, to take on stores, to change members of the ship's crew, or for ship repairs would be levied a discounted rate. In some ports vessels of the national flag or owned by the national government would be immune from any levy or granted more favourable rates. Pleasure craft such as yachts are granted a special scale of dues. Given below are the various types of ship's dues in existence – the level of ship's dues will vary:

(a) Vessel on service calling at a port to discharge/load cargo and/or passengers.

(b) Ships laid up at a berth/quay usually charged a daily rate.

(c) Ship calling at a port to be afforded shelter from a storm.

(d) Vessel calling at a port for bunkering, replenishment of stores, general victualling, or ship repair purposes.

Ship's dues are for the account of the shipowner, charterer or ship agents.

Additionally, a scale of charges is provided by the Institute of Chartered Shipbrokers relative to the port authority acting as the ship's agent while in port.

In most major ports of the world pilotage is compulsory unless the master has an exemption certificate. Pilotage arises in two prime areas: the seaway gaining access to the river estuary and the port area itself. The charge varies by application. It may be based on the gross registered tonnage of the vessel, or a charge per ship – the latter may vary by ship tonnage and type.

Goods dues

Dues levied on cargo passing over the quay/berth as import or export merchandise are known as cargo dues/dock rates/wharfage rates/quay rates depending on the port. They are normally levied on all goods shipped, unshipped or transhipped at the port and are chargeable by some unit of weight, volume or number, according to the nature of the goods.

They are paid by importers and exporters to the port authority and contribute to the revenue from which it has to meet the cost of providing and maintaining the requisite facilities such as berths/ transit sheds, examination sheds and warehouses, without which the goods could not be handled.

Given below are the types of dues levied on goods:

(a) Cargo dues based on tonnage which may vary according to commodity. In many trades it is called a wharfage charge involving the movement from the ship to the customs examination shed and vice versa.

(b) Cargo dues for livestock are assessed on a per head basis.

(c) Road haulage vehicles are calculated on a laden or unladen basis. This will be assessed on the total laden weight of the loaded vehicle. Further calculations are assessed on the accompanied and unaccompanied vehicle. The unaccompanied vehicle requires the services of port equipment such as the tug master. The tariff is assessed on a per vehicle basis.

(d) Import/export vehicles. These include cars, lorries, coaches, agricultural machinery either being exported from or imported through a port. The tariff is based on a per vehicle/agricultural machinery unit basis. Special tariffs exist for very large vehicles such as earth-moving equipment.

(e) Containerized cargo tariff is based on a container unit usually differentiating between the FCL and LCL container unit. The tariff will vary according to container length and whether the port lifting equipment (crane), ship's derrick or combination of the two are used. Tariffs vary according to the commodity in the container. Discounted rates may be negotiated for volume business annually. Alternatively, in some ports the tariff is based on the linear footage differentiating between the laden and unladen container unit. This is a less popular tariff structure.

(f) Palletized cargo and merchandise conveyed on slave trailers. Such cargo is charged on a tonnage or per unit basis. The latter is the more common with the variation for commodity.

CUSTOMS ENTRY CHARGES

Many ports offer a customs entry service involving the presentation and processing of consignments through customs. Details are given below:

(a) Preparation of the customs entry. This is charged on a per entry basis.

(b) Presentation of the prepared entry or carnet. This is on a per shipment basis and involves the port authority lodging all the documents/entry with customs for clearance purposes.

(c) The passing of the prepared full 'T' documents. Again this is on a per shipment basis.

(d) Assistance in preparation and/or passing prepared T2L documents. Such documents are relative to EEC consignments and are charged on a per set basis.

The foregoing applies to export consignments but for imports the following are available:

(a) Preparation and presentation of complete entry. The charge is on a per entry basis.

(b) Submission of complete entry or other document to customs. Again the charge is on a per entry basis.

Cargo handling is undertaken either by the port authority, master stevedores, master porters or master lumpers. The term varies according to the country and in many they are called porters or stevedores. A charge is levied on the shipowner or importer/exporter for the loading and discharging of the vessels. The practice of charging for this type of operation varies considerably from port to port. In some the shipowner pays for all the stevedoring cost while in others he pays a proportion. Many negotiations today involve a split in the costs of the activities depending upon the responsibility of the parties involved. The charge is usually based on the nature of the commodity and its ease of handling and is related to weight or measurement (W/M) (see p. 145). If the cargo has a high weight density, such as steel, it will be charged on weight, while if the commodity has a high volumetric density, such as bales of cotton, it will be charged on measurement. Hence the cargo-handling company will charge the W/M rate whichever will produce the highest revenue.

Details of the normal division for liner cargo services are given below:

(a) From receiving road vehicles or rail through shed or quay to ship's rail. This cost is met by the exporter.
(b) From ship's rail to stowed in hold or reverse for imports. This cost is met by the shipowner, charterer or ship's agent.

With regard to bulk cargo shipment, such as iron ore, grain, oil, and so on, the shipper usually pays for the cargo-handling services. A significant volume of such cargo is shipped under chartered tonnage and the responsibility for meeting such cargo handling cost is clearly defined in the charter party document (see *Elements of Shipping*, Chapter 15).

Details of cargo-handling tariffs are given below:

(a) Import/export cargo. Removal of cargo from a wharf apron to a transit shed or an adjacent open storage area where the vessel is berthed or vice versa, or where cargo is loaded on a vessel from a vehicle/lorry or vice versa. The tariff is likely to be two tier: one for palletized cargo, which is the cheaper, and one for non-palletized cargo.
(b) 'Shut out' cargo. Where cargo to be exported from a particular port is brought to a wharf for loading on to a vessel and is 'shut out' by the vessel, and subsequently delivered to another vessel for shipment, an additional charge is made. Again, the tariff would be based on palletized and non-palletized cargo.
(c) Where cargo is delivered for transhipment/re-export a separate scale of charges per tonne is provided, differentiating between palletized and non-palletized cargo.

The tariff strategy at a port with regard to cargo handling will vary with circumstance but most port authorities do not offer any concessionary rates. Higher negotiated rates usually apply to dirty obnoxious bulk cargoes and a surcharge above the published tariff can apply to heavy lifts and large awkwardly shipped cargoes requiring extra equipment and additional dock labour.

Passenger dues

These are levied by the port authority on the shipowner, charterer, ship's agent for the passenger/motorist, accompanied car, coach passing over the quay/berth with a ramp linking the ship with the shore. It is an important form of revenue at passenger ports such as in Dover and Singapore. Details of the types of passenger dues are given below, which are based on the facilities at the port provided for the passenger/motorist/coach operator including lounges, refreshment rooms, immigration, gangway, baggage facilities, and so on.

(a) Passenger dues based on the number of passengers passing over the quay which may be embarking or disembarking passengers. The tariff will be the same for adult or child. Lower rates usually exist for day excursion passengers. A differing rates scale would be available for the coach passenger and motorist.

(b) Coach tariffs are based on the coach unit plus the number of passengers including driver conveyed in it. Vehicles under 5.50 m in length such as a minibus would be regarded as a car.

(c) The accompanied car tariff involves the vehicle up to 5.50 m in length and is charged on a unit basis. The driver and passengers would attract the passenger dues tariff. Vehicles over 5.50 m length and carrying freight requiring customs documentation would be charged as a freight Ro/Ro vehicle. Touring caravans being hauled by a car would be charged as a caravan unit. Motor cycles and cycles would have a separate unit tariff, while the motor-cyclist would be charged passenger dues.

All the foregoing passenger dues and their associated port tariffs are for the account of the shipowner. In so far as the passenger/motorist, etc. is concerned, these are incorporated in the passenger fare or motorist, coach tariff.

Containerization now features very prominently in liner cargo trades and falls into three main definitions relative to the container tariff as detailed below:

(a) The Full Container Load (FCL) tariff applies (i) to a loaded or empty container discharged from a vessel, moved and stored in the container stacking area or marshalling yard for direct delivery or subsequently removed to the interchange area for delivery; or (ii) to a shipped loaded or empty container and the reverse operations to (i) are performed; or (iii) to an empty container discharged from a vessel moved and stored in the railway marshalling yard and subsequently removed to a container freight station or container base.

(b) The Less than Container Load (LCL) applies (i) to a loaded container discharged from the vessel and moved to the container stacking area or marshalling yard for storage and subsequently removed to a container freight station, or container base where the contents are unstuffed and the empty container is moved to the marshalling yard; or (ii) an empty container stuffed at a container freight station or container base and the reverse operations to (i) are performed.

(c) Transhipment/reshipment container tariff applies to an empty or loaded container under the following conditions:

(i) When it is discharged from the first carrier on to the port authority premises and remains in the custody of the port authority until it is transhipped or reshipped by the port authority.

(ii) When it is transhipped or reshipped in its original status within a period of 28 days from the time of completion of discharge of the first carrier to the time of berthing of the on-carrying vessel.

(iii) Loaded and empty containers need to be manifested or declared in writing for transhipment at least 24 hours before the first carrier's arrival.

It will be appreciated that the foregoing definitions will vary with the port authority and country. Details are given below of the actual tariffs.

FCL containers loading or discharging

The tariff is often based on the following:

Containership using container quay crane or conventional ship using ship's derrick				*Containership using ship's container crane*			
Wholly using port's machinery appliances and chassis		Using port's machinery and appliances and ship's chassis		Wholly using port's machinery appliances and equipment		Using port's machinery and appliances and ship's chassis	
Container		Container		Container		Container	
Up to 20 ft in length	Over 20 ft in length	Up to 20 ft in length	Over 20 ft in length	Up to 20 ft in length	Over 20 ft in length	Up to 20 ft in length	Over 20 ft in length

The rate involving the container ship providing her own cranage is the cheaper one. Many port authorities require 24 hours' notice of the container being received on the port authority premises.

LCL containers loading or discharging

Any break-bulk transhipment cargo received or reshipped in a container is usually entitled to a rebate per tonne even when the transhipment cargo stored originally in the container remains intact within the container. The same rate structure obtains as for FCL containers.

Transhipment containers loading or discharging

Any transhipment container sent to a container freight station or container base for stuffing/unstuffing will lose the concessionary rate and be charged the LCL container rate. Again the rate structure as for FCL containers applies.

Opening or closing hatch covers

This involves opening the hatch cover, placing it at the next hatch on board the vessel, and subsequently closing the hatch; or opening the hatch cover, placing it on the wharf, and subsequently closing the hatch at the same berth. The rate is based on a per operation principle and the lower rate obtains when the container vessel uses her own cranage.

Shifting containers

This arises within the same hatch or bay or level involving without landing and reshipping operation, or with landing and reshipping operation. Alternatively, it will involve shifting a container from a hatch or bay or level to another hatch or bay or level of the same vessel. The rate is based on per container per shifting operation with the lower rate applying when the vessel uses her own cranage.

Containers from lighterage/barges

This concerns the discharge or loading of containers from a lighter or barge. Differing rates apply to FCL, LCL and transhipment containers. Two main tariffs exist for containers up to 20 ft, and those above 20 ft.

Uncontainerized cargo, overheight containers and containers stored athwartship
This arises when the handling of any lift/container can only be performed with a container quay crane or van carrier spreader with special attachments or manual slings. The uncontainerized tariff would be up to 15 tonnes gross weight, 15 to 30 tonnes and above 30 tonnes.

Storage charges of containers/chassis/break-bulk cargo
The tariff is on a per day basis and has two categories of container length up to 20 ft and over 20 ft. Differing rates exist for the empty container, loaded container, overheight container and chassis with or without a container. A free storage period exists usually up to 72 hours, and beyond which demurrage arises on a daily basis. A similar situation applies to other cargo such as break-bulk consignments and trailer cargo. The demurrage charges are on a per day basis and usually arise through the failure of the shipper to clear the goods through customs. Such demurrage consignments create port congestion.

Reefer container services
This involves pre-trip inspection, connecting or disconnecting services on board vessels, and electricity supply. Tariffs are on a per container basis.

Standby charge for gangs and equipment for stuffing/unstuffing
The standby charge is applied from the time the service is originally required to the time the service is rendered. It is based on an hourly rate.

Standby charges for labour and equipment
This arises owing to the late arrival of the vessel which is deemed to have been confirmed not less than 8 hours in advance, up to the actual time of arrival.

Containers – physical examination import and export
In situations where the port authority undertakes on behalf of the shipper an examination of the goods a charge is raised. This arises through the customs requesting a 'turn out' to examine the container contents to ensure that they comply with the customs declaration.

Charges range from empty, partial turn-outs, tallies and full turn-out. The same criteria apply to a Ro/Ro vehicle.

MISCELLANEOUS CHARGES

A wide variety of other port charges exist and these will vary according to the type of port and nature of the traffic. Details are given below of the more common ones, but the list should not be regarded as exhaustive.

(a) Warehouse or transit shed rental for transhipment, re-export and valuable cargoes. Cargo in process of transhipment from one vessel to another would be subjected to a warehouse rental. It may be on a daily or weekly basis. The tariff may be on the metreage area occupied or the tonnage of the cargo. Similar arrangements would apply to cargo refused by the consignee and re-exported. Cargo-handling charges would be raised separately to move cargo into or from the warehouse based on tonnage handled. Cargo of a high value and requiring special security measures would be charged at a higher tariff than the foregoing general cargo tariffs and this may be based on a percentage of the value of the cargo usually, about 1%. The charges are for the account of the shipper or consignee.

(b) Warehouse or transit shed rental for bonded goods' dangerous cargo. Tariffs are provided separately for cargo accommodated in bonded warehouse on which customs duty is only paid when it is withdrawn. Cargo classified as dangerous is accommodated in an isolated area of the port and shippers are encouraged to restrict the rental period to the absolute minimum. Published or negotiated rates apply. Again, the charges are for the account of the shipper or consignee.

(c) Port equipment daily hire charge. Ports have a wide range of equipment which may be hired. This includes pallets, tarpaulins, tenders, barriers, camel fenders, gangways, letter boards for passenger baggage, platform for refrigerated cargo, set of four steel plates, tow rope, baskets, hand truck, steel roller, shackle, shackle for 5 tonne lifts or over, sling, sling with heavy wire, cluster or electric cargo lights, and so on.

These are charged on a daily hire basis.

(d) Weighbridge. A charge on a per object weighed basis is raised on use of the weighbridge.

(e) Fire service. Most major port authorities have a fire fighting vessel and a tariff exists for its use.

(f) Police service. Likewise, most major port authorities have a police force and charges are based on a per hour tariff.

(g) Cargo palletizing service. Some ports have a cargo palletizing service which includes use of mechanical appliances or machinery for palletizing and strapping cargo on pallets. The tariff, which includes dock labour charge, is based on a tonnage scale.

(h) Removal of refuse from port authority premises. The collection of refuse is on a per trip basis.

(i) Ambulance service. This is on a per ambulance basis.

(j) Anti-pollution and/or salvage operations. This involves anti-pollution and/or salvage operations and/or assistance rendered to a vessel in difficulty. Additionally, it can involve launches, barges and oil booms. Charges vary according to whether it is within or outside port limits. A scale of charges also exist relative to cleaning up oil spill and/or salvage operations from or on land.

Most modern ports have computerized accounting and each tariff is allocated a code such as T1007 on the computer master file tariff. This is identified on the invoice billed to the client.

PORT AUTHORITY RATES AND CHARGES POLICIES

During the past 15 years there has been a dramatic change in many ports throughout the world in the method of international trade distribution. It has had a profound effect on the method of handling goods passing through a port. A number of the relevant points are detailed as follows:

The most major factor has been the transfer from the break-bulk loose cargo shipments involving 'tween-deck tonnage to the container ship. It has resulted in massive investment in containerized berths and equipment throughout the world and enabled a new rates structure to be devised of a much simplified nature (see pp. 157–160).

The era of 'tween-deck tonnage required an intensive dock labour operation to handle the cargo. The port authority in such circumstances compiled their handling cost on a commodity basis. This tended to be complex to apply and cumbersome to administer. It could involve a port tariff listing different rates for some 4000 commodities. Many ports handling break-bulk cargoes have rationalized their commodity classification as an aid to simplifying the rates structure. An increasing volume of break-bulk cargoes is non-palletized. Many ports have a palletized cargo tariff.

Dues on ships and passengers are relatively straightforward, although the number of voyage categories have been reduced.

An increasing number of ports are consolidating their wharfage rates and simplifying them into a limited number of categories.

The development of the Ro/Ro market in the short sea voyage markets has introduced a new port rates structure (see p. 153).

The purpose-built bulk cargo carrier is very prominent in many ports. It may be an oil tanker, ore carrier, car carrier, liquefied gas carrier, and so on. Many of such berths are leased from the port authority and the provision of such facilities is the responsibility of the shipowner. Accordingly, the shipowner would pay the usual ship's dues, but no wharfage charge would be raised as the handling of such cargo would be undertaken by the shipowner.

Computerization. Many ports worldwide are developing computerization in all areas of their business. Computerized billing features strongly in this area and accordingly all the port tariffs are allocated a number such as C1006 to identify the rate level on the invoice. Computerization has put pressure on many port authorities to rationalize/modernize their rates structure to aid marketing and simplify the computerized billing system on a cost-efficient basis.

As we progress through the next decade the development of combined transport will become more prominent. This will continue to facilitate the rationalization and modernization of the rates system. It is unlikely that the existing structure on ship's dues will change, but wharfage tariffs will continue to be modernized.

CHAPTER 10

Finance of international trade

In our study of the port industry, it is most desirable that we examine the finance of international trade. It is an area where the port operator needs to comprehend the implications of any tran-shipment delays through the port and the financial implications which follow to the buyer/seller.

In the days when the UK had extensive overseas investments and a dominant position in world trade, business was fairly straightfor-ward for British exporters. They encountered few foreign exchange problems, as most transactions were conducted in sterling, and the seller's market that prevailed allowed them to dictate terms and to grant or refuse credit as they wished.

Today the picture is entirely different. The UK's overseas invest-ments have been dispersed to pay for two wars, her products have to compete with those of equally efficient and sometimes more effi-cient producers in a buyer's market and sterling is no longer the dominant currency but, like other currencies, is subject to consider-able exchange rate fluctuations. Moreover, the ability to sell goods abroad no longer depends solely on quality, delivery and price; a new factor of growing importance is the ability and willingness to grant credit. The granting of credit terms, which are lengthening as the dominance of buyers increases, means that the exporter must wait longer for payment. This automatically reduces cash flow and sooner or later forces the exporter to seek assistance from his bank. Hence, the financial aspects of selling goods abroad are likely to assume increasing importance and, as a consequence, influence the fortunes of the shipping and port industries.

EXPORT AND IMPORT PRICES

In the periods when rates of exchange remained stable for many years, import and export prices tended to find their own level; they probably owed little to serious research and careful consideration but just emerged naturally. However, in the present period of exchange rate instability, which may be said to have begun with the devaluation of the pound sterling in November 1967, the setting and adjustment of prices has become a serious problem.

In 1967 few traders had a pricing policy to contend with a devaluation. Some held their sterling prices level, thus passing the 'full benefit of devaluation' on to their overseas dealers and customers. In consequence, they were flooded with orders that they were unable to fulfil, finance, or deliver on time, with the result that they lost many orders and customers. Others kept their overseas prices unchanged and thus upset their customers, who thought they were entitled to a price reduction.

It should be borne in mind that a 10% devaluation does not lead to a 10% change in the local price of a commodity, as the export price is only one element in the final cost to the consumer. Customs duty, import and distribution costs and local mark-ups, which are expressed in local currency, account for about half the retail price of many goods. Hence a 10% devaluation may at best lead to a change of about 5% in local price.

In establishing prices, firms must decide whether to charge 'what the market will bear' in each case or to set prices that cover costs and give a reasonable return on the capital employed. It may be argued that if a manufacturer does not charge as much as the market will bear, other operators in that market will add the difference and make an easy profit; according to this view, it is unlikely that the final consumer will be charged any less. On the other hand, there is little point in charging what the market will bear if this fails to show a return.

Hence the question of pricing will revolve around:

(a) The extent to which costs and returns on capital can be related to the price that the market will pay. This will involve a close study of the size and potential of the market, the strength of competitors and the elasticity of demand for the product.

(b) The extent to which exchange rate changes can be used to advantage.

(c) The credit terms that are usual in the market and whether the cost of the credit is borne by the buyer.

(d) Sources of raw materials and possible price changes.

The practice of expressing export prices in the customer's currency is a marketing principle that has much to recommend it; from the buyer's point of view the price is clear and relatively stable and there are no problems with exchange rates. By selling in foreign currency, the exporter has assumed the exchange risk himself, but he can protect himself against any exchange rate fluctuations by selling the currency in the forward market.

PAYMENTS ON 'OPEN ACCOUNT'

Credit terms and the method of payment are agreed when the sales contract is concluded. If relations between the buyer and seller are good, they may agree to trade on 'open account' terms. This means simply that the seller will dispatch the goods directly to the buyer, send him an invoice and await payment, as in domestic trading.

The debtor may use a number of means to pay his supplier:

Personal cheque
This is not very satisfactory from the creditor's point of view. Apart from the usual risk that the cheque may be dishonoured, it has to be sent through banking channels to the buyer's country for collection, thus incurring additional expense.

Banker's draft
This would be a draft drawn by the buyer's bank on its correspondent bank in the exporter's country. As such it is a good means of payment, but there is always the danger that the draft may be lost in the post; a new draft could be issued only against indemnity, as bank drafts cannot be 'stopped'.

Mail transfer (MT)
This is the most common method of payment. The debtor instructs his bank to request its correspondent bank in the exporter's country to pay the specific amount to the exporter. The whole procedure is effected by accounting entries; the buyer's bank debits his account and credits the account of the correspondent bank which, on receipt of the payment instructions, passes a reciprocal entry over its account with the remitting bank and pays the money to the exporter. The instructions between the banks may be sent by ordinary mail or air mail.

Telegraphic transfer (TT)
The procedure is essentially the same as for mail transfers, except that the instructions are sent by cable, thus ensuring that payment is effected more quickly.

BILLS OF EXCHANGE

If 'open account' terms have not been agreed, the exporter has to arrange for collection of the amount due. One way in which this can be done is by drawing a bill of exchange, the traditional instrument for claiming that which is due from a debtor. Bills of exchange can be used in international trade involving practically all countries of the world. Indeed, in some countries a trader would be unwise to forgo the protection a bill can provide.

The use of bills of exchange presents several advantages:

(a) The bill of exchange is an instrument long recognized by trade custom and by the law, so that it is governed by an established code of practice.

(b) A bill is a specific demand on the debtor, which the latter refuses at his peril.

(c) The bill is a useful instrument of finance.

(d) The bill provides a useful mechanism for granting a prearranged period of credit to an overseas buyer. Thus if an exporter has to offer his client a period of credit of 90 days, the bill can be drawn at 90 days after sight.

(e) The bill permits the exporter to maintain a degree of control over the shipping documents by making their release subject to payment or acceptance of the bill. Nevertheless, it should be noted that the drawing of a bill of exchange does not guarantee payment; bills too can be dishonoured.

In normal circumstances the exporter draws a bill of exchange, attaches the shipping documents to it and lodges the whole with his bank, giving very precise and complete instructions as to the action to be taken in certain circumstances: whether to forward the bill by air mail and ask for the proceeds to be remitted by cable or air mail; whether the documents are to be released against payment or acceptance of the bill; whether the bill is to be 'protested' if dishonoured; whether the goods should be stored and insured if not taken up by the buyer; whether rebate may be given for early payment;

the party to whom the collecting bank may refer in case of dispute.

The exporter's bank will forward the bill and documents to its correspondent bank in the buyer's country, passing on exactly the instructions received from the exporter. Acting as collecting bank, the correspondent will present the bill to the buyer and release the documents in accordance with the instructions received. If the arrangement called for payment to be made immediately, then the bill of exchange will be drawn at 'sight' and the instructions will be to release the documents against payment (D/P). If a period of credit has been agreed, then the bill will be drawn at, say, '90 days sight' and the instructions will be for the documents to be released against acceptance of the bill by the buyer (D/A). In this case, the buyer signs his acceptance across the face of the bill, which now becomes due for payment in 90 days, and he receives the documents of title to the goods. The collecting bank will advise the remitting bank of the date of acceptance and hold the bill until maturity, when it will present it to the buyer for payment. In the event of dishonour, the collecting bank will arrange 'protest' by a notary if it has been instructed to do so. This procedure provides legal proof that the bill was presented to the drawee and was dishonoured, and enables action to be taken in the courts without further preliminaries.

The procedures and responsibilities of the banks and other parties are laid down in the Uniform Rules for the Collection of Commercial Paper issued by the International Chamber of Commerce and accepted by major banks throughout the world.

The method of collecting payment described above is based on the documentary bill, but in certain circumstances use may be made of a 'clean' bill, that is, a bill to which no documents are attached. Such bills may be drawn for the collection of monies for services or for any debt which does not relate to goods. A clean bill may also be used to obtain payment for goods sent on 'open account', especially where payment is overdue.

DOCUMENTARY CREDITS AND ALLIED DOCUMENTS

Apart from requiring 'cash with order', the most satisfactory method of obtaining payment is by means of a documentary credit. It provides security of payment to the exporter and enables the buyer to ensure that he receives the goods as ordered and delivered in the way he requires. It is an arrangement whereby the buyer requests his bank to establish a credit in favour of the seller. The buyer's bank (the issuing bank) undertakes, or authorizes its correspondent bank in the exporter's country, to pay the exporter a sum of money (normally the invoice price of the goods) against presentation of specified shipping documents. It is a mandatory contract and completely independent of the sales contract. It is concerned only with documents and not with the goods to which the documents refer. Liability for payment now rests with the issuing bank and not with the buyer. Such credits are usually 'irrevocable', which means that they cannot be cancelled or amended without the agreement of the beneficiary (the exporter) and all other parties. The exporter can thus rely on payment being made as soon as he has shipped the goods and produced the necessary documents. The security provided by an irrevocable credit may be further enhanced if the bank in the exporter's country (the advising bank) is requested by the issuing bank to add its 'confirmation'. The exporter then has a 'confirmed irrevocable credit' and he need look no further than his own local bank for payment. If a credit is not 'confirmed', liability for payment rests with the issuing bank abroad, although the advising bank would usually be prepared to negotiate with recourse.

A documentary credit contains a detailed description of the goods: price per unit and packing; name and address of the beneficiary; the voyage, that is, port of shipment and port of destination; whether the price is Free on Board (FOB), Cost and Freight (C & F) or Cost, Insurance Freight (CIF); and whether part shipments and transhipment are allowed. In some cases, the ship will be named. Details of insurance (if CIF) and the risks to be covered will also be shown. The credit will specify a latest date for shipment and an expiry date, which is the latest date for the presentation of documents. It will also stipulate a time limit for presentation measured from the issue date of the bills of lading; in the absence of such a stipulation, banks refuse to accept documents presented later than 21 days after issuance of the bills.

The basic documents usually required, invoice, bills of lading, and insurance, are as follows:

Invoice

The amount must not exceed the credit amount. If terms such as 'about' or 'circa' are used, a tolerance of 10% is allowed (in respect of quantity the tolerance is 3%). The description of the goods on the invoice and the packing must be precise and agree with the credit. An essential part of the description is the marks and numbers on the packages. These must appear on the invoice, which should be in the name of the buyer.

Bills of lading

These are the document of title to the goods, without which the buyer will not be able to obtain delivery from the shipping company. The credit will call for a full set; they are usually issued in sets of three. They must be clean, that is to say bear no superimposed clauses derogatory to the condition of the goods such as 'inadequate packing', 'used drums' or 'on deck'. Unless the credit has specifically permitted the circumstances contained in the clause, the negotiating bank will request an indemnity. The bills of lading must show the goods to be 'on board'. Bills marked 'received for shipment' are not acceptable unless they bear a subsequent notation, dated and signed, stating that the goods are 'on board'. Under the new regulations set out in the Uniform Customs and Practice for Documentary Credits the following bills of lading will be accepted:

(a) Through bills issued by shipping companies or their agents, even though they cover several modes of transport.

(b) Short form bills of lading which indicate some or all of the conditions of carriage by reference to a source or document other than the bill of lading.

(c) Bills covering unitized cargoes such as those on pallets or in containers.

Unless specifically authorized in the credit, bills of the following type will not be accepted:

(a) Bills of lading issued by forwarding agents.
(b) Bills which are issued under and are subject to a charter party.
(c) Bills covering shipments by sailing vessels.

The bills must be made out to the order of the shipper and endorsed in blank. If the sales contract is CIF or C & F, then the bills must be marked 'freight paid'. The general description of the goods including marks and numbers must match the details given in the invoice. The voyage and ship, if named, must be stated in the credit.

Unless transhipment is expressly prohibited in the credit, bills indicating transhipment will be accepted provided the entire voyage is covered by the same bill. Part shipments are permitted unless the credit states otherwise.

Insurance
The policy or certificate must be as stated in the credit and must have been issued by an insurance company or its agent. Cover notes issued by brokers are not acceptable. The details on the policy must match those on the bills of lading – it must also be in the same currency as the credit and endorsed in blank. The amount covered should be at least the invoice amount – credits usually call for invoice value plus 10%. The policy must be dated not later than the date of shipment as evidenced by the bill of lading. The risks covered should be those detailed in the credit. If cover against 'all risks' is called for but is unobtainable, a policy covering all insurable risks will be acceptable.

According to circumstances, the credit may call for other documents, such as certificate of health, certificate of inspection, phytosanitary or veterinary certificate, certificate of origin, railway Convention Internationale *Concernant le Transport des Marchandises par Chemin de Fer* (CIM) or road Convention Marchandises Routiers (CMR) consignment notes or post office receipts.

The credit may stipulate a last shipment date and the bill of lading must show shipment by that date. Extension of the shipment date automatically extends the expiry date, but not vice versa.

It is very important that exporters immediately check the details of credits established in their favour to see that the goods and terms agree with the sales contract and that all the necessary documents are at hand. If any amendment is required, they can approach the advising bank in good time for action to be taken before expiry.

Besides the basic irrevocable credit there are revocable credits which, as the name implies, can be cancelled or amended at any time without notice to the beneficiary. They do not constitute a legally binding undertaking by the banks concerned. Once transmitted and made available at the advising bank, however, their cancellation or modification is only effective when that bank has received notice thereof and any payment made before receipt of such notice is reimbursable by the issuing bank. The value of these credits as security for payment is plainly doubtful. They are used mainly between parent and subsidiaries companies, where a continuing series of shipment is concerned, or as an indication of good intent.

Where a buyer wishes to provide his supplier with the security of payment afforded by a documentary credit, but at the same time requires a period of credit, he may instruct his bank to issue a credit calling for a bill of exchange drawn at so many days after sight instead of the usual sight draft – this would, of course, be an irrevocable credit. In this case the beneficiary would not receive immediate payment upon presentation of the documents as under a sight credit, but his term bill would be accepted by the bank. It could then be discounted in the money market at the finest rates. Thus the beneficiary would still receive payment, but the buyer would not be called upon to pay until the bill matured.

The subject of Export Documentation is dealt with in Chapter 12 of *Elements of Export Practice.*

TRANSFERABLE CREDITS

These arise where the exporter is obtaining the goods from a third party, say the actual manufacturer, and as middleman does not have the resources to buy outright and await payment from his overseas customer. The credit is established in favour of the middleman (the prime beneficiary) and authorizes the advising bank to accept instructions from the prime beneficiary to make the credit available, in whole or in part, to one or more third parties (the second beneficiaries). The second beneficiary is then notified of the credit on the original terms and conditions, except that the amount and unit price are reduced and the shipment and expiry dates shortened. The original credit relates to the price the buyer is paying to the prime beneficiary, but the latter will be obtaining the goods at a lower price, hence the reduction in amount. When the second beneficiary presents the shipping documents, he obtains payment for his invoice price, and the prime beneficiary is called upon to substitute his own invoice and receive the difference (his profit). The negotiating bank then has documents in accordance with the original credit.

Where more than one second beneficiary is involved the credit must permit part shipments. If the prime beneficiary does not wish his buyer and supplier to be aware of each other, he may request that his name be substituted for that of the opener on the transfer credit, and that shipping documents be in the name of a third party blank endorsed.

BACK-TO-BACK CREDITS

Back-to-back credits arise in circumstances similar to those of the transferable credit and particularly where both the supplier and the buyer are overseas. In this case, the middleman receives a credit in his favour from the buyer and asks his bank to establish a credit in favour of his supplier against the security of the credit in his own favour. Hence there are two separate credits instead of one as in the case of a transferable credit, and this can create problems in the matching of documents and credit terms.

REVOLVING CREDITS

Revolving credits are used where a series of shipments are made at intervals and the parties wish the programme to proceed without interruption. A credit is established for a certain sum and quantity of goods with a provision that, when a shipment has been made and documents presented and paid, the credit is automatically renewed in its original form so that another shipment can be made.

RED CLAUSE CREDITS

Red clause credits are sometimes called packing credits. These are mainly encountered in connection with shipments of wool from Australia, New Zealand or South Africa. A clause (in red) inserted into the credit authorizes the negotiating bank to make an advance by way of loan or overdraft to the beneficiary to enable him to purchase the wool, collect and warehouse it and prepare it for shipment. The loan is repaid out of the amount due upon presentation of the shipping documents.

ACCEPTANCE CREDITS

Acceptance credits were originally provided by merchant banks but they are now also available through clearing banks. The bank opens a line of credit in favour of the exporter, who is then able to draw bills on the bank, which are accepted by the latter and can then be discounted in the money market at the finest rates. Such credits usually run parallel with the bills drawn by the exporter on his overseas buyer and are drawn on the same terms as the latter. In due course the payment received for the commercial bills will meet the amount due to the bank on its acceptance. This facility is a means of obtaining export finance and can occasionally be cheaper than ordinary bank accommodation.

FACTORING

Although 'factoring' had its origins in the conduct of sales and collection of payments by the representatives sent to North America by English textile manufacturers, in its present form it is regarded as an American idea that has been introduced to the UK in recent years. The main function of a factoring service is the maintenance of suppliers' sales ledgers on the basis of copy invoices received from the suppliers themselves. Factors neither make sales nor issue invoices at the time of delivery of the goods; these functions are performed by the suppliers against the background of the factors' credit approval. The willingness of factors to make advance payments in respect of outstanding receivables increases suppliers' cash flow; usually 70% of amounts awaiting collection can be drawn in this manner. The factoring of export sales, which is a relatively recent development, provides a comprehensive package of export services to exporters requiring short-term finance. The collection of payments overseas is handled either by the UK factor's own offices or by correspondent factors. This network provides factors with a broad knowledge of payment patterns for credit control purposes and enables them to deal with overseas buyers in their own language and handle sales expressed in foreign currency. Credit cover of 100% is provided for approved buyers.

BANK FINANCE FOR EXPORTS

Theoretically, a company should be able to finance all its operations from the resources available to it, that is, its capital and any funds it is able to borrow from the bank. Its capital will depend on the amount that the members of the company are prepared to invest in the enterprise, and its borrowing from the bank will depend on such factors as balance sheet figures, the profit and loss account, turnover or the security it can offer by way of mortgages, life policies and stocks. Both these sources are subject to strict limitations and, for reasons already mentioned above, they are bound to prove inadequate for a company expanding its export trade. To meet the cash-flow problems engendered by long credit terms, extra sources of finance must be tapped over and above the basic sources of capital and bank lending. This finance can best be found in ways related to the export transactions themselves and, in particular, to the method of payment. Let us examine the various methods by which payment is made and the types of finance associated with them:

(a) Sales on open account. The exporter is entirely dependent on the goodwill of the buyer to remit payment when due. Admittedly, the outstanding debts will increase the receivables item in the company's balance sheet and may therefore enable it to obtain additional overdraft facilities from the bank. However, the best answer to the problem of finance in this case would be use of the services of a factoring company (see above).

(b) Collection by means of a bill of exchange drawn on the buyer. Finance may be obtained by discounting the bills with the bank or obtaining loan accommodation against bills outstanding for collection. The bank has some element of security in the documents pertaining to the goods, which are attached to the bills. The possibility of obtaining bank finance in this way is enhanced if the export sale is covered by a policy issue by the Export Credits Guarantee Department (ECGD), as the rights under the policy may be assigned to the bank. See Chapter 10 of *Elements of Export Practice*.

(c) Documentary credits. An irrevocable credit assures the exporter of payment immediately he has shipped the goods and presents correct documents to the bank, so that his need for finance is reduced. He may, however, be able to obtain some extra help from his bank to produce and ship the goods on the strength of the payment assured under the credit.

LESS COMMON FORMS OF TRADE

Consignment trade
Goods are sent by an exporter to a nominal importer in another country, that nominal importer being, in fact, a nominee or agent of the exporter. The intention is that the merchandise shall come into the physical possession of the agent, whose duty it is to sell it on the exporter's behalf and remit to his principal the proceeds of the sale, less all expenses of handling, storing and transport, customs duties, fees and his commission.

Participation
Joint venture in which a UK manufacturer and a foreign concern co-operate in marketing the exporter's product, assembling it or manufacturing it abroad.

Licensing
A licence may be granted to an overseas company to manufacture products on a royalty basis under either the UK manufacturer's brand name or the name of the licensee.

Barter or compensation trade – counter trade
This arises from the restrictive effects of exchange control and the shortage of foreign exchange in some countries. For instance, an importer may be unable to obtain an allocation of sterling or other acceptable currency, so that he offers goods in payment of those he wishes to buy. This has been quite a common practice in trade with some countries in the Eastern bloc, South America and Africa, but it is fraught with problems: the goods offered may not be required by the other party or may not be easy to sell, the trader may find himself involved in trades with which he is not acquainted and it may be difficult to agree the quantities to be exchanged. A number of the larger international banks in London have set up a type of 'clearing' system for exchanging goods and finding outlets for the goods received in settlement. Today it is called counter trade.

CHANGING METHODS OF PAYMENT

Transfers of funds from one centre to another arise from a variety of transactions in international trade, such as the collection of bills of exchange, payments for goods received on 'open account', payments under documentary credits, transfers of funds to subsidiaries and the settlement of balances within multinational companies. The ways in which such transfers are made have not changed in principle, but improvements in banking arrangements and technology have enabled the banks to expedite them. For example, the Society for Worldwide Interbank Financial Telecommunication (SWIFT) has set up a highly sophisticated communications network which enables its members to send authenticated messages to one another automatically. The system caters for international payment instructions in a variety of currencies, funding advices, account statements, debit and credit confirmations and a range of foreign exchange transactions. It is cheaper than telex and has two levels of priority – normal and urgent. A normal message is expected to take 10 minutes for transmission and an urgent message 1 minute. Systems such as this and the general improvement in the methods of interbank transfers should go some way towards meeting traders' demands for the more rapid execution of payments.

Other developments have also had an effect on the way in which payments for goods are made. The increased speed of modern transport has meant that on shorter sea voyages bills of lading have to be sent in the ship's bag to avoid demurrage at the port of destination. As there is therefore no document of title to support a documentary bill, banks will regard such a bill lodged for collection as tantamount to a clean bill and be less prepared to provide finance. The development of container transport and groupage has created a problem in that individual consignments are the subject of a forwarding agent's certificate referring to the bill of lading covering the container. Certificates issued by forwarding agents of repute are accepted, but in the case of documentary credits, banks are unable to pay against such certificates unless the credit authorizes them to do so. Payment delays may therefore result pending confirmation from the buyer that the documents are acceptable.

A growing market is now emerging relative to counter trade and by 1990 it could represent some 10% of world trade. (See also *Economics of Shipping Practice and Management*, 2nd edition, in preparation.)

CHAPTER 11

Port management structure and dock labour

SIZE AND SCOPE OF THE PORT AUTHORITY

Ports provide a fairly wide range of different services. There are, in fact, not one but several markets for their products. The demand for the bulk dry cargo shipment market is different from the carriage of bulk liquid cargoes. This in turn requires differing port facilities not only in terms of berths, but also in distribution arrangements. Likewise, the demand for containerized shipments is different from the passenger market involving a cruise liner, or the motorist travelling on a car ferry service. Again, such differing shipping services need the appropriate separate berthing facilities and 'back-up' resources including customs, immigration, distribution arrangements, and so on.

The size of the port authority, its organization and cost structure and the pricing of the tariffs are influenced largely by the type of facilities provided/offered. For example, this may include the provision of stevedoring, control of tug operations, operation of a container complex, provision of a conservancy authority, or the operation of a port authority's own police force. Hence there is a great variation in the size of port authorities, which range from the small private company to the giant groups.

Another factor is that port authorities are themselves of different institutional types. These include part of a local authority structure as found in Bristol; a private company as found in Manchester Ship Canal; a public trust as exists in the Port of London Authority; an estuarial situation covering several ports as found in the Forth Port Authority, or a public limited company as exists in the port of Felixstowe, called the Felixstowe Dock and Railway Company. Another public limited company is found in the Associated British Ports, which controls some nineteen ports. In contrast, British

Ferries Ltd, a private company, own and operate both ships and ports: the latter total seven.

In France a number of ports are owned and operated by the local chamber of commerce on a government agency basis. This includes Boulogne, Calais and Dieppe. The larger port of Dunkerque is government owned, financed and managed. Many other large Continental ports including Antwerp, Rotterdam and Hamburg are state owned and managed, either directly or through local government arrangements. This arrangement applies on a worldwide scale: examples include Lagos in Nigeria, Aqaba in Jordan, Singapore in Malaysia and Bombay in India. All Eastern Bloc countries own and control their major ports and practise flag discrimination extensively.

A further aspect determining the organizational structure is the geographical spread of the port area, which may include a complex of docks each some distance from one another. Examples are Grimsby and Immingham; Portway and Bristol; and the New South Wales ports of Newcastle, Sydney involving Port Jackson and Botany Bay, and Kembla.

Hence there is a great variation in size amongst port authorities. From an economic standpoint the entrepreneur will try to maximize his profits and therefore expand his output, so long as the increase in his total cost is less than the increase in his total revenue. He will therefore continue to expand to the point where his marginal additional cost is equal to his marginal additional revenue.

Increased profits generally arise from lower cost due to operating on a larger scale, or from the ability to control the price of the product. There are certain economies which occur in a large-scale operation. The large firm may be able to specialize and to use elaborate machinery, the cost of which can be spread over a large number of units of output.

The tendency in recent years is for the number of ports to be rationalized and for the larger and some older ports to be modernized and rationalized. This has resulted in some closed docks being sold for industrial/residential development, as is found in the Port of London. The income therefrom has facilitated the funding of the remaining dock areas to accommodate modern tonnage. A further aspect is the tendency to develop the modern port at the mouth of the river estuary and not at the head of the river as is found with earlier docks systems. No longer does the port have to rely on a hinterland in the immediate port environs. Finally, shipowners conscious of the need to maximize ship utilization tend to favour particularly those ports which are conveniently situated on a shipping lane.

The reasons for such rationalization and modernization are numerous. They include the fact that economies are realized on administration cost; prospects are improved of raising more capital for port modernization/development through the sale of redundant dock systems; the rationalization of facilities through fewer berths more intensively used lowers unit costs; the concentration of port facilities tends to rationalize the number of offices required for agents, port authority offices, etc.: port modernization lowers cost, and encourages modern tonnage, thereby improving business expansion prospects; and finally, modern technology, including berths, port facilities, computers and port facilities which facilitates more competitive tariffs to be available/negotiated.

To conclude our review of the size and scope of the port authority, it is essential that the organization is so structured as to exploit/develop the maximum business opportunities of the port and its facilities.

PORT AUTHORITY ORGANIZATION

In our examination of the port authority organization we will first of all consider some existing organization structures which will give us a measure of the varying types in being today. This includes the Ports of Rotterdam, Antwerp, Sydney and Singapore.

Port of Rotterdam

The Port of Rotterdam, as is fairly usual in western Europe, is controlled by the local City Council. The municipal port operation includes the planning, construction and operation of dock basins, quays and sites, and the ensuring of order and safety. Port policy is decided by the Rotterdam City Council. This policy aims at improving all the functions of the port, and at selective industrial expansion. It is put into effect by the Port of Rotterdam Authority in collaboration with other local authority departments. The Dutch government also has certain responsibilities in the Rotterdam port area because the Nieuwe Maas, the New Waterway and the entrance to the port are state-controlled. The relevant authorities are the State Pilotage Service and the State Docks Service. The storage and handling of goods are entirely in the hands of private enterprise. A large number of private firms provide services in the port, including towing, repairs and provisioning of ships, and the maintenance of containers.

The City Council has entrusted the management of the port to one specific municipal port management department. Port users mainly have to deal with this particular department.

The municipal port management, under the name of 'Port of Rotterdam' is responsible for the planning, construction and operation of the infrastructure of the port. The Port of Rotterdam Authority also handles safety in the port, the efficient movement of the very dense traffic and adherence to port regulations. Dock and industrial sites, quays and parts of the dock basins are leased to private firms.

The local authority and trade and industry pursue the same objective in the development and organization of the port area: to further the productivity and the versatility of Rotterdam. The Port of Rotterdam Authority does not handle goods itself but tries to attract traffic and to promote the establishment of industrial and commercial firms via marketing and information activities. The port authority publishes statistical reports and detailed studies.

The Dock and Pilotage Service department of the Port of Rotterdam Authority ensures that the right procedures are used. It also controls traffic and ensures safety in the port. A special Dangerous Goods Bureau is entrusted with supervising toxic cargoes and explosives (which have to be notified 24 hours in advance). The Pilotage Service is authorized in the dock basins only. The State Pilotage Service pilots sea-going vessels into and out of the port. The activities of the municipal Dock and Pilotage Department, the State Pilotage Service and the State Dock Service are controlled from the Captain's Room of the Port, the Port Co-ordination Centre, which is run from the port authority building.

The chamber of commerce and industry for Rotterdam and the Lower Maas is an official body. It has been watching over the interests of commerce and industry (for employers and employees) in the Rotterdam Europoort area for 178 years. It is the officially recognised top organization for the region's commerce and industry. All the 38 000 businesses in the Rijnmond area are compulsorily registered in the chamber's trade register.

The aim of the Rotterdam Port Promotion Council is to promote good relations between Rotterdam industry on the one hand and customers and prospective customers of the Rotterdam Port and the New Waterway area on the other.

To bring industry to the Rotterdam region and interested national and international parties closer together the Rotterdam Port Promotion Council is active in a variety of ways: internationally and in its own area. By way of illustration: port/shipping delegations pay regular visits to groups of current and potential customers in the hinterland. These delegations act as representatives for the entire Rotterdam industry operating in the port.

In Rotterdam itself the council makes and strengthens contacts by entertaining Dutch and foreign visitors. All these activities are organized in close co-operation with SVZ (Port of Rotterdam Employers' Association), the chamber of commerce and the local authority. To support these activities and for purely informative reasons all sorts of promotional material are published: maps, statistics and leaflets containing general information on the port area situated between the Van Brieneoord bridge and the Maasvlakte. A sailing list of the regular shipping lines is published fortnightly.

The waterway from the North Sea into Rotterdam is maintained by the state. The state is also responsible for the buoys, beacons and piloting along this waterway.

The dock basins, quays and similar facilities in the port are managed by the Port of Rotterdam Authority. This authority's general task is to run the port, and more specifically to design, build and maintain new basins and quays, to build dockyards and allocate them, to pilot sea-going vessels in the docks and to maintain order and safety.

Most of the dockyards and quays are leased on a long-term basis (25 years or more) to private firms. The sheds, cranes and equipment all belong to these private firms, who also operate them. The Port of Rotterdam Authority has nothing to do with the handling of goods as such. This is dealt with entirely by private enterprise: shipowners, stevedores, forwarders and warehousing and storage firms.

Besides the typical port firms providing services having an immediate bearing on sea-going vessels and their crews – towing, ship's-chandling, etc. – there are various types of business concerned with the handling of goods: stevedores load and discharge vessels direct into or from barges, railway wagons, trucks, coasters or other sea-going ships, or indirectly via the quay or shed where the goods are kept in short-term storage in their own sheds pending onward transport; warehousing and storage firms are geared to indefinite storage. As a rule goods will be stored by one of these firms if the time of production or arrival does not coincide with the time of sale or consumption. They are frequently called on to store buffer stocks from certain parts of the world and thus act as a distribution centre of as yet unknown destinations.

Warehouses and stores include cold stores, silos for bulk goods and storage tanks for liquid cargoes. Besides storage, custody and delivery of goods these firms provide a wide range of services such as weighing, gauging, sampling, taring, sorting, inspecting, palletizing, reconditioning, arranging customs clearance, transport and insurance.

For goods stored by warehousing/storage firms, documents called warehouse receipts are issued entitling the holder to have these goods available at the desired moment. Stevedores have dockyards with deep water berthing, fully equipped with sheds, cranes and transport. Generally speaking, Dutch stevedores have a more comprehensive job than similar firms in foreign natural harbours. They are concerned not only with loading and discharging cargoes from sea-going vessels but also with work on the quayside and in the sheds. A great advantage is that all the handling operations can be better co-ordinated, which makes for greater handling efficiency – and that benefits everyone.

Shipbrokers look after shipowners' interests and cargo interests – in the broadest sense of the word. On the one hand they act as confidential agents for shipowners, taking charge of all the matters affecting the ship, crew and cargo, and on the other they co-ordinate discharging and loading in the service of those interested in the cargo: the receivers and shippers of goods or the forwarders, operating on their behalf. The shipbrokers' principal activities include canvassing for and booking cargoes; publication of sailings; notification of shippers and receivers or their forwarders as to when and where they can deliver or receive their goods in the docks; arranging temporary storage; supervising the discharging and loading of sea-going vessels; making out and dispatching shipping and export documents; acting as intermediary in the authentication of these documents; effecting customs formalities; arranging for pre- or post-transport; assisting in the settlement of insurance claims; and collecting freight and other charges.

The freight forwarder's task is to arrange for the transport of goods at the request of third parties, providing all the documents necessary for the operation. As experts on transport they advise on the most suitable mode of transport and route, taking their principals' wishes and the nature of the goods into account. Along the path from seller to buyer the freight forwarder's numerous other tasks include the processing of import, export and transit formalities; arranging and supervision of loading/discharging/storage of goods; and following any insurance claim; the weighing, tallying and sorting of goods. Several forwarders act as groupage forwarders and have their own shed space.

To conclude our review of the Port of Rotterdam and its organization, one must stress that it is one of the world's leading ports and is fully integrated with the City of Rotterdam business interest/ community. It plays a decisive part in the Dutch economy.

Port of Antwerp

The management of the port is a part of the city administration. The City of Antwerp is the owner of the docks and the entire port area. The city also owns and operates the larger part of the port equipment.

The port installations are located within the territory of the City of Antwerp and every time the port area is extended the city borders are shifted. The River Scheldt belongs to the domain of the state administration and management. The Scheldt quays (about 5 km) are state property; the equipment, however, is city property. Management of the port is based on the laws on the administration of the Belgian municipalities.

The executive control/management of the port is performed by the City Council, consisting of 51 elected representatives. The burgomaster is appointed by the King on the proposal of the City Council.

All municipal councils in Belgium are subject to the guardianship of the Provincial Government and the King. Some decisions of the City Council therefore require the approval of these authorities, including the regulations on port operation and harbour police. The daily administration of the city and the port is in the hands of the board of the burgomaster and aldermen, elected by the City Council.

The municipal services which are directly involved in the administration and management of the port, are grouped in the 'Port Administration' (Havenbedrijf) under the general manager. He is responsible for administration and co-ordination of the port services and also liaises with port users and public bodies. The general manager has two departments. One is primarily concerned with the management and operation of the business, while the other deals with marketing and management information.

The 'port administration' includes several services for the operation, extension and upkeep of the port installations as detailed below:

(a) Harbour Master's Office. This includes two branches: the nautical department, and the department quays and sheds. The head of this department is the harbour master.

(b) Nautical Department. This department is responsible for the police force, quick turn-round of vessels and barges, and provision of adequate berthing space. Other responsibilities include tug service, traffic co-ordination of vessels, allocation of berths, and operation of enclosed dock system.

(c) Department quays and sheds. The role of this department is the leasing of quays, sheds and hire of cranes. It also undertakes the management of warehouses and control of cargo storage on the quays or in the sheds.

(d) Technical services of the port. This department is under the control of the chief engineer and has two divisions:

- (i) Harbour works. This is concerned with the planning, construction, and upkeep of docks, locks, bridges, quaywalls, sheds, warehouses and premises.
- (ii) Port Equipment and Dredging. This department undertakes the planning, control and construction of mechanical and electrical port equipment including cranes, tugs, dredgers, grain elevators, and so on. It also includes maintenance of bridges, locks and port equipment. Port dredging and supplies of ship stores are entrusted to this department.

(e) Port Finance. This is under the control of the Financial Director. Its prime responsibilities include port revenue collection, expenditure control and budgeting.

To conclude our brief review of the Port of Antwerp, it is important to bear in mind the reliance on the State for its funding and the important role it plays in the Belgian economy.

Port of Sydney

Sydney Harbour is a ria, or drowned river system, into which flow several streams, the Parramatta River being the longest, with the northern shores generally more rugged than the southern, and only one ocean entrance, approximately 1500 m wide. The harbour foreshores, extending over 250 km, enclose an area of 5500 ha or 55 km^2.

The natural depths within the port area are generally adequate for shipping needs and relative to other major ports, little dredging has been required.

The port has the advantage of two separate channels, the western channel, 210 m wide, with a minimum depth of 13.7 m, and the eastern channel, 180 m wide, with a minimum depth of 12.2 m. The minimum depth at the Heads is 24 m and the major wharfage within the port area has 11 m depth of water alongside.

Approximately 16 km of commercial wharfage within the port is available to shipping. In addition to general cargo berths, special berths are available for the container and unit cargo trades. Other facilities are provided for bulk cargoes such as oil, wheat, timber and coal.

Almost 150 000 passengers embark or land at the port each year through four passenger terminals. These are situated at Sydney Cove, No. 13 Pyrmont, No. 20 Pyrmont and No. 7 Woolloomooloo. The Sydney Cove passenger terminal regularly caters for the largest passenger ships operating today and is capable of a throughput of more than 2000 passengers at one time.

Sydney is one of Australia's leading ports in trade volume, handling nearly 24 million tonnes during 1984. Over 2400 vessels visited the port in 1984.

To assist in the safe and efficient movement of these ships, the board's port operations and communications centre, situated in a tower 87 m high on the foreshore of Millers Point, has been in operation since 1974. Pilotage is compulsory within the Port of Sydney. The board employs pilots who board inward ships approximately 1 mile east of the Heads, and are transported to and from ships by pilot vessels stationed at Watsons Bay.

In its control of the ports and navigable waters of the State, the Maritime Services Board of New South Wales is the port authority, the pilotage authority and the navigation authority. Briefly, its functions comprise:

(a) Control and administration of wharves and other harbour facilities at all the commercial ports of the State.

(b) Provision and maintenance of adequate wharfage, channels and port facilities at all such ports.

(c) The operation of bulk coal-handling facilities at the ports of Sydney, Newcastle and Port Kembla.

(d) General control of ports and harbours and the conservation, management and prevention of oil pollution of all navigable waters within the State.

(e) Collection of rates and charges on goods and vessels.

(f) Administration of the navigation laws of the State, including
- (i) Control over interstate shipping;
- (ii) The survey and certification of vessels; and the conduct of examination for the issue of certificates of competency;
- (iii) Maintenance and administration of pilotage and other navigation services;
- (iv) Recreational boating.

(g) Administration and maintenance of properties – including a bond and warehouse and other business premises – at the Port of Sydney.

The principal Acts administered by the board include the Maritime Services Act, 1935; the Navigation Act, 1901; the Sydney Harbour Trust Act, 1900; the Port Rates Act, 1975; the Prevention of Oil Pollution of Navigable Waters Act, 1960 and the Pilotage Act, 1971.

Many of the board's statutory powers and functions are exercised by the implementation of Regulations made pursuant to these Acts.

The income of the board is derived mainly from port rates, comprising harbour rates on goods handled through the ports, tonnage rates on vessels using the wharves, together with coal loading charges, licences, and rents or other revenues from properties, including bond store charges, wharf rentals, etc.

At present, major works such as the construction of new wharfage, the dredging of new channels or the provision of other forms of major port facilities, are financed from loans raised by the Board under its statutory borrowing powers or from loan money made available to the board by the State Government, together with funds generated from its own earnings. The board is responsible for the payment of statutory charges in addition to the repayment of the loans.

In common with the Ports of Rotterdam and Antwerp, the Port of Sydney plays a major role in the economy of New South Wales.

PORT AUTHORITY ORGANIZATION, CONTINUED

The structure of a port authority is determined primarily by the nature of the trade(s) in which it operates and by the scale of its activities. Irrespective of the size of the company, its structure would be designed to permit swift decision making. A cumbersome organization tends to lead to procrastination, which does not contribute to general competitiveness. Furthermore, the line of responsibility should be precise and self evident, with each person having a well-defined job specification. It is also important to ensure that responsibility is delegated wherever possible. Centralized organizations tend to frustrate initiative and discourage an *esprit de corps*. Port authorities operating as a self-contained unit under their own management board with extensive autonomous powers offer major advantages. These include prompt decision making, reduced administrative cost, and a more precise orientation towards specific targets. The greater the delegation of responsibility also simplifies the task of measuring the competence of employees.

In the main most port authorities are composed of a single port embracing a complex of dock systems. There are few countries which have a group of ports controlled by one port company as found in the UK, where the Associated British Ports controls some nineteen ports. A further example is the seven ports owned and managed by British Ferries Ltd, which is a subsidiary of Sea Containers Ltd.

Accordingly, most major ports worldwide are state owned and managed. The structure of the port authority organization varies as has been exemplified in the three ports examined earlier – Rotterdam, Antwerp and Sydney. An interesting organizational structure is found in the Port of Singapore Authority (Diagram XV).

A commentary now follows on the role of each element of the

organizational structure, and it is stressed that the observations are of a general nature to enable the reader to compare it with other ports, especially those within his/her own country.

Chairman and members of the authority

The chairman's role is one of ultimate control and management of the port authority. He is responsible for company policy and development of the business in collaboration with members of the authority who overall form the most senior management team. They work very closely with the general manager. In some authorities they are called directors, with the general manager being described as the managing director (see Diagram XV). In the case of a State owned/controlled port authority, the chairman and his board would be appointed by the state. Each board member would have special responsibilities/interest such as finance, industrial relations, marketing, technical operations, and so on. Additionally, representatives from the Trade Union Congress, port users' council, and a senior civil servant may also be board members – all of which would be appointed by government and usually on a part-time basis.

The general manager role tends to be the liaison link in general management terms between the members of the authority and senior managers. He is essentially concerned with the day-to-day running of the business, particularly with its development, and formulates policy in consultation with the members of the authority. It is a very key post in the port authority, and a good general manager can greatly influence the port authority's favourable financial results.

Departments of the authority

A commentary on each of the departments now follows:

Marine division

This embraces the Port Master, and deals with hydrographic matters, chemistry, fire and safety, tug services and marine craft, and the environmental control unit. Overall, it deals with all the marine aspects of the business and especially with the movement of vessels within the port area.

Commercial division
This deals with the marketing and commercial aspects of the business including rates and charges. As indicated in Diagram XV it also deals with estate matters, and with the port authority subsidiaries and free-ports.

Operations division
This in particular involves the management and operation including berth allocation within the port complex and liaison with all the parties concerned to ensure prompt turn-round of vessels and the provision of a quality service.

Audit and Systems division
This involves primarily internal audit.

Administration division
The prime function of this division is the administration of the port authority. It would have a secretariat and works very closely with the general manager and the members of the port authority. It contains a public relations officer. The control of the police comes under this division together with corporate planning of the business and legal matters.

Personnel division
This division deals with staff recruitment and training, industrial relations and port establishment.

Engineering division
An important spending division within the port authority. It deals with marine, electrical, mechanical and civil engineering; building and plant services; contracts; planning and design, major projects; planning and design, construction and maintenance and research and development.

Finance division
This deals with all the financial aspects of the port authority business and also with computerization.

In contrast to the foregoing organization, a privately owned port organization is outlined in Diagram XVI.

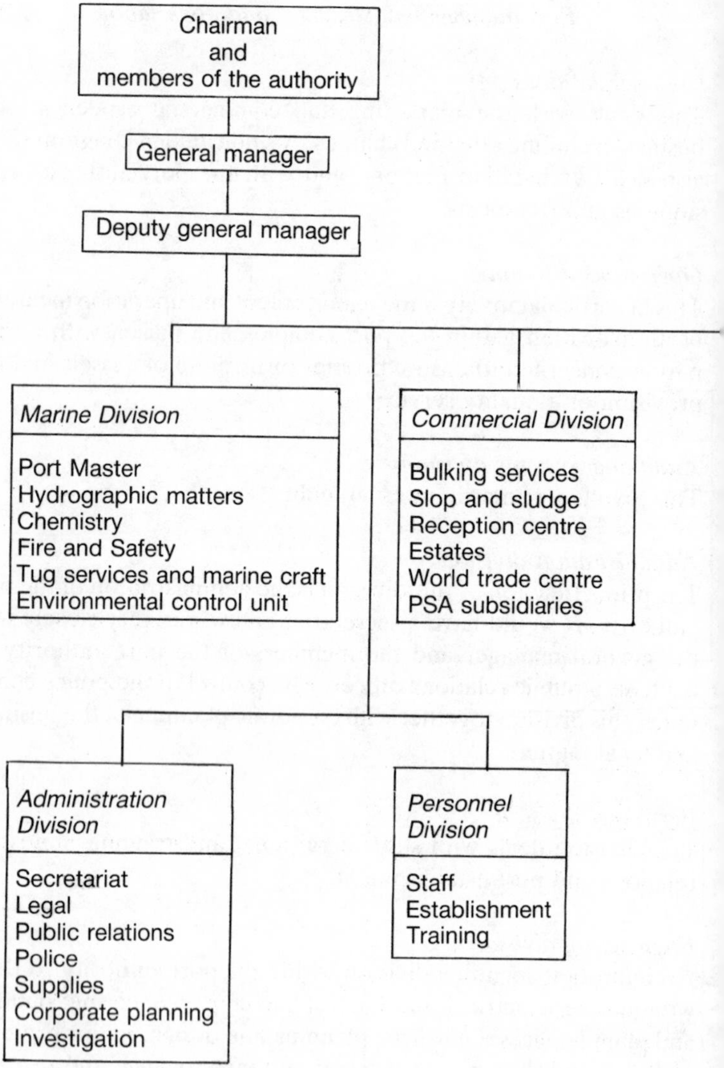

Diagram XV A government/State owned port organization (reproduced by kind permission of the Port of Singapore Authority)

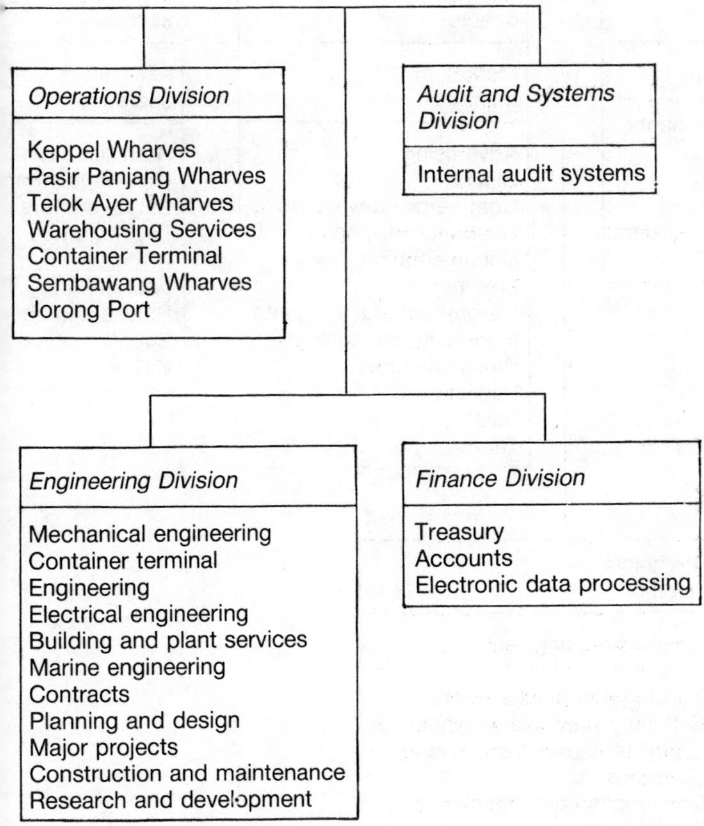
Operations Division
Keppel Wharves
Pasir Panjang Wharves
Telok Ayer Wharves
Warehousing Services
Container Terminal
Sembawang Wharves
Jorong Port
Audit and Systems Division
Internal audit systems
Engineering Division
Mechanical engineering
Container terminal
Engineering
Electrical engineering
Building and plant services
Marine engineering
Contracts
Planning and design
Major projects
Construction and maintenance
Research and development
Finance Division
Treasury
Accounts
Electronic data processing

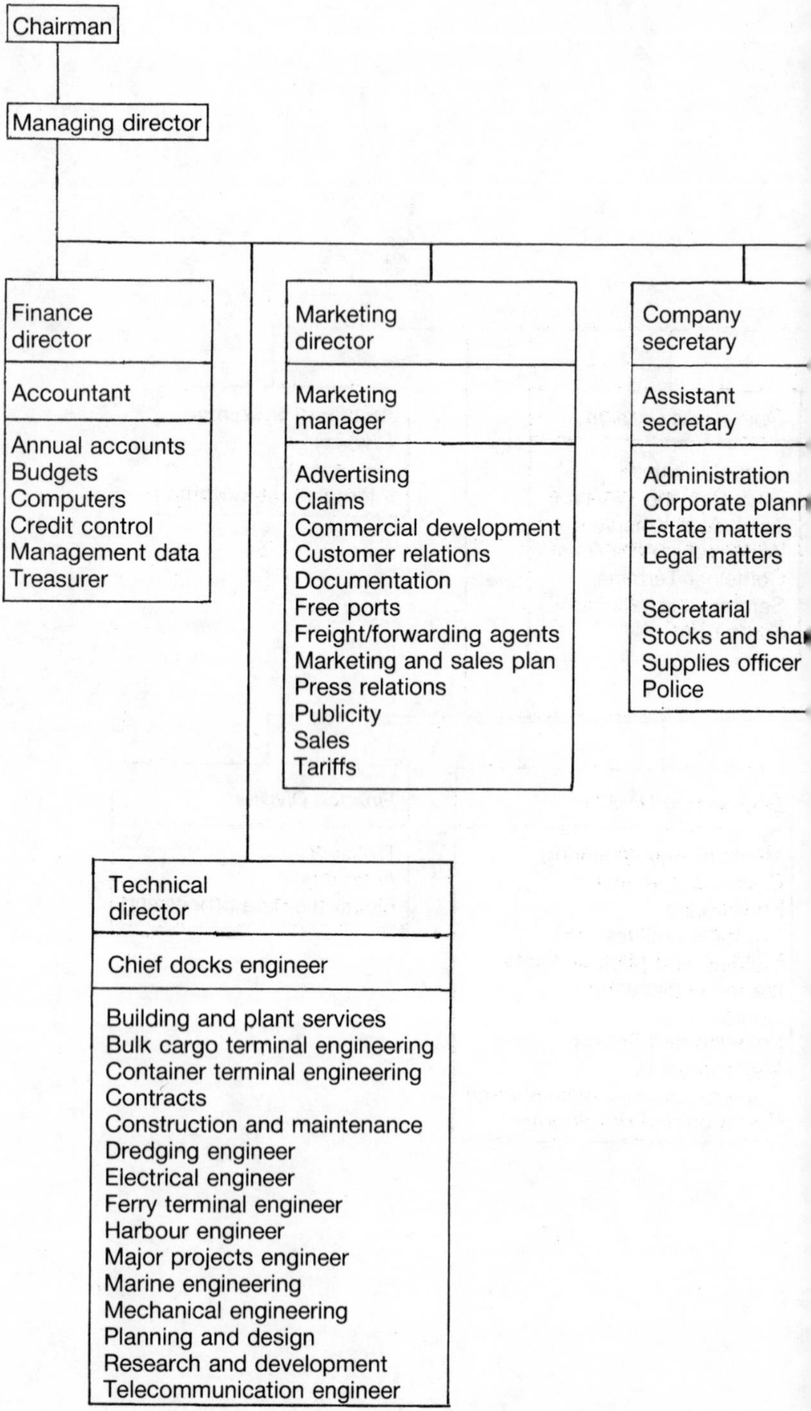

Chairman
Managing director
Finance director
Accountant
Annual accounts
Budgets
Computers
Credit control
Management data
Treasurer
Marketing director
Marketing manager
Advertising
Claims
Commercial development
Customer relations
Documentation
Free ports
Freight/forwarding agents
Marketing and sales plan
Press relations
Publicity
Sales
Tariffs
Company secretary
Assistant secretary
Administration
Corporate plann
Estate matters
Legal matters
Secretarial
Stocks and sha
Supplies officer
Police
Technical director
Chief docks engineer
Building and plant services
Bulk cargo terminal engineering
Container terminal engineering
Contracts
Construction and maintenance
Dredging engineer
Electrical engineer
Ferry terminal engineer
Harbour engineer
Major projects engineer
Marine engineering
Mechanical engineering
Planning and design
Research and development
Telecommunication engineer

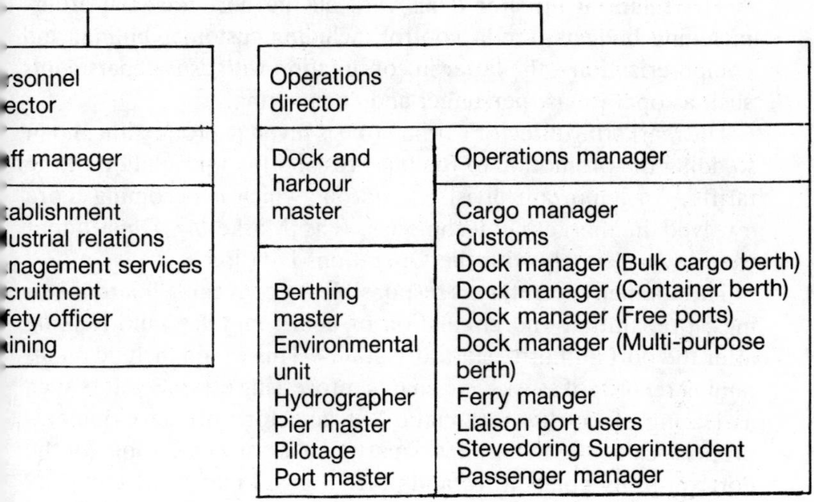
rsonnel
ector
aff manager
tablishment
lustrial relations
nagement services
cruitment
fety officer
ining
Operations
director
Dock and
harbour
master
Berthing
master
Environmental
unit
Hydrographer
Pier master
Pilotage
Port master
Operations manager
Cargo manager
Customs
Dock manager (Bulk cargo berth)
Dock manager (Container berth)
Dock manager (Free ports)
Dock manager (Multi-purpose
berth)
Ferry manger
Liaison port users
Stevedoring Superintendent
Passenger manager

gram XVI A privately owned port organization.

The following observations on the self-explanatory diagram are relevant:

The organization is headed by a chairman with seven directors, including the managing director and secretary.

The financial director deals with all the port financial affairs including budgets, credit control including customer billing, and computerization – the latter in consultation with user departments such as operations, personnel and engineering.

The marketing director's prime role is revenue production and in so doing the promotion of the business and the formulation of the tariffs. An important division, and one which is becoming more involved in marketing techniques. The Marketing Department would work closely with the Operations Division.

The company secretary is responsible for convening board meetings, preparation and circulation of board minutes, and looking after the port authority statutory affairs. This would include maintaining records of stocks and shares, processing estate matters such as leasing of berths, reclamation of land for port development, property sale, and so on. This department is also responsible for the port authority police force and ports stores. Finally, the company secretary is responsible for the general administration of the port and corporate planning including the 5 year business plan.

The personnel director's responsibilities cover all aspects of staff. The staff manager is responsible to the personnel director. This post covers training, education, recruitment, career development, appointments, redundancy, discipline, wages and salaries negotiation, industrial relations, service conditions, staff safety, etc. Management services provide a consultancy service with the port authority embracing studies in operational research, organization and methods (O & M), work study, etc. The Staff Manager works in close liaison with other departments.

The operations director has the responsibility of producing the optimum performance from the work force under him. This primarily involves all the dock labour engaged in berthing of vessels and their deployment, processing of cargo/passengers, liaison with customs agents, shippers, transport operators, planning of berth occupancy schedules and related resources in terms of transport requirements, cargo-handling equipment, dock labour, customs, and so on. The operations manager would be responsible for the shore-based resources and the dock and harbour master for the waterborne activities such as ship berthing, lighterage, tugs, police, and so on.

The technical director is responsible for all the port authority installations and equipment, and their maintenance. An important and big department with a large expenditure budget: it involves many activities. These include harbour dredging; maintenance and survey of equipment and installations in accordance with statutory obligations as found in lifting apparatus; contracts for new projects and development, and their supervision; research and development of new technology; the obligation to ensure that all the equipment is maintained at an optimum cost and to the requisite safety standard; and so on. It requires close liaison with other port authority departments and port users.

To conclude our examination of port organization, one cannot stress too strongly that each organizational structure will tend to be different to reflect the varying needs and circumstances. Ideally it should be reviewed every two to three years, to ensure that it caters adequately for market needs especially in terms of efficiency, quality of service and presentation of a favourable image to develop the business. In the longer term it is quite possible that some ports will diversify their business on an increasing scale. This includes, for example, development of marinas, and high-class flats in favourable positions. Such a policy is largely determined by the need to lessen the impact of trade recessions and low profitability levels, and to create an adequate cash flow.

DOCK LABOUR

The arrangements relative to the management of dock labour vary worldwide and, in an endeavour to place the subject in perspective, we will examine the situation in Rotterdam, and the National Dock Labour Board scheme in the UK.

Rotterdam Port Employers' Association (SVZ)

Rotterdam's importance as a world port is due not only to its favourable geographical position but also, primarily, to the policy of an inspired local authority and dynamic private enterprise. In 1907 port and transport business combined forces to form

Scheepvaart Vereeniging Zuid (Port Employers' Association) now comprising 250 transport and port companies. In the year of its foundation the association's terms of reference were limited: the establishment of controlled conditions in port operation and the prevention of disputes between employees and employers.

From these terms of reference the SVZ developed to become a co-ordination centre for the social, economic, technical, commercial, administrative and educational sectors. The Port of Rotterdam is supported by three bodies: the local authority, the employees and the employers, who all have their own tasks, responsibilities and organizational structures. They consult regularly on the numerous varied programmes which are of importance to the economic and social climate of the port.

The SVZ serves to pool its members' interests. Members consist on the one hand of port operating companies and on the other of several associations which watch over the interests of a group of special businesses. Additionally, the SVZ watches over the interests of the shipowners whose vessels call at Rotterdam. It keeps in touch with the local authorities and official bodies in the preparation and implementation of statutory measures in the nautical and customs sectors and in respect of pilotage and port dues. The basic aim is the speedy, reliable turn-round of ships. Some of the work is delegated to special committees, e.g. the safety committee and the hazardous cargoes committee, which have worked uninterruptedly to help improve safety in the Port of Rotterdam. In this respect chemists have been brought in to run daily consultations and provide information on chemical matters.

Among its tasks there is the job of maintaining and consolidating relations with shippers and receivers, forwarders, hauliers and the railways. There is close collaboration with the Rotterdam Port Promotion Council.

One of the SVZ's major tasks is to negotiate with trade unions. The SVZ aims at well-balanced labour relations in the port and the avoidance of labour unrest. In personnel matters it advises on terms and conditions of employment.

The National Dock Labour Board (NDLB) and registered dock workers in the UK

The UK port management scene is complicated by the special position of 'registered dock workers' and the 'National Dock

Labour Board'.

In the early 1940s HM Government introduced the compulsory registering of dock workers and employers, together with other professions, and introduced the concept of attendance money. The latter guaranteed payment to men reporting for duty but without work. To administer the scheme, a National Dock Labour Corporation was formed together with local boards, for the purpose of joint control between employers and unions.

In 1946, port employers and unions could not voluntarily agree on the terms of continuing the scheme, but under the *Dock Workers (Regulation of Employment) Order 1947*, a National Dock Labour Board and Scheme were created with effect from 1 July, 1947, preserving the 1940 principles. The 1947 scheme has continued although amended to some extent in 1960, 1961 and 1967, the latter amendments being to give effect to decasualization.

The objectives of the 1967 scheme are 'to ensure greater regularity of employment for dock workers and to provide an adequate number of dock workers for the efficient performance of dock work'. The scheme is administered by the NDLB. Overall there are eight members: each side is equally represented. In more specific terms, the function of the NDLB are as follows:

(a) To ensure the full and proper utilization of dock labour, in order to give speedy transit of cargo and rapid and economic turn-round of ships.

(b) To regulate recruitment and discharge of dock workers, their allocation to and transfer between employers.

(c) To give or withhold consent to the termination of employment of a dock worker by an employer.

(d) To determine and review the size of local registers, with regard to the circumstances of each port.

(e) To keep, adjust and maintain employers' registers and to enter, remove or suspend any employer as required.

(f) To keep, adjust and maintain registers of dock workers, and where required remove the name of any worker.

(g) To make provision for the training and welfare of dock workers including port medical services.

(h) To levy and recover from employers the cost of operating the scheme.

At port level, most of these functions devolve on to local Dock Labour Boards, which consist of equal numbers of employers' and workers' representatives, usually nominated by the local Joint Port Committee and approved by the NDLB. It is usual for the chairman to be drawn alternately from each side. Particular functions of the local boards are to control and allocate supplementary and temporarily unattached workers, to arrange inter-employer transfers on a daily basis according to demand, to run training and welfare facilities, and to administer the disciplinary procedure for both employers and employees. The last function gives the local board the ability to uphold, amend or cancel any dismissal or suspension of a dock worker by an employer.

The scheme applies in 80 ports in the UK ranging in size from London to Porthleven and Portreath in Cornwall.

The ports were included on the basis of their importance in 1947, since when many have declined, especially Bristol, Liverpool and London. Conversely, some ports outside the scheme have grown, such as Dover, Harwich and Felixstowe. The scheme applies strictly to loading, unloading, movement or storage of cargoes in or in 'the vicinity of' these ports.

Dock labour worldwide

In our study of dock labour worldwide there is no doubt that in many countries it is strongly unionized. The NDLB in the UK is a good example but it is significant that the more modern and developing ports of Harwich, Felixstowe and Dover are not part of this scheme. Other unions are involved and are of broader base.

The following points are relevant with regard to the future development of dock labour worldwide.

(a) The development of containerization, Ro/Ro vessels, combi-carriers, bulk carriers and other modern tonnage will continue. This will encourage capital-intensive cargo transhipments arrangements, purpose-built modern berths, and complete emphasis on quicker turn-round of vessels in port coupled with overall port efficiency.

(b) Unions are likely to continue to play their role in the dock labour scene. However, emphasis will be placed on the flexibility of working practices; higher productivity, and greater versatility in the type of work any dock labour employee would become involved in.

The aspects dealt with under item (a) are very relevant.

(c) Ports long term will place increasing emphasis on quality of service, and the need to have a good industrial relations image is paramount in the competitive market place.

(d) The development of free ports and ICDs will continue, especially the former in many countries. Additionally, the concept of the combined transport operation. All of these will have a profound effect on dock labour resources and work practices. Management and unions must be prepared to accept change on the most productive dock labour resources terms. Cargo mechanization will continue to play an increasing role.

To conclude, the need to have an efficient dock labour force worldwide is paramount in the interest of maintaining efficiency and developing trade internationally. Management and unions must work closely together to achieve this objective and in so doing meet the needs of the market embracing shippers and shipowners – the latter with increasing emphasis on modern tonnage and quick, efficient turn-round.

CHAPTER 12

Budgetary control and marketing

REVENUE, EXPENDITURE AND INVESTMENT BUDGETS

Effective budgeting is the key to maximum profitability in the port industry, which in turn helps attract the investment that is vital to the long-term future of the port authority. There are several ways in which the existence of a budget can be advantageous:

(a) The forecast of revenue and expenditure expressed in the budget enables management to predict the cash flow during the year and hence to make the best use of monthly cash surpluses or to meet any expected deficits. Knowledge about the pattern of income makes it possible to finance the company's investment programme efficiently and to make optimum use of the port authority resources. The budget should also reveal the profit centres within the port's activities and thus help avoid non-productive expenditure.

(b) The budget acts as a yardstick against which to judge performance at regular intervals and hence allows management to adapt their policies to changing events. For instance, a fall in revenue below the forecast level may give early warning of the need to reduce expenditure in the face of a decline in business. The achievements of management and staff may also be gauged objectively against the budget.

(c) The targets that a budget necessarily implies encourage the development of an *esprit de corps* among managers, who are then better able to win the support of their staff. Having such targets also encourages cost consciousness, especially among senior and middle managers, who are most deeply committed to realization of the budget.

(d) The budget facilitates the formulation of tariff increases in line with predicted rises in expenditure and ensures that the company's profitability remains adequate.

Budgets are generally compiled for one year and the income and expenditure are then spread over the period, usually on a monthly or four weekly basis, so that the results can be assessed at regular intervals. Tables II, III, and IV show the budget for January 1986 of a fictitious port authority handling general cargo, bulk cargo, containers, Ro/Ro traffic and passengers; subsequently monthly tables would probably also show the cumulative results for the year to that date alongside the month's figures. The budget headings, layout and contents of the table will vary according to the type of port and nature of the trade/cargo involved.

Revenue budget

The revenue budget is drawn up by the port authority traffic officers and represents their commitment to fulfil the predictions. Failure to achieve the expected revenue results would cause serious cash flow problems which in turn would affect not only profits but also future investment and development of new facilities. The projections are usually formulated in September and October for the following year on the basis of the circumstances expected to prevail. These include the following:

(a) Competition. If competition is intense between neighbouring ports, port authorities tend to hold down their 'average' tariff rate in an effort to sustain or generate business.

(b) The international economic situation. The relaxation of trade barriers could increase trade but a rise in oil prices might cloud the prospects of an expansion of trade.

(c) The political situation worldwide. The risk of hostilities may have a bearing on trade prospects.

(d) The fiscal policies of the countries served. Countries with serious balance of payments problems tend to impose severe restrictions on trade, which in turn has an adverse effect on traffic volume passing through the port. In some situations they operate on a trade quota basis.

(e) Any government controls on port tariffs. An increasing number of countries keen to develop their own maritime fleet tend to have a more favourable port tariff for national flag tonnage than foreign flag vessels and their cargoes.

(f) Additional port revenue expected to accrue from the provision of new berths; improvements to existing berths; new port facilities in the form of container standage area or introduction of modern cargo-handling equipment; development of a computerized cargo clearance system; introduction of new shipping lines or expansion of existing sailing schedules; improved port marketing; and tariff charges geared to market pricing and designed to attract more volume business. All such factors have a profound effect on traffic flows.

(g) Fluctuations in exchange rates. Passenger ports can be favourably affected when the national currency level depreciates, thereby making it cheaper for the overseas visitor. Likewise, it tends to boost exports provided the goods are competitive.

(h) Quality of service. The ability of a port to keep pace with modern tonnage needs in terms of deep water berths, modern cargo-handling techniques and a productive dock labour force is paramount in the development of the business through the port. Good industrial relations and access to the port at all times coupled with continuous working on the berth throughout the 24 hours daily and seven days per week also play their role in port development.

Port development

The draft budget is considered collectively by the chief officers and ultimately by the board of directors. Each revenue area is scrutinized objectively with a view to improvement, and the basis of the figures examined particularly where there are significant variations from the previous year's results.

The revenue budget consists of two main elements: the physical facts, i.e. the volume of business to be handled including number of ships, volume/tonnage of cargo (see Table II): and the gross receipts, each expressed in terms of actual results in the particular period; the budget forecast and any discrepancy between the two (see Table III). Further columns are provided to explain such variations in pricing (e.g. changes in tariff levels), investment schemes (e.g. new berths, or cargo-handling equipment); service disruption (docks strike); traffic volume (e.g. extra traffic secured by virtue of additional sailings, or new contracts) and other variances.

The headings for the various items in the physical facts budget Table II are largely self explanatory. Overall the figures are split between national and foreign flag tonnage merchandise carryings as the port authority has differing tariff levels favouring the national

Table II XYZ Port Authority: Physical facts budget January 1986

	National flag Tonnage			Foreign flag Tonnage		
	Actual	*Budget*	*Discre-pancy*	*Actual*	*Budget*	*Discre-pancy*
Total number of ships						
Gross tonnage						
Passengers						
Cargo bulk						
Crude oil						
Mineral oil products						
Ores						
Coal						
Other bulk cargo						
Cargo general						
Lash						
Lighterage						
Other general cargo						
Containers (TEUs)						
Ro/Ro units						

flag shipowners and their cargoes. Physical facts include the number of ships and overall gross tonnage; number of passengers; tonnage of bulk cargo, and general cargo, the number of containers (TEUs) and finally the number of Ro/Ro units. The figures found in this table would 'key in' with the revenue budget and thereby form the basis on which the revenue budget would be compiled. Likewise, the expenditure budget would represent the cost to provide the resources to handle the budgeted business.

Table III is the revenue budget which is largely self explanatory. For example the passenger income from national flag tonnage was £2000 below budget due to reduced volume and lower tariffs. Containers, however, were above budget, yielding an improvement of £4000. Again, this was due to improved volume and pricing, involving higher tariff levels. The Ro/Ro services were adversely affected due to an industrial dispute involving suspension of the service for seven days in January. This resulted in reduced revenue of £3000 for foreign flag tonnage. Overall revenue totalled £436 000 which was £32 000 (+5%) above budget.

Revenue budget results such as these can be regarded as reasonably satisfactory, bearing in mind traffic fluctuations between periods and that the next one could produce a decline below budget predictions. Items showing a variation in excess of 2.5% will require particular scrutiny when the following year's budget is compiled in order to ascertain whether any further refinements are necessary.

Expenditure budget

The expenditure budget is compiled at the same time as the revenue budget by all the departmental officers, each of whom thus becomes committed to achieving the predicted results. A port authority has direct control over expenditure, but less influence over income, so that much thought must be given to the type and level of expenditure to ensure that the principle of 'value for money' is applied. Close liaison must be maintained with the traffic departments, particularly as regards immobilization of equipment/berths for maintenance/modernization/development to ensure that traffic disruption is kept to a minimum, revenue production is preserved, quality of service maintained and optimum use is made of resources. The port operations manager plays a decisive role to ensure that the port resources are economically deployed and that adequate cost consciousness permeates all levels of management involved in the day-to-day operations.

The layout of an expenditure budget will obviously depend on the needs of the individual port authority. The example given in Table IV relates to the month of January 1986. As in the case of revenue, there are columns of actual and projected expenditure variations and explanations of the latter under various headings.

Let us examine the various items recorded in the expenditure budget:

(a) Operating and handling expenses: general dock services. This item involves the repair and depreciation of the berths/quays/dock in the port together with the dock labour cost.

(b) Handling and other services. This concerns dock labour handling cost and cargo-handling equipment provision, repairs and depreciation.

(c) Maintenance of structures and buildings. This involves the repair and amortization of the port authority buildings/structures. Items included are office accommodation, workshops, roadway maintenance, and so on.

(d) Dredging. This embraces the cost of dredging the port including staff cost, repair work and general depreciation.

(e) Miscellaneous. Items included are publicity/advertising cost, compensation including settlement of claims, and insurance premiums.

(f) Administration. Such cost represents administration expenses incurred in the general administration of the port authority.

(g) General expenses. Items included are local rates, rent payments, wayleaves and police cost.

The results of the period relating income to expenditure will reveal a trading profit or loss which must be compared with the budget forecast. Experience has shown that it is easier to effect expenditure cuts quickly than to generate additional income at short notice, but both courses must be pursued vigorously in the event of a serious shortfall.

The budget results should be reviewed monthly by a meeting of departmental officers as soon as the data are available, ideally two weeks after the period to which they relate. Departmental officers should be aware much earlier of the results achieved by their own department and be able to take remedial action where necessary. It is usual to conduct a major budget review in the sixteenth and thirty-second weeks of the year, or in April and August, in order to ascertain whether adjustments are required in the light of changed circumstances. In this way the management ensures that its objectives are up to date and that financial control of the port authority remains tight, particularly with regard to cash flow.

Investment budget

The investment budget is formulated along similar lines and is regularly reviewed as an integral part of the financial management of the company. If the revenue and expenditure predictions are not fulfilled, the investment budget is usually subjected to more critical scrutiny, as failure to realize an adequate trading surplus will affect cash flow and the arrangements for financing the investment programme.

Table III XYZ Port authority: budgeted trading results for January 1986

Revenue *Harbour receipts*	*Gross receipts*			*Explanations*				
	Actual	*Budget*	*Discrepancy*	*Pricing*	*Investment schemes and services charges*	*Service disruption*	*Traffic volume trends*	*Other variances*
Harbour dues	£ *(000)*	£ *(000)*	£ *(000)*	£ *(000)*	£ *(000)*	£ *(000)*	£ *(000)*	£ *(000)*
National flag tonnage								
Ships – national flag	8	8	—				−1	
Passengers	12	14	−2	−1				
Cargo – bulk	14	13	+1				+1	
Cargo – general	10	8	+2				+2	
Containers	24	20	+4	+2			+2	
Ro/Ro units	6	8	−2				−2	
Handling/Wharfages and other services								
Passengers	2	2	—					
Cargo – bulk	20	19	+1				+1	
Cargo – general	30	26	+4				+4	
Containers	50	42	+8	+4			+4	
Ro/Ro units	14	18	−4			−4		
Foreign flag tonnage								
Ships – foreign flag	6	6	—					

Containers	36	30	+6	+3			+3
Ro/Ro units	7	10	−3			−3	
Handling/wharfage services							
Passengers	1	1	—				
Cargo – bulk	16	15	+1				+1
Cargo – general	26	22	+4				+4
Containers	70	60	+10	+5			+5
Ro/Ro units	20	22	−2				
Miscellaneous							
Pilotage fees and other services	40	37	+3				+3
Total revenue	£436 000	£404 000	+£32 000				

Table IV XYZ Port Authority: budgeted trading results for January 1986

Expenditure	*Gross expenditure*			*Explanations*				
Operating and handling expenses	*Actual*	*Budget*	*Discrepancy*	*Staff costs*	*Investment schemes and services changes*	*Service disruption*	*Traffic volume trends*	*Other variences*
	£	£	£					
General dock services								
Operating:								
Staff expenses								
Other expenses								
Repairs								
Depreciation								
Handling and other services								
Operating:								
Staff expenses								
Other expenses								
Repairs								
Depreciation								
Maintenance of structures and buildings								
Repairs								
Amortization								

Dredging
Operating:
Staff expenses
Other expenses
Repairs
Depreciation
Miscellaneous
Compensation, etc.
Publicity
Insurance
Others
Administration
Staff expenses
Other expenses
General expenses
Rents, wayleaves, etc.
Local rates
Police
Others
Total expenditure
Net trading surplus or loss

MARKETING

Marketing is an extensive and rather specialized subject that cannot be examined in depth within the scope of this book. Nevertheless, it is appropriate to touch upon the major elements of marketing strategy that are relevant to port management and economics. Moreover, it is a subject of growing importance in the ports industry as competition increases and marketing techniques come more into play in the successful management of the business. Furthermore, one must bear in mind that the port authority is reliant on its users for development and profitability. This involves particularly shipowners and shippers. This requires market information not only in the home country, but also overseas involving those countries which trade with the port and commodities involved. Close liaison should be maintained with government and their agencies regarding trade agreements.

The promotion of a port authority business involves four basic elements:

(a) Advertisement of the product or service.

(b) Pricing policy with regard to tariffs in terms of those for both the shipowner's and shipper's accounts.

(c) Publicity, embracing press releases and general relations with the press.

(d) Direct selling of the company's services by salesmen negotiating contracts with shipowner/shipper or by agents.

The marketing policy pursued by any port authority has a profound influence on the overall annual results of the company. It is an area where more and more time is being devoted by management at all levels in an era of increasing competition and the need to develop the business profitably. Furthermore, ports are essentially an international product depending for their existence on international trade, involving strong marketing and selling, both at home and overseas, are vital to the development of port business, particularly at middle and senior management levels. One has only to analyse the results of the major ports of the world and their expansion in recent years to determine the role effective marketing has played in their success on a profitable basis.

The key to effective marketing is the provision of a marketing plan which should be devised at the same time as the budget and should match the aspirations expressed therein; it is, after all, the key instrument in securing the traffic predicted in the budget itself. The plan should 'key in' with the budget both in terms of sales (including advertising and staff expenses) and income. The object of the marketing plan is to identify the products that the port authority wishes to provide and to win the maximum market share consistent with adequate profitability.

The plan outline is found in Diagram XVII and it must be stressed that each port authority will give varying emphasis to parts of it, according to circumstances. Above all, it must set realistic goals. Like the budget, the objectives of the plan must be reviewed about every four months.

The marketing and sales plan should be regarded as the expression by the management of the techniques to be used to secure the business predicted in the plan and sales budget. All personnel involved in its execution should ideally have a copy, especially those in direct selling. Furthermore, such personnel should be given the opportunity to contribute to its formulation and be present when the marketing director/manager reviews it from time to time. The marketing director/manager should give a presentation of the plan to relevant company personnel, including those engaged in the operating and commercial side of the business. This ensures that such personnel are well aware of their obligations to fulfil the plan either in product selling or operating the business efficiently and to a high standard compatible with market needs.

The general features of the plan are given below. It will vary with port, country and circumstances.

The plan is drawn up for a particular port, or group of ports – if the port authority own a number of ports – as in the case of Associated British Ports.

Details are given of the traffic forecast and analysis shown in the budget. The breakdown may be by commodity type; by country of origin and destination; by berth or type of berth such as grouping all the container berths; by type of vessel such as Ro/Ro, container vessel, ore carrier, combi-carrier, and so on.

The plan should include a brief description of the port(s), its schedules/services, and range of facilities.

Details should be given of significant changes in the port facilities in the previous year or planned in the future. These could include

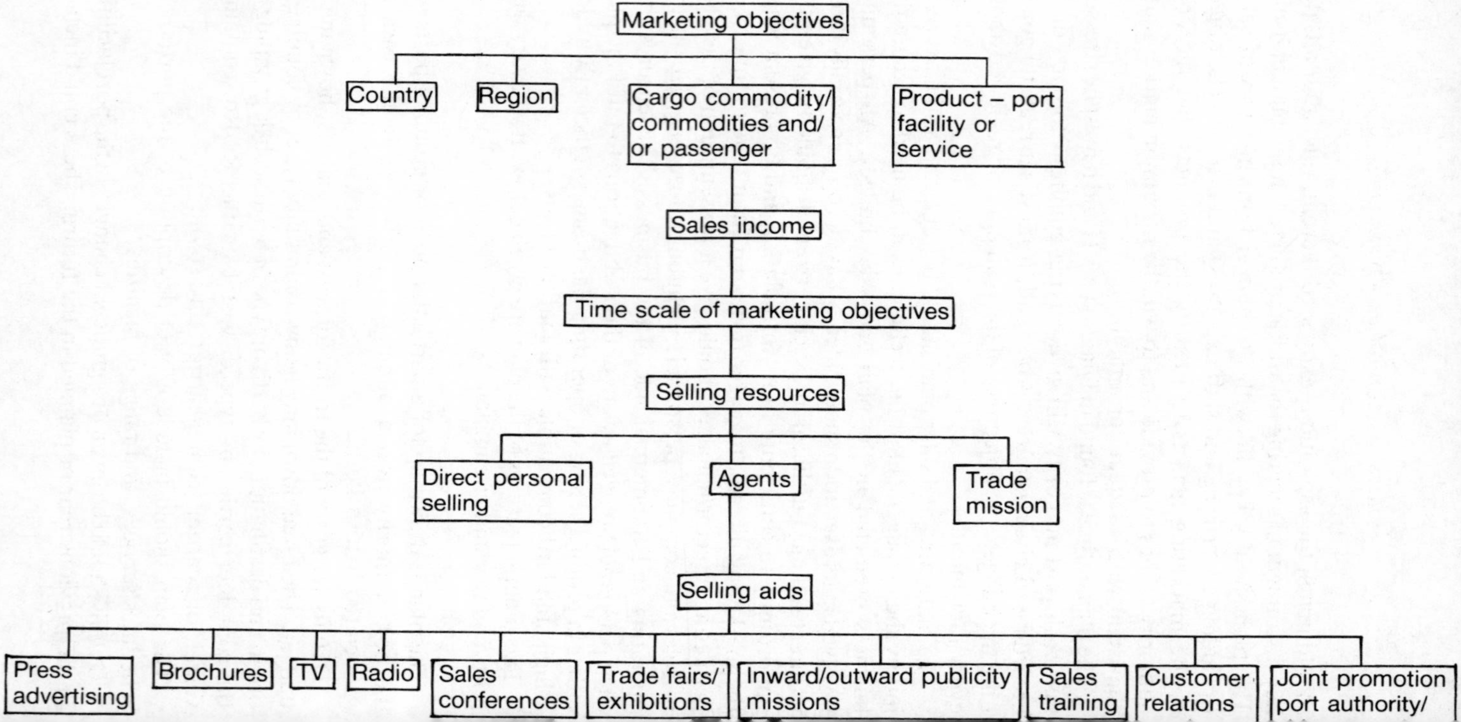
Marketing objectives
Country
Region
Cargo commodity/ commodities and/ or passenger
Product – port facility or service
Sales income
Time scale of marketing objectives
Selling resources
Direct personal selling
Agents
Trade mission
Selling aids
Press advertising
Brochures
TV
Radio
Sales conferences
Trade fairs/ exhibitions
Inward/outward publicity missions
Sales training
Customer relations
Joint promotion port authority/

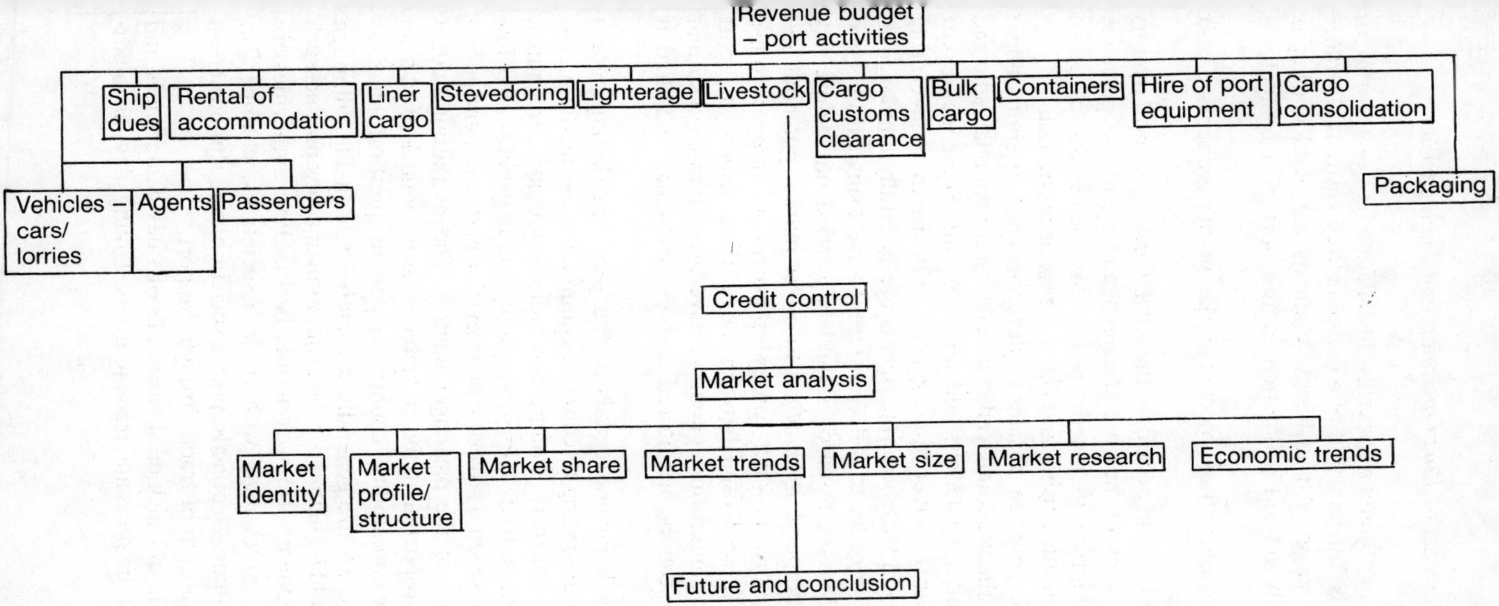

Diagram XVII Marketing and sales plan of a port authority.

provision of new container berths, installation of a new portal for Ro/Ro vessels, introduction of a computerized customs clearance system, and so on. All such developments are good marketing points and should aid promotion of the port in a competitive environment.

The pricing policy: the subject of market pricing is discussed later in this chapter.

Great stress should be laid on the advantages of the port over its competitors, thereby helping salesmen and agents to persuade shipowners/shippers to use the port. This should also be given prominence in advertising and other forms of promotion.

Details will be given of sales conferences and any promotional campaigns in the press and trade journals, on commercial radio and television, and at trade fairs and similar events. Some major port authorities engage advertising agencies to devise their advertising and promotion plans; separate agents are generally employed in each country in order to reflect different advertising customs and techniques. Market research should be carried out before any advertising campaign is launched to assess market potential and determine the factors which cause shipowners and shippers to use the port(s). Close liaison between advertising agency and port authority is essential throughout an advertising campaign so that the response can be monitored and the campaign modified if necessary.

The plan will include details of the year's marketing budget broken down according to country, commodity and media: newspapers, trade journals, commercial radio, television, brochures, sales conferences, trade fairs promotions, etc. In general, very few port authorities would advertise on television and radio, and generally only those in the passenger market. The marketing budget should be in proportion to the budgeted gross revenue derived from the particular commodity, country or port in question; amounts between $\frac{1}{2}$ and 3% are generally considered reasonable, although the figure would be higher for the promotion of a new product such as the development of new container berths. Port authorities are collaborating increasingly with trade associations, chambers of commerce, shippers' councils, port associations and shipowners in the joint promotion of trade through the port.

The plan should include a timetable of sales conferences and promotions in the press and trade journals. Timing plays an important role in achieving the maximum impact so that note should be taken of competitors' programmes. An attempt should be made to keep the company in the public/trade eye throughout the year. Particular attention should be paid to the lead time to formulate the media programme. In the case of new products/facilities at a port, it is advantageous to have the media plan commencement some months before the actual availability of the product. This enables the trade to examine the feasibility of using the facility before it is completed rather than wait until it is operational. In so doing it maximizes market impact and encourages maximum trade patronage of the new facilities.

Agents and personnel responsible for executing the plan should be allotted realizable revenue targets. Reports on achievements in individual countries or commodities should be prepared at regular intervals wherever practicable.

A commentary follows on the constituents of a marketing and sales plan for a port authority (see Diagram XVIII):

The marketing objectives must be clearly outlined. This can be done on the basis of country or cargo commodity, or mixture of these, to suit the selling techniques of the port authority. Alternatively, it may be based on the product facilities at the port by berth, type of traffic, etc.

The budgeted sales income may again be categorized by country, region or commodity. This will 'key in' with the sales budget, and individual sales personnel should be identified with their contributions to the sales budget.

The time scale of the marketing objective is specially important for the promotion and any new facilities such as a new Ro/Ro berth or extension of the free trade zone.

The available selling resources form an important part of the plan. They may involve one or more of the following: direct personal selling using staff employed by the port authority based either at home or overseas; engagement of agent; formulation of a very small group such as a trade mission of possibly four people from the port authority who visit overseas territories for the purpose of obtaining new business – this would involve senior managers, concerning sales, and port operation, harbour/dock engineer and estate; and finally attendance at trade fairs or similar overseas missions involving port authority personnel representation. To

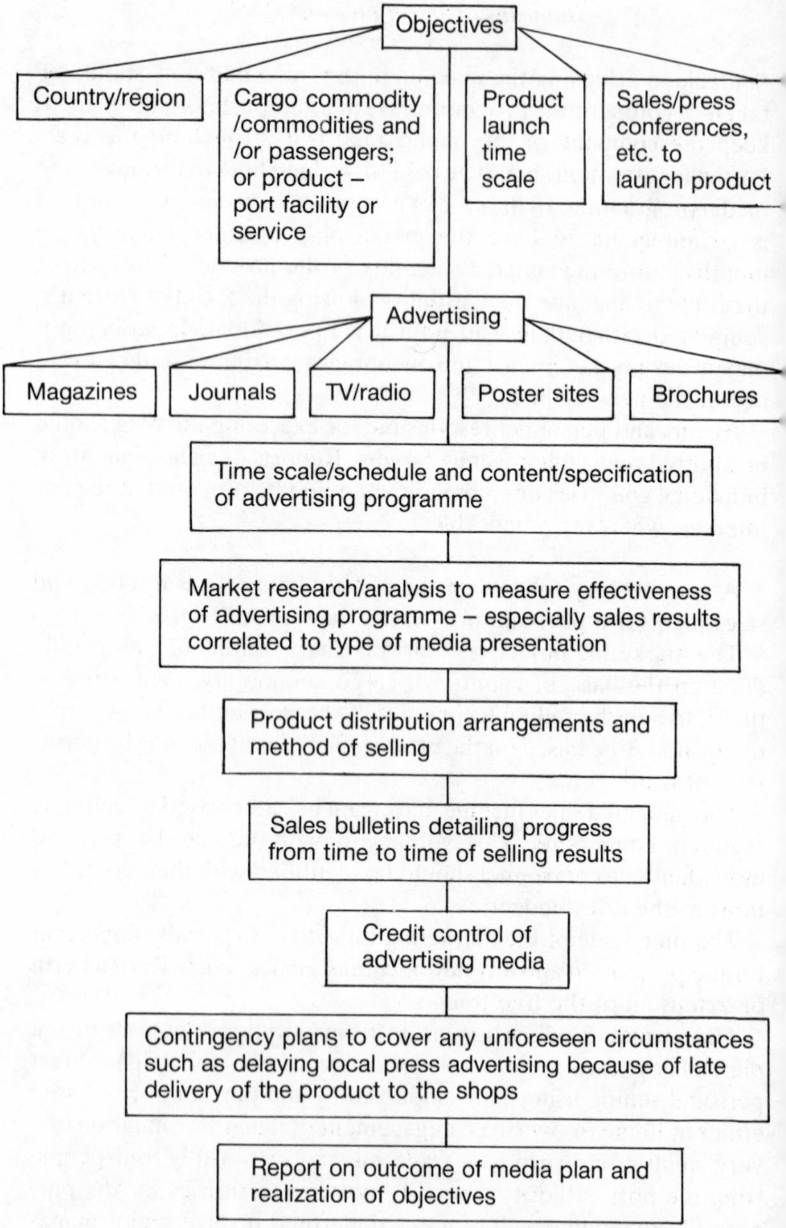

The media plan should be costed against the market potential and be closely in accord with the budget predictions. Advertising agencies are usually able to obtain discounts for press advertising.

Diagram XVIII Media or campaign plan of a port authority

ensure that sales personnel are aware of their objectives, a broad indication of the income and/or volume of each selling resource should be quoted, if practicable. Overseas trade missions are tending to become a popular means of developing/promoting the port in overseas markets.

Extensive selling aids to promote the product are available today. The scale of the use of such techniques will depend on the cost and predicted market response, the facilities available both at home and overseas, the market potential and the port authority sales budget. Items available include press advertising; brochures; television commercials, and radio commercials and cinema presentations, both of which have limited use for port authority promotions; sales conference/presentation to launch or develop the product; participation in trade fair exhibitions; joint promotion with an agent; inward or outward missions involving trade associations, shippers' councils, agents, shipowners, chambers of commerce; general publicity involving press releases, etc.; and sales training. Each featured item should be costed and the expenditure should not be exceeded. A customer relations department may exist to deal with customer complaints.

The revenue production/income for the port will be primarily based on the cargo/trade/commodities passing through it. It will also reflect the type of tonnage involved and the associated distribution arrangement which will be rail, road or inland transport. Close liaison is desirable on any port promotion especially bearing in mind the growing development of the combined transport operation. At all times the port authority must be in close touch with major port users and conduct regular meetings of mutual interest. The port authority should also liaise on stevedoring, customs clearance, consolidation, and so on.

The credit control deals with the billing of the customer and the credit terms.

The market analysis gives a broad assessment of existing markets and their opportunities, together with forthcoming developments which could improve the company's market share.

To conclude our review of the marketing and sales plan, one cannot stress too strongly that it will vary with the individual port(s). The major ports will have more specialized staff resources engaged on marketing and will work through advertising agencies both at home and overseas. The plan should point the way to opportunities for future business development. It should also encourage maximum support and co-operation from all concerned with the plan. Trade missions tend to become increasingly popular with some major ports.

MARKET ANALYSIS

A port authority must have a good knowledge of the market in order to exploit it to the most profitable advantage. This requires thorough market analysis not only prior to entering the market to determine prospects on any new venture, but also as a continuous assessment to keep pace with its trends and opportunities.

Prior to considering the various elements involved in market analysis, we will establish its objectives:

(a) To identify suitable markets with a view to their profitable development.

(b) To aid profitability of the port authority. The ultimate aim of selling in a market must be profit, although this may not always be attained in the short term. In some ports which are State owned a loss may be acceptable for several years until the market volume is adequate to bring it into a profitable situation.

(c) To keep in touch with market developments and opportunities both at home and overseas. This can be achieved through regular market reports produced by overseas agents, and through other sources including the press, journals and trade associations.

(d) To produce a trend of market developments and aid long-term market sales prospects. This helps develop sales strategy within the market. For example, if another competitor is planning to enter the market by opening up a new container or Ro/Ro berth the following year, the port authority may decide to strengthen its advertising campaign.

(e) To aid preparation of more meaningful market reports. This may be produced by overseas agents, economic institutions or trade associations and includes data on market trends, market shares, size of the market, profile of the market, and so on.

(f) To aid development of more competitive facilities including tariff structure. The more information one has about one's competitors, especially of future plans, and market reaction thereto, the greater the ability of the port authority to remain competitive.

(g) To produce more effective management information. The decision-making process is facilitated by current and relevant statistical data.

(h) To keep in touch with technical trends. This involves technical product development by competitors such as in the area of computerization.

(i) To identify new developments and market opportunities. This would emerge through regular market reports and continuous vigilance by agents.

MARKET STRUCTURE

Knowledge of the composition, profile or structure of the market both at home and overseas enables the port authority to plan the promotion and development of port facilities and tariff structure in a particular market(s). The following are the salient questions which must be answered when determining market structure:

(a) Who are the main port operators in the market and what are their strengths and weaknesses?

(b) Which are the main trading countries and/or commodities and details of their distribution/transport arrangements? For example, is it container, Ro/Ro, break bulk, combined transport operation, etc.?

(c) Which are the most important trading countries and/or commodities and do they have an increasing or diminishing share of the market?

(d) What is the quality of service of the main competitive port authorities? This includes tariff structure, industrial relations, dock labour efficiency, general port efficiency, development of computerization, and so on.

(e) Which are the competitors' main markets? Do such port authorities operate within a trade, or concentrate on a particular specialized market such as all requiring specialized berths and storage/distribution facilities?

(f) What are the geographical variations in the market?

(g) What are the seasonal/cyclical variations in the market? Can they be extended through improvement in storage facilities such as grain silos; skilful promotional techniques such as extending the passenger market season, and/or market pricing. The seasonal/

cyclical variation tends to push up unit cost and an attempt to extend the season/cycle could aid the competitiveness of the product by spreading the cost over a longer period. This involves the fullest co-operation/liaison of exporter/importer/transport operator/port authority, etc.

(h) What factors, currently or in the longer term favour the emergence of new competition? An example arises where a particular port is constructing a new container berth/terminal and rationalizing an existing break-bulk 'tween-deck tonnage trade involving some four ports on a seaboard to one central port equipped with container facilities.

(i) What factors are likely to lead to the reduction of competition? This may emerge through the competitor lacking capital to fund new technology; the presence of too many ports chasing too little traffic on a profitable basis; the absence of modern berths causing traffic to be re-routed through modern ports; the development of landbridge tariffs and movements; (see *Economics of Shipping Practice and Management*, Chapters 6 and 9) government legislation; or the absence of good port management, which results in poor quality of service and deteriorating levels of profitability.

(j) Do any trading practice(s) exist which makes it more difficult to break into a market? For example, government legislation may exist which compels certain traffics to be routed through a particular port.

(k) Do any shippers receive any government grants/subsidies in using a particular port? Alternatively, do any competitive ports receive government grants for investment or operating subsidies purposes?

MARKET SHARE

Market share is an important consideration in a general market analysis, but the paramount concern, long term, must always be the degree of profitability each market share commands. The long-term motive for entering the market must remain one of profit attainment unless compelling commercial reasons dictate otherwise. The following questions are relevant.

(a) What share of the market for a particular trade/commodity/transport mode (Ro/Ro, containerization, etc.) does the port authority command? This requires very careful evaluation.

(b) What are the market shares of the main competitive ports and is there likely to be much change in the foreseeable future?

(c) What is the port authority share of the market when analysed in terms of commodity/trade/transport mode?

(d) What is the main competitors' share of the market when analysed in the same terms?

(e) To what extent – if any – is the present market share influenced by tariffs, government controls/regulations, flag discrimination, etc?

(f) What percentage, in volume terms, is from established/historical trades and new trades?

(g) How concentrated or dispersed are the trades/commodities/transport modes?

MARKET RESEARCH

We have already touched briefly on the need for market research to establish the characteristics of a market that the port authority is already serving or may wish to enter if it proves economically viable. Market research can be used to ascertain market shares and other aspects of the business. In a progressive major port authority entity the individual commercial, operating and technical departments should request the market research department to undertake specific projects in order to maximize the profitable development of the business.

Relatively simple surveys may be carried out to discover, for instance, why shippers use a particular port, and the good and bad points relative to the port quality of service. At the other end of the scale specialist consultants may conduct research that will result in far-reaching developments, as in the case of the market research used to determine shippers'/container operators' needs at a proposed container berth.

Simple market research surveys may be carried out in a number of ways:

(a) By questionnaire distributed by mail. This may be to all agents/shippers using the port to determine their evaluation of tariff structures, facilities available, clearance of cargo, and so on.

(b) By desk research, in other words by extracting statistics and other information from trade journals, newspapers, government reports and publications of chambers of commerce and the like.

(c) By direct personal interview in a field survey; this is the most expensive but most reliable method of obtaining data from respondents.

MEDIA PLAN

In an era when more and more money is being spent on press and television advertising, it is most important that a media plan is devised so that it reaches the right people for the product. A major media plan is usually produced by the advertising agency in consultation with the advertising or publicity department of the promoter. It is essential that it is launched to coincide with the availability of the product and this could involve a lead time of up to 12 months from the time the plan is first discussed. Ideally all concerned with the promotion should attend a briefing to discuss objectives and strategy.

The following factors are relevant to the compilation of the media plan:

The objectives of the media plan must be clearly defined and all personnel associated with the formulation and execution of the plan must be aware of them. It may involve for example trade journal advertising giving details of new computerized cargo clearance facilities which should speed up the system.

The media plan should be costed against the market potential and be closely in accord with budget predictions. Advertising agencies are usually able to obtain discount for press advertising.

The plan should specify separately the various forms of advertising contained in the programme. The advertising agency should be foremost in producing the format of the advertising programme, in consultation with the client. Full use should be made of any research material and statistical data on market or customer profile and any commercial intelligence data relating to the product which is available. It is often sensible to test market the advertising material to gauge the response to it. This also gives the sales personnel an opportunity to comment on the programme.

The media schedule should be cleared with the department involved in the product promotion which may concern provision of new facilities, revised tariff structure, and so on.

Once the media plan has been launched it should be reviewed at regular intervals when any necessary alterations can be made in the content of the advertising programme and/or dates when press advertisements appear.

It is sometimes the practice to run a market research survey concurrently with the advertising programme to establish its effectiveness. This is usually on a small scale and enables the promoters to make adjustment to any subsequent plan.

In compiling future media plans, opportunity should be taken to discuss the survey results with sales personnel and agents.

Any advertising code of practice must be taken into account.

Consideration should be given to the strengths and weaknesses of existing promotions by competitors.

Above all the cost of the plan must be related both to the long-term and short-term market potential of the product.

COMPUTERIZATION

In the years to come the increasing use of computers in the port industry will contribute towards greater efficiency and profitability by facilitating the optimum use of available resources. The introduction of computers is not to be undertaken lightly, however. A feasibility study should first be made by systems analysts to ascertain whether the work in question is suitable for computerization and to compare the costs of the existing methods with those of the proposed computer application. All departments likely to use the computer should be consulted to ensure that any scheme ultimately adopted contains the data. Scope should also be provided for future development.

In the port industry computers can be used in the following fields:

(a) Stores control. By recording in the computer details of stores in stock, their value and consumption, and statements of consumption over a given period. Also an inventory of stocks by quantity and value can be produced at regular intervals, thus keeping consumption and stocks down to an economic minimum and facilitating ordering.

(b) Personnel records. Details of all the port authority labour force can be recorded on the computer master file, including name, address, date of birth, education, qualifications, staff appraisals, training courses attended, salary level, career development, and so on.

(c) Wage bills. Staff salaries including national insurance contributions, overtime, productivity bonuses, pension contributions and tax deductions can be calculated by the computer.

(d) Container control. The use of computers to record containers entering the port and leaving the port; those occupying standage area, those awaiting customs clearance, and so on, enable the container movement to be monitored. It also enables shippers seeking the whereabouts of the container to enquire through the port authority computer system. Overall it encourages the optimum use of the container and infrastructure.

(e) Preparation of bills. Port authorities can bill their customers at regular intervals with the aid of a computer thereby ensuring prompt dispatch, automatically reminding late payers, and identifying potential bad debts.

(f) Formulation of allocation of berths/slots schedules to shipowners.

(g) Documentation. The design of many port documents has been transformed in recent years. An increasing number can be electronically produced for dispatch to the client.

(h) Customs clearance. Computers now play a large part in the customs clearance procedures as found in the direct trader input scheme (see *Elements of Export Practice*, pp. 147–8). This enables the imported cargo details to be fed into the computer by the shipper/agent for presentation to customs for clearance.

(i) Cargo manifest through the use of electronic data processing transmission technique. Many shipowners send the cargo manifest details to the destination port. This gives details of the ship, expected time of arrival, cargo specification details, container number, name of consignee/consignor, and so on. The ship's agent receiving such details can plan adequate port resources accordingly, including port equipment, stevedoring resources, customs, tallyings, transport distribution, and so on. Moreover, the agent can inform the importer of the anticipated arrival date of the goods and prepare all the requisite documentation for customs.

(j) Tariffs. Details of all port tariffs and individual client's tariffs are contained on a computer master file. This enables the port authority to computerize this invoice procedure for all traffic passing through the port. See item (c).

(k) Management information. Statistical data on the many subjects mentioned above (e.g. staff numbers, number of sailings, berth utilization, cargo-handling cost and productivity, cost analysis, and so on) can be obtained from the computer whenever required and used to generate further information, such as average handling cost per cargo ton at a particular berth. Such general data availability is very useful when a choice has to be made between various options.

The use of computers within the port industry is likely to grow, particularly as financial management techniques improve and routine clerical work is automated. Port authorities should examine their procedures continually to determine whether management areas that hitherto have used traditional methods would benefit from computerization. Close attention should be paid to the cost and benefit to be derived from the use of computers, particularly any financial savings.

CHAPTER 13

Role of British and international port and cargo-handling organizations

Our study of the elements of port operation would be incomplete without an examination of the role and increasing influence of some of the numerous national and international organizations in the fields of ports and cargo handling. Many of them work in close association with governments and they are undoubtedly making an increasing contribution towards the facilitation and development of international trade, thereby contributing to port expansion/modernization.

With regard to the principal shipping and international trade organizations, these are found in Chapter 8 of *Elements of Shipping* and Chapters 12 and 13 of *Economics of Shipping Practice and Management*.

BRITISH PORTS ASSOCIATION (BPA)

The British Ports Association (BPA) is an organization which represents at both national and international level the British ports industry. It has two prime objectives, detailed below:

(a) To promote, further and protect the general interests of port authorities and conservancy authorities.

(b) To afford opportunities for the discussion and consideration of general questions affecting all members of the association.

BPA has a well-developed committee structure. All types and sizes of port are represented, and all principal areas of interest in port affairs are covered.

BPA is the catalyst in the discussion of port-related topics and provides a central organization which represents the views of all ports to external bodies. There is a continuing dialogue with HM Government and other sectors of industry which have an interest in port affairs. International matters are represented through membership and services are performed for the International Association of Ports and Harbours.

The membership of BPA includes all British ports and harbours of commercial significance. They are diverse in size and character, ranging from the largest ports to small fishing and yacht harbours.

INTERNATIONAL ASSOCIATION OF PORTS AND HARBOURS (IAPH)

The International Association of Ports and Harbours (IAPH) is a worldwide association of port authorities with a membership of nearly 400 situated in 75 countries. The principal aim of IAPH is found in its constitution 'to develop and foster good relations and collaboration among all ports and harbours of the world.' The IAPH seeks to achieve its aim through the following areas:

(a) The association strives to promote and increase the efficiency of all ports and harbours by exchanging information connected with new techniques and technology relating to port development, organization, administration and management.

(b) Common viewpoints, policies or plans are encouraged where members share a mutual interest.

The association is also concerned to protect the legitimate interest and rights of its members within intergovernmental and other organizations in order to improve port conditions and efficiency on a worldwide basis. IAPH seeks the co-operation of shipowners, liner conferences and other parties involved in international trade in its efforts on behalf of ports and harbours to assist in the development of waterborne transport and marine industries in general.

The IAPH was granted non-governmental consultative status with the following three world organizations on the dates indicated and actively participates in their programmes.

(a) ECOSOC (United Nations Economic and Social Council, 8 July 1966).

(b) IMO (International Maritime Organisation, 26 October 1967).

(c) UNCTAD (United Nations Conference on Trade and Development, 31 August 1973).

The association makes recommendations from time to time either at the organization's request or on its own initiative through specially appointed liaison officers.

Additionally, to deal with the current issues of international importance, the IAPH maintains close contact with the following: BIMCO (Baltic and International Maritime Conference); CMI (Comite Maritime International); IACS (International Association of Classification Societies); IALA (International Association of Lighthouse Authorities); ICB (International Container Bureau); ICHCA (International Cargo Handling Co-ordination Association); ICS (International Chamber of Shipping); IMPA (International Maritime Pilots Association); INTERTANKO (International Association of Independent Tanker Owners); ISF (International Shipping Federation); ISO (International Organization for Standardization); IUMI (International Union of Marine Insurance); OCIMF (Oil Companies International Marine Forum); PIANC (Permanent International Association of Navigation Congress); UINF (Union Internationale de la Navigation Fluviale); UNIDROIT (International Institute for the Unification of Private Law).

In order to maintain a close relationship with the foregoing as well as with other international maritime organizations located in Europe, the British Ports Association (BPA) represents IAPH interests under a special agreement with IAPH. The BPA endeavours to facilitate effective concerted action, either wholly or partly, to protect ports and port interests whenever deemed necessary.

The work of IAPH is carried out through the Head Office in Tokyo in close contact with the President, Vice-Presidents and Executive Committee as well as the Chairmen of the various internal and technical committees. These committees report, advise, make recommendations and take such action as may be authorized by the association. The areas of work covered by the technical committees are as follows:

Committee on Cargo Handling Operations

The examination and continuous review of matters relating to the planning, development and operation of cargo-handling facilities and systems. These include general cargo, containerization, Ro/Ro, barging, equipment and manpower training.

Committee on Port Safety
Environment and construction. The consideration of matters relating to the construction, maintenance and safe marine operation of ports and harbours and to the protection of the port environment, including vessel traffic services, the control of dangerous substances, pollution control and management.

Committee on Trade Facilitation
The handling of procedures and documentation relating to the facilitation of trade through ports and harbours, including the communication and processing of data on a local, national or international basis, as may be required.

Committee on International Port Development
The proposing, developing, and administering of schemes for the provision of training, education and technical assistance to develop ports and the stimulation of co-operation between developing and developed ports.

Committee on Legal Protection of Port Interests
The examination and review of provisions of international law affecting port interests. IAPH works closely with many representatives of intergovernmental and other international maritime organizations.

Committee on Public Affairs
The encouraging of the development of all ports and harbours which in turn means the development of the whole port community. The identification of community attitudes to port development, operations and industrial growth in port areas. The determining of areas of public concern as well as the assessment of the economic impact of the port on the daily lives of the community and the development of a public relations strategy to deal with problems that may arise.

Besides the meetings of the Executive, Internal and Technical

Committees, official conferences are held every two years.

IAPH seeks to increase co-operation by inviting further membership, so as to be able to function more efficiently as well as being able to aid those who seek the association's expertise and knowledge for the development of their own ports and harbours.

There is no doubt the IAPH is aiding the development of ports throughout the world and through improved efficiency will contribute to international trade expansion.

INTERNATIONAL CARGO HANDLING CO-ORDINATION ASSOCIATION (ICHCA)

The International Cargo Handling Co-ordination Association was established in 1951 with the aim of facilitating improved handling techniques in the world transport system. Its headquarters are in London (see Appendix B) and some 90 countries are members. Membership is drawn from organizations and individuals involved in every aspect of the transport of goods.

The aims of the ICHCA are to increase efficiency and economy in the handling and movement of goods by all modes of transport and at all stages of the transport chain. It achieves this by generating contacts amongst members, by presenting opportunities for membership dialogue and information exchange, by collecting and disseminating information from all available sources, and by participating in technical and regulatory activities which significantly affect cargo handling in practice.

ICHCA is administered by a Council composed of the chairmen of each national section. Its policies are reported to a biennial General Assembly, where members vote on the proposals before them. National and regional sections, each with their own group of honorary officers, organize activities of national interest in many countries. An international secretariat in London co-ordinates the work of the national and regional sections under the direction of Council, and provides services to members in all countries.

ICHCA organizes a wide range of national and international meetings, from luncheons, short workshops and seminars, to major conferences on important subjects. These activities culminate in the ICHCA Biennial Conference, which coincides with the General Assembly of members.

ICHCA representatives participate in many other conference

and similar activities, ensuring that a consensus of member opinion is heard wherever people are brought together to discuss cargo handling.

ICHCA has consultative status with the major regulatory bodies and training agencies affecting the transport industry. By taking part in their meetings and monitoring their activities, it ensures that members' interests are represented when regulations and institutional customs are being developed, and also that its members hear about new regulations and practices quickly.

ICHCA conducts international study projects in response to identified needs for information within the membership, and publishes the results as reports and technical papers. Recent titles include 'The Securing of ISO Containers: Theory and Practice', 'Developments in the Air Cargo Industry', 'The Handling of ISO Containers in Low Throughput Situations', and 'An International Survey on Handling Iron and Steel Products'.

ICHCA operates a technical enquiry service, whereby members with a problem in one country or region may gain access to the solutions of members with specialized knowledge in other countries.

ICHCA scans all published material on cargo handling and maintains a data base of relevant information for the use of members. It also arranges introductions and technical visits for members visiting another country, providing the opportunity for continued contact and dialogue.

Cargo handling covers raw materials and manufactured goods from point of origin to final destination. It also embraces packaging, marking, modes of transport, vehicles, terminal operations and management, equipment, engineering, information channels and data processing.

There is no doubt that the ICHCA is making a world wide contribution to the modernization of cargo handling techniques.

INTERNATIONAL LABOUR ORGANIZATION (ILO)

The International Labour Organization was set up in 1919 to bring governments, employers and trade unions together for united action in the cause of social justice and better living conditions everywhere. It is a tripartite organization, with worker and employer representatives taking part in its work on equal status with those of governments. The number of ILO member countries now stands at 151. In 1969 the organisation celebrated its fiftieth anniversary and was awarded the Nobel Peace Prize. Its secretariat is based in Geneva, Switzerland (see Appendix B).

Historically, the ILO stems from the social thought of the nineteenth century. Conditions of workers in the wake of the industrial revolution were increasingly seen to be intolerable by economists and sociologists. Social reformers from Robert Owen onwards believed that any country or industry introducing measures to improve working conditions would raise the cost of labour, putting it at an economic disadvantage compared with other countries or industries. That is why they laboured with such persistence to persuade the powers of Europe to make better working conditions and shorter hours the subject of international agreements.

The first concrete result of these efforts was an international conference held in Berlin in 1890 and attended by representatives of 14 countries. They put forward suggestions, but did not make any commitments. In 1897 another conference was held, this time in Brussels; it adopted a resolution providing for an international bureau for the protection of labour. This bureau never materialized, but three years later a new international conference in Paris succeeded in creating the International Association for Labour Legislation. This forerunner of the ILO, with its headquarters in Basle, undertook the translation and publication of labour laws of many countries. The Legislative Series begun then, was taken over by the ILO and is still published.

By 1946, the ILO became the first specialized agency associated with the United Nations. Since then, a system of close co-operation has grown up between international organizations which attempt to deal with the grave inequalities and imbalances among the world's various regions. In the field of social policy the ILO plays an active part in one of the most striking changes since the Second World War: the large-scale development of international technical co-operation. New problems continue to arise as a result of technological, economic and social change. While improved working and living conditions and the promotion of full employment remain central aims of the ILO, it now has to deal also with such matters as migrant workers, multinational corporations, the working environment and the social consequences of monetary instability.

The ILO remains a standard-setting body, but today there is also marked emphasis on operational programmes and on educational work, in the broadest sense. This led to the creation of the International Institute for Labour Studies (Geneva) in 1960 and the International Centre for Advanced Technical and Vocational Training (Turin) in 1965, and to the launching of the World Employment Programme. The operational programmes have also been largely responsible for the current effort to decentralize responsibilities from Geneva headquarters to the various regions of the world.

The ILO has 161 member States, compared with 42 in 1919. Its budget has grown from $4.5 million in 1948 to £127 million in 1984. Growth has been accompanied by considerable changes in policy and geographical representation. The former preponderance of industrial countries with market economies has given way to a more varied mixture in which the centrally planned economies of Eastern Europe, the newly independent lands and the Third World in general also play an important part.

The International Labour Organization is composed of a yearly general assembly, the International Labour Conference; and executive council, the governing body; and a permanent secretariat, the International Labour Office. The organization also works through subsidiary bodies such as regional conferences, industrial committees and panels of experts. The ILO engages in research and publishes documents on a wide range of labour and social matters.

The main task of the ILO is to improve conditions of life and work by building up a comprehensive code of law and practice. The organisation's founders felt that standards laid down through the joint efforts of governments, management and labour would be realistic, solid and widely applicable.

This standard-setting function is one that the ILO still performs. The number of international labour instruments – Conventions and Recommendations – adopted by the International Labour Conference since 1919 has now reached 327 (159 Conventions and 168 Recommendations). Over 5000 ratifications of Conventions have been registered.

Each Convention is a legal instrument regulating some aspect of labour administration, social welfare or human rights. Its ratification involves a dual obligation for a member state: it is both a formal commitment to apply the provisions of the Convention, and an indication of willingness to accept a measure of international supervision. A Recommendation is similar to a Convention except that it is not subject to ratification, and provides more specific guide-lines. Both Conventions and Recommendations define standards and provide a model and stimulus for national legislation and practice in member countries.

ILO Conventions cover a wide field of social problems, including basic human rights matters (such as freedom of association, abolition of forced labour, and elimination of discrimination in employment), minimum wages, labour administration, industrial relations, employment policy, working conditions, social security, occupational safety and health, dock labour and employment at sea. A number of the agreements deal with women workers.

Conventions adopted at two recent sessions of the International Labour Conference covered maintenance of rights in social security, and termination of employment at the initiative of the employer (1982) and vocational rehabilitation and employment (1983).

Technical co-operation is concentrated in the following major areas:

(a) Training: assistance in the formulation of training policies and systems; management training; industrial, rural and commercial vocational training, and development of teaching methodologies and materials. Special attention is given to vocational rehabilitation of the disabled and training for women and out-of-school youth.

(b) Employment and development: definition of national policies and strategies; manpower planning; special labour-intensive public works programmes; alleviation of rural poverty; choice of technology; and small-scale industry development.

(c) Sectoral activities, comprising in particular development of co-operatives and training for the hotel and tourism industry.

(d) Conditions of work and the working environment; occupational safety and health; conditions of work and life.

(e) Industrial relations (including labour administration), social security; workers' education and assistance to employers' organizations.

The modernization of ports and associated cargo-handling techniques involving a much reduced dock labour force features increasingly in the work of the ILO.

The question of technical and social changes in the world's ports and their effects on job opportunities for port labour was discussed at an ILO technical meeting held in Rotterdam, the Netherlands in 1969. It was discussed further by the International Labour Conference in 1973 which adopted a Convention and a supplementary Recommendation concerning the social repercussions of new methods of cargo handling in docks. These instruments set out standards for national authorities to improve the working conditions of their respective port labour force and to solve redundancy problems resulting from new cargo handling methods, it being borne in mind, however, that port performance will improve due to capital investments being made to adapt ports to these modern developments. These instruments call, among others, for appropriate safety, health, welfare and vocational training being applied to the port labour force. Since 1969 the ILO's technical assistance programme in the port field has been directed mainly towards assisting governments in establishing port training centres. Such assistance has been given to Singapore (1969), Peru (1975) and to the Philippines (1976). In Peru, however, the ILO assisted in the assessment of training needs, the selection of instructors and fellowships abroad, and in the design of the project document which served as a basis for the execution of this project by the Government of the Netherlands. From 1980 until 1984, a UNDP/ILO project in the field of port management and training was undertaken in Turkey. Project activities included the training of trainers, preparation of training curricula, fellowship programmes and the organization of three seminars for senior and middle port management which were held in close co-operation with UNCTAD. In 1985 the ILO is assisting the Governments of Costa Rica and Mauritius to strengthen and establish port training centres with a view to introducing and further developing permanent training schemes for port personnel.

During the past few years a number of short-term missions have also been carried out at the request of governments for the purpose of giving technical advice on specific port matters. Such advice has been given on labour legislation for port workers (Cameroon 1981), problems existing in various sectors of the harbours authority including specific recommendations and project proposals to assist in the solution of these problems (Tanzania 1981), assessment of training needs for port workers (Ivory Coast 1981), training requirements for various ports (India 1982), requirements for establishing a cargo-handling corporation (Mauritius 1983), new labour arrangements to be considered on account of developments in modern cargo-handling techniques (Cyprus 1983), improvement of dock safety regulations taking into account new working methods which have been introduced since the time these regulations were adopted (Malta 1983), new labour arrangements to be considered on account of redundancy problems originated by the development of cargo being shipped by container (Peru 1984) and measures to be taken for establishing a port training centre (Paraguay 1984).

In 1979, an ILO sub-regional port consultant was stationed in Trinidad to provide advice on port operations, manpower development and training to port authorities and port workers' organizations of the Caribbean region. Similar technical assistance is being provided to the Asian countries by the ILO Regional Adviser and the Associate expert in maritime activities stationed in Bangkok. Services are also available for the African and Central and Latin American regions.

The assistance that may be provided by the ILO's technical co-operation programme in the field of training port personnel may entail the assessment of training needs, the training of instructors, fellowship programmes and curricula development complemented with the necessary audio-visual aids. Activities in the field of port training are also carried out in co-ordination with the ILO International Centre for Advanced Technical and Vocational Training.

The design, purchasing, shipment and installation of necessary equipment for establishing a port training centre, as well as its organization and management, are fields of technical assistance that the ILO may provide.

The importance for all industries to develop a core of well-trained supervisors is widely recognized. Based on an analysis of supervisory training programmes throughout the world, the ILO has completed a series of 34 modules for supervisory training. These modules have been subjected to rigorous testing and, in close collaboration with the ILO Regional Adviser for Maritime Activities stationed in Bangkok, work has started to adapt them for the training of port supervisors in India. The ILO has also recently sent out a questionnaire to a large number of port authorities in order to obtain their views and their interest in collaborating in the further adaptation of these modules for the training of their supervisors.

The traditional standard-setting activities of the ILO and its newer technical co-operation activities complement one another and are inseparable from its research and publishing work. Without the modernization of social structures and increasing economic development of production, ILO standards would be only a distant hope in many of the emerging countries rather than reasonable and immediately applicable measures.

INTERNATIONAL MARITIME ORGANIZATION (IMO)

The International Maritime Organization (IMO) is the specialized agency of the United Nations concerned solely with maritime affairs. Its interest lies basically in ships used in international services. This also extends to oil pollution, dangerous cargo, containers, and so on. Some 86 states are members of the IMO including shipowning nations, countries which use shipping services and countries in the course of development.

Its objectives are to facilitate co-operation among governments on technical matters affecting shipping to ensure the achievement of the highest possible standards of life at sea and of efficient navigation. This entails providing an exchange of information between nations in technical maritime subjects and concluding international agreements.

IMO is a forum where its members can exchange information and endeavour to solve problems connected with maritime, technical and legal matters. It makes recommendations on maritime questions submitted by the member state or by other members of the United Nations family. IMO is responsible for covering and preparing international conferences in subjects within its sphere of action for the purpose of concluding international conventions or agreements.

Details of some of the IMO conventions are found in Chapter 8 of *Elements of Shipping* and Chapter 12 of *Economics of Shipping Practice and Management*.

The ILO works closely with the IMO in areas of mutual concern. An increasing number of IMO conventions concern the port industry.

NATIONAL ASSOCIATION OF PORT EMPLOYERS (NAPE)

The National Association of Port Employers (NAPE) is an organization involved in dock labour and represents the UK port authorities. It has three main objectives detailed below:

(a) To ensure the fullest consultation and co-operation between all interests concerned in the employment of port transport workers.

(b) To provide a medium for the attachment to it (NAPE) of appropriate organizations of employers with a view to co-operative action and common effort.

(c) To operate the conciliation machinery of the port transport industry.

NAPE's members are local associations of port employers which are divided into eight geographical groups, each with its own Group Secretary. The Association's affairs are the responsibility of the Council which has 50 members from all groups.

NAPE negotiates with the trade unions through the National Joint Council for the Port Transport Industry on terms and conditions of employment for registered dock workers. It represents the employers' interests with HM Government and other external bodies.

NAPE, as representing the port employers on the National Joint Council, operates jointly the industry's national procedure for settling disputes referred from port level. Although not directly represented on the National Dock Labour Board NAPE is, in practice, closely concerned with the dock labour scheme.

THE FUTURE

Our study of the elements of port operation and management would not be complete without a broad evaluation of likely future developments in the next decade. One can say at the outset that the future will be one of challenge and opportunity. It will demand higher professional standards in all areas of the business, and a greater degree of business acumen. Above all it will require greater perception of business opportunity and development. This requires much improved liaison between port authorities, shipowners and shippers – the latter involving trade associations, chambers of commerce, agents, governments and so on. Ports and their infrastructure will feature more in government long-term economic planning and development within the context of international trade development and, in some countries, tourism.

We will now consider likely future developments:

The expansion of containerization of liner cargo services is likely to continue with further penetration in developing countries trades and the expanding oriental market. It will have a profound effect on all areas of the port business.

Computerization will play a more decisive role in the management and operation of the port (see pp. 223–225). It will help to aid much improved efficiency.

Dock labour will continue to be rationalized through cargo mechanization. The more dramatic changes will emerge in the developing countries as modern tonnage displaces the 'tween deck ship.

Customs documentation and the processing/clearance of cargo through customs will tend to become more simple. Some rationalization in customs documentation will also occur. Computerization will feature more strongly in the lodgement of entries through customs.

The expansion of free port/free trade zones will accelerate especially in non-manufacturing economically based countries.

To facilitate increased throughput of cargo volume through the port the development of inland clearance centres/container freight stations will continue. This will have the added benefit of reducing port congestion often attributable to late presentation of documents.

The throughput per berth will continue to rise. This is coupled with continuous modernization of berth layout/facilities involving capital-intensive cargo-handling systems and modern tonnage.

Governments will play an increasing role in the development and management of ports. This will be very much in the context of developing their economy and improving their external trade balance.

ILO, IAPH, ICHCA, UNCTAD and OECD will continue to play a significant role in port expansion, modernization and so on. The ILO especially will become involved in the social and redeployment problems inherent in the rationalization of the dock labour force. Their influence will also include dock labour training programmes.

Port traffic control systems are becoming more common as the volume of business and especially ship movements increase annually in ports. See pp. 124–145. Computerization and radar will feature more strongly in the port control systems.

Port management techniques will continue to be rationalized and modernized. In particular greater emphasis will be given to budgetary and marketing controls.

The role of the port long term will change in many countries. No longer will it be a terminal where consignments originate or terminate their transit, but part of a link in a transport chain thereby providing an interface between two transport modes. This will be achieved through the development of the combined transport operation.

The development of the combined transport operation will continue involving containerization, Ro/Ro, train ferry and bulk cargo rail/ship movements (see Chapter 9 of *Economics of Shipping Practice and Management*). This will demand continuing port investment to take full advantage of such quality international distribution networks.

The tendency to encourage the shipowner to lease the berth and manage it will continue. This will involve warehouse accommodation, cargo-handling equipment, dock labour resources, and so on.

Governments are likely to provide/facilitate more capital availability for port modernization/development on proven projects. This will be more confined to the actual berth provision with the user operating under leasehold arrangement and funding/managing the facilities.

The development of passenger ferry will continue in many short sea and estuarial trades involving the coach, car and associated passengers. It will attract a continuing improvement in facilities to handle such traffic especially within the context of raising the quality of such passenger facilities and quick turnround.

High professional standards are essential if the port industry is to remain viable and foster international trade, thereby raising standards throughout the world. It is hoped that this book will make a modest contribution towards attainment of that objective and that it will form the basis of further study.

Appendix A

FURTHER RECOMMENDED TEXTBOOK READING

Branch, A. E. (1981). *Elements of Shipping*, 5th edn Chapman and Hall, London.

Branch, A. E. (1982). *Economics of Shipping Practice and Management*. Chapman and Hall, London. (2nd edition in preparation).

Branch, A. E. (1984). *Elements of Export Marketing and Management*. 1st edn Chapman and Hall, London.

Branch, A. E. (1985). *Elements of Export Practice*, 2nd edn Chapman and Hall, London.

Branch, A. E. (1982). *Dictionary of Shipping/International Trade Terms and Abbreviations*. 2nd edn (3rd edn in preparation, 8000 entries). Witherby and Co. Ltd, London.

Branch, A. E. (1984) *Dictionary of Commercial Terms and Abbreviations* (6000 entries), 1st edn Witherby and Co. Ltd, London.

Branch, A. E. (1986). *Dictionary of Multilingual Shipping/International Trade/Commercial Terms in English – French – German – Spanish* (10 000 entries), 1st edn Witherby and Co. Ltd, London.

Branch, A. E. (1986). *Dictionary of Multilingual Shipping/International Trade/Commercial Terms and Abbreviations in English – Arabic* (3000 terms), 1st edn Witherby and Co. Ltd, London.

Schmitthoff, C. M. (1976). *The Export Trade*, 8th edn Sweet and Maxwell, London.

Watson, A. (1985). *Finance of International Trade*, 3rd edn Institute of Bankers, London.

Appendix B

ADDRESSES OF ORGANIZATIONS AND INSTITUTES ENGAGED IN THE FIELDS OF SEAPORTS AND INTERNATIONAL TRADE

Baltic and International Maritime Conference,
19 Kristianiagade,
DK – 2100 Copenhagen,
Denmark

Baltic Mercantile and Shipping Exchange,
St Mary Axe,
London EC3

British Ports Association,
Commonwealth House,
1/19 New Oxford Street,
London WC1A 1DZ

Chartered Institute of Transport,
80 Portland Place,
London W1N 4DP

Council of European and Japanese National Shipowners' Associations (CENSA),
17/18 Bury Street,
London EC3A 5AH

Freight Transport Association (FTA),
Hermes House,
157 St John's Road,
Tunbridge Wells,
Kent TN4 9UZ

General Council of British Shipping (GCBS),
30/32 St Mary Axe,
London EC3A 8ET

Institute of Bankers,
10 Lombard Street,
London EC3

Institute of Chartered Shipbrokers,
25 Bury Street,
London EC3A 5BA

Institute of Export,
64 Clifton Street,
London C2A 4HB

Institute of Freight Forwarders Ltd,
Suffield House,
9 Paradise Road,
Richmond,
Surrey TW9 1SA

Institute of Marine Engineers,
76 Mark Lane,
London EC3

Institute of Marketing,
Moor Hall,
Cookham,
Maidenhead,
Berks SL6 9QH

Institute of Materials Handling,
Cranfield Institute of Technology,
Cranfield,
Bedford MK43 0AL

Institute of Packaging,
Sysonby Lodge,
Nottingham Road,
Melton Mowbray,
Leicester LE13 0NU

Institute of Road Transport Engineers,
1 Cromwell Place,
Kensington,
London SW7 2JF

Institute of Transport Administration,
32 Palmerston Road,
Southampton SO1 1LL

International Association of Independent Tanker Owners,
(INTERTANKO),
Radhusgaten 25,
PO Box 1452 – VIKA,
Oslo,
Norway

International Association of Ports and Harbours
Kotohira Kaikan Building,
2–8 Toranomon 1–Chome,
Minato-Ku,
Tokyo 105,
Japan

International Cargo Handling Co-ordination Association
(ICHCA),
1 Walcott Street,
London SW1P 2NY

International Chamber of Commerce (ICC),
38 Cours Albert 1 er,
75008 Paris,
France

International Labour Office (ILO),
CH – 1211 Geneve 22,
Switzerland

International Maritime Organization (IMO),
101–104 Piccadilly,
London WIV 0AE

International Monetary Fund (IMF),
Washington DC,
20431,
USA

Lloyd's Register of Shipping,
71 Fenchurch Street,
London EC3M 4BS

Organization for Economic Co-operation and Development (OECD),
Maritime Transport Committee,
2 Rue André Pascal,
75775 Paris Cedex 16,
France

Organization of the Petroleum Exporting Countries (OPEC),
Obere Donaustrasse 93,
1020 Vienna,
Austria

Simplification of International Trade Procedures Board (SITPRO),
Almack House,
26–28 King Street,
London SW2

United Nations Commission on International Trade Law (UNCITRAL)
United Nations,
New York,
NY 10017,
USA

United Nations Conference on Trade and Development (UNCTAD),
Palais des Nations,
CH – 1211 Geneve 10,
Switzerland

Appendix C

MAJOR PORTS OF THE WORLD AND THEIR LOCATION

Port	Country
Aarhus	Denmark
Aberdeen	United Kingdom
Abidjan	Ivory Coast
Abu Dhabi	United Arab Emirates
Acajutla	El Salvador
Adelaide	Australia
Alexandria	Egypt
Algeciras	Spain
Algiers	Algeria
Alicante	Spain
Amsterdam	Netherlands
Antofagasta	Chile
Antwerp	Belgium
Apapa	Nigeria
Aqaba	Jordan
Arica	Chile
Ashdod	Israel
Assab	Ethiopia
Asuncion	Paraguay
Auckland	New Zealand
Baghdad	Iraq
Bahia (Salvador)	Brazil
Bahrain	Bahrain Islands
Balboa	Panama
Bangkok	Thailand
Banjul	Gambia
Bar	Yugoslavia
Barcelona	Spain
Barranquilla	Colombia
Basrah	Iraq
Basseterre	St Kitts (Leeward Islands)
Beira	Mozambique
Beirut	Lebanon
Belawan Deli	Indonesia
Belem (Para)	Brazil
Belfast	United Kingdom
Benghazi	Libya
Bergen	Norway
Bilbao	Spain
Bislig	Philippines
Bissau	Guinea-Bissau
Boca Chica	Dominican Republic
Boma	Zaire
Bombay	India
Bordeaux	France
Boulogne	France
Bremen	Germany
Bremerhaven	Germany
Bridgetown	Barbados
Brisbane	Australia
Bristol	United Kingdom
Buchanan	Liberia
Buenaventura	Colombia
Buenos Aires	Argentina
Bugo	Philippines
Burgas	Bulgaria

Port	Country
Burnie	Australia
Busan (Pusan)	Korea
Butuah	Philippines
Cabinda	Angola
Cadiz	Spain
Cagayan de Oro	Philippines
Calabar	Nigeria
Calcutta	India
Calais	France
Callao	Peru
Capetown	South Africa
Cartagena	Colombia
Casablanca	Morocco
Castries	St Lucia (Windward Islands)
Catania	Italy
Cebu	Philippines
Chalna	Bangladesh
Chanaral	Chile
Cherbourg	France
Chisimayo	Somali Democratic Republic
Chittagong	Bangladesh
Coatzacoalcos	Mexico
Cochin	India
Colombia	Sri Lanka
Colon	Panama
Conakry	Republic of Guinea
Constanza	Romania
Copenhagen	Denmark
Coquimbo	Chile
Corinto	Nicaragua
Cork	Ireland
Cotonou	Republic of Benin
Cristobal	Panama
Curacao	Netherlands Antilles

Port	Country
Cutuco	El Salvador
Cuxhaven	Germany
Dakar	Senegal
Dammam	Saudi Arabia
Dar-es-Salaam	Tanzania
Davao	Philippines
Derince	Turkey
Djakarta	Indonesia
Djibouti	Djibouti Republic
Doha	Qatar
Douala	Cameroon
Dover	United Kingdom
Drammen	Norway
Dubai	United Arab Emirates
Dublin	Ireland
Dumai	Indonesia
Dunedin	New Zealand
Dunkerque	France
Durban	South Africa
East London	South Africa
Eilat	Israel
Eregli	Turkey
Esmeraldas	Ecuador
Felixstowe	United Kingdom
Fortaleza	Brazil
Fos	France
Freeport	Bahamas
Freetown	Sierra Leone
Fremantle	Australia
Funchal	Madeira Islands
Garston	United Kingdom
Gdynia	Poland
Geelong	Australia
Genoa	Italy
Georgetown	Guyana
Ghent	Belgium
Glasgow	United Kingdom

Port	Country	Port	Country
Gothenburg	Sweden	Kingston	Jamaica
Grangemouth	United Kingdom	Kingstown	St Vincent (Windward Islands)
Greenock	United Kingdom	Kobe	Japan
Guam	Guam	Koper	Yugoslavia
Guanta	Venezuela	Kuwait	Kuwait
Guatemala City	Guatemala	Lagos	Nigeria
Guayaquil	Ecuador	La Guaira	Venezuela
Haifa	Israel	Las Palmas	Canary Islands
Hamburg	Germany	Latakia	Syria
Hamilton	Bermuda	Launceston	Australia
Harwich	United Kingdom	Legaspi	Philippines
Helsingborg	Sweden	Leghorn	Italy
Helsinki	Finland	Le Havre	France
Hilo	Hawaii	Leixoes	Portugal
Hobart	Australia	Leningrad	USSR
Hodeida	Yemen Arab Republic	Libreville (Owendo)	Gabon
Hong Kong	Hong Kong	Limassol	Cyprus
Honolulu	Hawaii	Lisbon	Portugal
Hsingkong	PRC	Liverpool	United Kingdom
Hull	United Kingdom	Livomo	Italy
Ilweus	Brazil	Lobito	Angola
Ilo	Peru	Lome	Togo
Inchon	Korea	London	United Kingdom
Iquique	Chile	Luanda	Angola
Iskenderun	Turkey	Lyttelton	New Zealand
Istanbul	Turkey	Macapa	Brazil
Izmir	Turkey	Madras	India
Jakarta	Indonesia	Majunga	Malagasy Republic
Jebel Ali	United Arab Emirates	Malaga	Spain
Jeddah	Saudi Arabia	Malmo	Sweden
Jubail	Saudi Arabia	Managua	Nicaragua
Kaohsiung	Taiwan (Formosa)	Manaus	Brazil
Kandla	India	Manchester	United Kingdom
Karachi	Pakistan	Mangalone	India
Keelung	Taiwan (Formosa)	Manila	Philippines

Port	Country
Manta	Ecuador
Maputo	Mozambique
Maracaibo	Venezuela
Mariveles	Philippines
Marseilles	France
Masao	Philippines
Massawa	Ethiopia
Matadi	Zaire
Matanzas	Venezuela
Matarani	Peru
Melbourne	Australia
Mersin	Turkey
Milan	Italy
Mogadiscio	Somali Democratic Republic
Moji	Japan
Mombasa	Kenya
Monrovia	Liberia
Montevideo	Uruguay
Mtwara	Tanzania
Muscat	Oman
Muttrah	Oman
Nacala	Mozambique
Naha	Japan
Nagoya	Japan
Nakhodha	USSR
Napier	New Zealand
Naples	Italy
Nassau	Bahamas
Natal	Brazil
Newcastle	United Kingdom
Norrkoping	Sweden
Odense	Denmark
Odessa	USSR
Oporto	Portugal
Oranjestad (Aruba)	Netherlands Antilles
Osaka	Japan
Oslo	Norway
Owendo	Gabon
Palermo	Italy
Palma de Majorca	Majorca (Spain)
Palva	Venezuela
Panama	Panama
Paramaribo	Surinam
Paranagua	Brazil
Pasajes	Spain
Patras	Greece
Penang	Malaysia
Piraeus	Greece
Plymouth	Montserrat (Leeward Islands)
Pointe Noire	Congo Republic
Polloc	Philippines
Ponta Delgada	Azores
Port Allen	Hawaii
Port Alma	Australia
Port-au-Prince	Haiti
Port Elizabeth	South Africa
Port Gentil	Gabon
Port Harcourt	Nigeria
Port Kelang	Malaysia
Port Kembla	Australia
Port of Spain	Trinidad
Port Said	Egypt
Port Sudan	Sudan
Port Suez	Egypt
Porto Alegre	Brazil
Porto Grande	St Vincent (Cape Verde Republic)
Progreso	Mexico
Puerto Barrios	Guatemala
Puerto Cabello	Venezuela
Puerto Cortes	Honduras
Puerto Limon	Costa Rica
Puerto Ordaz	Venezuela
Puntarenas	Costa Rica
Pusan (Busan)	Korea
Rangoon	Burma

Port	Country
Ras-al-Mishab	Saudi Arabia
Recife Pernambuco)	Brazil
Reykjavik	Iceland
Rijeka	Yugoslavia
Rio de Janeiro	Brazil
Rio Grande (Do Sul)	Brazil
Rio Haina	Dominican Republic
Riyadh	Saudi Arabia
Roseau	Dominica (Windward Islands)
Rota	Spain
Rotterdam	Netherlands
St Barthelemy	Guadeloupe
St Croix	Virgin Islands
St George	Grenada (Windward Islands)
St John	Antigua (Leeward Islands)
St Maarten	Netherlands Antilles
St Thomas	Virgin Islands
Salonika	Greece
Salvador (Bahia)	Brazil
San Antonio	Chile
San Fernando	Philippines
Sangi	Philippines
San Jose	Costa Rica
San Juan	Puerto Rico
San Pedro Sula	Honduras
San Salvador	El Salvador
Santa Marta	Colombia
Santo Domingo	Dominican Republic
Santos	Brazil
Santo Tomas de Castilla	Guatemala
San Vincente	Chile
Savona	Italy
Semarang	Indonesia
Shanghai	PRC
Sharjah	United Arab Emirates
Shimizu	Japan
Singapore	Singapore
Sousse	Tunisia
Southampton	United Kingdom
Soya	Angola
Split	Yugoslavia
Stavanger	Norway
Stockholm	Sweden
Subic Bay	Philippines
Surabaya	Indonesia
Sydney	Australia
Taipei	Taiwan
Takoradi	Ghana
Talara	Peru
Talcahuano	Chile
Tamatave	Malagasy Republic
Tampico	Mexico
Tanga	Tanzania
Tangier	Morocco
Tartous	Syria
Tema	Ghana
Tenerife	Canary Islands
Timaru	New Zealand
Tocopilla	Chile
Tokyo	Japan
Tortola	British Virgin Islands (Leeward Islands)
Trieste	Italy
Tripoli	Libya

Port	Country	Port	Country
Tsingtao	PRC	Volso	Greece
Tunis	Tunisia	Walvis Bay	South West Africa
Turku	Finland		
Tuticorin	India	Warri	Nigeria
Umm-Qasr	Iraq	Wellington	New Zealand
Valencia	Spain	Willemstad	Curacao (Netherlands Antilles)
Valetta	Malta		
Valparaiso	Chile		
Varna	Bulgaria	Yanbu	Saudi Arabia
Venice	Italy	Yokkaichi	Japan
Vera Cruz	Mexico	Yokohama	Japan
Vitoria	Brazil		

Appendix D

SEAPORT AND INTERNATIONAL TRADE TERMS AND ABBREVIATIONS

Assembly area	Place where cargo awaits shipment or inland distribution situated usually at a seaport, ICD, CFS, etc.
Berth	Place where a vessel loads/discharges cargo.
Berth allocation	The allocation of berths at a specified port for particular sailings.
Bonded warehouse	Accommodation under customs surveillance housing dutiable cargo such as tobacco or spirits which may be stored on importation and withdrawn at importer's convenience on payment of relevant duty for individual quantities.
C & F	Cost and freight – cargo delivery term.
Cargo dues	Charges raised by port authority on cargo passing over the quay usually based on tonnage or specified unit method, i.e. per vehicle.
Cargo-handling equipment	Equipment provided at a port or freight depot to handle cargo such as cranes, pallet trucks, pallets, fork lift trucks, straddle carriers, and so on.
Cargo manifest	Inventory of cargo shipped.
Cargo plan	Plan depicting space in a ship occupied by cargo.
Cargo superintendent	Person in charge of stevedores involving loading/discharging a ship.
CFS	Container (ISO) freight station.
Chartering	Process of hiring a vessel under charter party terms for voyage or period of time.
CIF	Cost Insurance Freight–cargo delivery term.
Closed dock system	A dock system within a seaport which main-

	tains a constant water level at all times and access to which by ship is through lock gates.
Cold store	Accommodation housing cargo to a refrigerated condition.
Combined transport operation	The provision of a through transport service involving a combination of transport modes with the goods being conveyed in a transport unit throughout and thereby usually being able to offer a door-to-door service.
Container berth	A berth at a seaport transhipping containers. Usually such a berth is purpose built and handles only containers.
Container stowage area	Place where containers are stored – usually empty.
Conveyor systems/belt	Equipment enabling bagged cargo, cartons, and in some ports bulk cargo, to be loaded/discharged on an automatic electrically operated conveyor belt.
Deep water harbour	A harbour offering deep water facilities including deep water berths thereby being able to accommodate vessels of up to 20 m draught.
Demurrage	Money paid by the shipper for occupying space at a port or warehouse beyond the specified period – usually pending cargo customs clearance. It also applies to delay incurred in loading/discharging a ship, container, road vehicle or road trailer, beyond the agreed period.
Destination port	The specified port of destination for a ship or consignment.
Dock labour	The labour force in a seaport handling cargo.
Direct delivery	Process of discharging cargo direct from the ship to inland transport system such as a bulk cargo shipload of rice which has been cleared by customs.
Discharging berth	Place where cargo is discharged from a ship in a seaport.
Distribution arrangements	The transportation of goods to/from the sea-

	port by road, rail or inland waterway.
Dredging	Process of recovering silt, etc. from a river bed, port estuary, etc.
Dry cargo	Goods not requiring controlled temperature protection and not of a liquid composition.
Dry dock	Dock in which ships may be repaired or built – the water being pumped out as required.
Export shed	Covered accommodation at a seaport or agent's premises housing cargo awaiting exportation.
FCL	Full container load.
FLT	Fork lift truck.
FOB	Free on Board–cargo delivery term.
Fork lift truck	Cargo-handling equipment designed particularly for palletized cargo to lift the pallets vertically/horizontally and transport them.
Free trade zone	A defined area where trade is based upon the unrestricted international exchange of goods, with customs tariffs used only as a source of revenue and not as an impediment to trade development.
Freight manifest	Inventory of cargo shipped on board a specified vessel.
Fuel oil tank farm	An area accommodating fuel in storage tanks near a berth/quay/jetty connected by pipeline.
Graving dock	Dock in which ships may be repaired or built, the water being pumped out as required.
Green channel	Process of passenger customs examination at a seaport whereby those with no goods to declare to customs will pass through the green channel.
GRT	Gross Registered Tonnage.
Harbour Master	The person in charge of all the operational/navigational aspects of a harbour.
HWOST	High Water Ordinary Spring Tide.
IAPH	International Association of Ports and Harbours.
ICC	International Chamber of Commerce.
ICD	Inland Clearance Depôt.

ILO	International Labour Organization.
Immigration	Process of examining a person's passport and other relevant documents such as a visa or health certificate – usually at an international frontier point – to establish whether all the documents are in order for the person to proceed on their journey.
IMO	International Maritime Organization.
Import shed	Covered accommodation at a seaport housing imported cargo usually awaiting distribution.
Incoterms 1980	International rules for interpretation of terms frequently used in foreign trade (export sales) contracts. These rules are drawn up by the International Chamber of Commerce and include FOB, CIF, etc.
Inwards clearance	The process of clearing a vessel through customs on arrival at the port to enable cargo discharge to commence.
ISO	International Standards Organization.
LCL	Less than full container load.
Lighterage	A barge.
Loading berth	Place where cargo is loaded on to a ship in a sea port.
Loading port	Port at which cargo is loaded on to a ship.
LWOST	Low Water Ordinary Spring Tide.
Marshalling area	Place where cargo/vehicles are assembled in a port area awaiting shipment or inland distribution.
Multi-port itineraries	A sailing schedule of a vessel involving a number of ports of call during a voyage conveying eg. a bulk cargo of oil.
Multi-purpose berth	A seaport berth able to handle a wide variety of cargoes/commodities in varying forms, i.e. pallets, containers, break bulk; vehicles, unitized shipments, involving vessels of differing specification.
NRT	Nett Registered Tonnage.
OBO	Oil/bulk/ore carriers – multi-purpose bulk carriers.

Oil/bulk terminal	A berth/terminal at a seaport equipped to handle oil and bulk cargo transhipments.
Oil terminal	A berth/terminal at a seaport equipped to handle oil transhipments.
Open dock system	A dock system in a seaport which is subject to tidal variations.
Opening date	The earliest date on which cargo is accepted for shipment by (liner) shipment for a specified sailing.
Overside discharge	Process of discharging cargo direct into barges/lighterage over the ship's side using the ship's derricks.
Out-turn report	A report detailing the condition of cargo(es) stripped/unloaded from a container.
Outwards clearance	The process of clearing a vessel through customs prior to the ship sailing from a port.
Passenger terminal	A terminal/seaport provided with facilities to handle passengers which at a seaport involves immigration and customs examination, accommodation, passenger lounges, refreshment facilities, and so on.
Pallet	A mounted steel or wooden platform of 1000 mm × 1200 mm dimensions designed to accommodate and facilitate merchandise transhipment, stowage, and through conveyance.
Port dues	A charge raised on a vessel entering a port usually based on ship's gross registered tonnage.
Port of refuge	A port at which vessels may safely anchor in times of adverse weather conditions at sea such as a storm.
Port traffic operation	An operating system which regulates/controls the passage of ships into and out of the port; also in some ports it extends to the overland cargo distribution arrangements to and from the port by road and rail.
Pre-slinging	The process of assembling loose bundled cargo on the quayside/berth in slings prior to

	the commencement of loading the cargo on to the ship.
Quay	Place where vessel loads/discharges cargo.
Ramp	A vehicle transhipment facility at a berth/quay providing access to and from the vehicular ferry at a port, thereby enabling vehicles to be driven on or off the ship.
Red channel	Process of passenger customs examination at a seaport whereby those with some goods to declare to customs proceed through the red channel.
Roll-on/roll-off terminal	A seaport terminal accommodating/berthing roll-on/roll-off (Ro/Ro) vessels whose vehicle and/or unitized cargo is transhipped by means of a ramp.
Sailing list	A list of sailings of a particular shipowner(s) from a specified port(s).
Sailing schedule	A ship's timetable detailing ports of call including arrival and departure time, the requisite dates, name of vessel and other relevant details.
Ship arrival time	The arrival time of a particular vessel at a specified berth in a named port.
Ship departure time	The departure time of a particular vessel at a specified berth in a named port.
Ship's derrick	Ship's lifting apparatus.
Slave trailer	A low-sided trailer used to convey/transport containers in the port area, or stow them on a vehicular deck of a Ro/Ro vessel.
Spotting	The process of identifying the cargo in the ship's hold or on the quayside by the crane/derrick operator prior to transhipping/lifting the cargo from the ship's hold to the quayside/berth or vice versa.
Stacking area	Place where containers are stacked/parked which may be at a port or container freight station.
Stevedores	Dockers engaged on cargo/baggage transhipment at a seaport.
Storage area	An area designated for the storage of cargo.

Straddle carriers	Shore-based mechanized cargo-handling equipment used to convey pipes, timber or containers.
Stripped	The process of unloading a container of cargo.
Stuffing	The process of loading a container of cargo.
SWL	Safe working load.
Tallying	The process of checking cargo in the course of being unloaded from a ship to the berth or cargo loading from the berth to the ship.
TEU	Twenty foot equivalent units.
Tractors	A driving unit used primarily to move trailers in a port area or container freight station.
Trailer	A non-motorized unit accommodating/ conveying a container or other cargo load.
Transit shed	Covered accommodation at a port near a berth/quay housing cargo pending shipment or inland transport distribution.
Tug master	A tractor unit at a port which hauls trailers conveying cargo/containers or slave trailers, usually operative in a port area or container freight station.
ULCC	Ultra large crude carrier.
Vegetable oil tank farm	Area accommodating vegetable oil in storage tanks usually near a berth/quay and connected by pipe line.
VLCC	Very large crude carrier.
Warehouse	Accommodation housing cargo. It may be at one floor level or a number of floor levels.
Wet bulk cargo	Merchandise conveyed in bulk and of a liquid nature/specification such as oil, wine, gas, and so on.

NB: Readers are also recommended to study the *Dictionary of Shipping/International Trade Terms and Abbreviations*, 2nd edn 1982 (3rd edition in preparation) (see Appendex A).

Index